THE MISSISSIPPI GULF COAST

THE MISSISSIPPI GULF COAST: PORTRAIT OF A PEOPLE

AN ILLUSTRATED HISTORY BY CHARLES L. SULLIVAN

PICTORIAL RESEARCH
BY
MURELLA HEBERT POWELL

"PARTNERS IN PROGRESS"
BY
NEDRA A. HARVEY

PRODUCED IN COOPERATION
WITH
THE MISSISSIPPI COAST HISTORICAL
AND
GENEALOGICAL SOCIETY

WINDSOR PUBLICATIONS, INC.
NORTHRIDGE, CALIFORNIA

Page six: A view of Biloxi during the 1890s shows Pass Christian Avenue. It was renamed Howard Avenue in honor of the Howard family, Biloxi benefactors. Courtesy, Biloxi Public Library

Windsor Publications, Inc.
History Book Division

Publisher: John M. Phillips
Editorial Director: Teri Davis Greenberg
Design Director: Alexander D'Anca

Staff for *The Mississippi Gulf Coast*:
Senior Editor: Laurel H. Paley
Editorial Development: Annette Igra, Lissa Sanders, Pamela
    Schroeder
Director, Corporate Biographies: Karen Story
Assistant Director, Corporate Biographies: Phyllis Gray
Editor, Corporate Biographies: Judith Hunter
Editorial Assistants: Kathy M. Brown, Patricia Cobb, Gail Koffman,
    Jerry Mosher, Lonnie Pham, Pat Pittman

Layout Artist: Christina McKibbin
Designer: Ellen Ifrah

Library of Congress Cataloging in Publication Data

Sullivan, Charles L.
    The Mississippi Gulf Coast.

    Produced in cooperation with the Mississippi Coast Historical and
Genealogical Society.
    Bibliography: p. 195
    Includes index.
    1. Gulf Region (Miss.)—History. 2. Gulf Region (Miss.)—Description and travel. 3. Gulf Region (Miss.)—Industries. I. Mississippi
Coast Historical and Genealogical Society. II. Title.
F347.G9S84   1985   976.2'1   85—5293
ISBN 0-89781-097-X

CONTENTS

M. James Stevens, a native of New Jersey, arrived on the Mississippi Gulf Coast in 1948. Although his college degree was in business administration, he possessed an avid interest in history. Combining his vocation and avocation, he established the Confederate Inn at Biloxi and proceeded to collect Civil War memorabilia. The artifacts led to questions, and Stevens went after the answers with a vengeance. In 30-odd years of searching and compiling he has amassed a treasure trove of documents detailing the grand sweep of coast history from earliest times to the present.

The preservation of documents led Stevens into historical activism, which has resulted in the official marking of important sites and the salvation of such coast landmarks as Fort Massachusetts. Recognition of his efforts came in 1980 with his selection as the first Northern-born president of the prestigious Mississippi Historical Society.

When Stevens learned that the Mississippi Coast Historical and Genealogical Society intended to sponsor this work to be produced by Windsor Publications, he volunteered his services as editorial consultant and placed his entire collection

at the disposal of the society. In doing so he afflicted this author with a malady rarely experienced by writers of local history— too much magnificent primary material to use. This book represents only the tip of Stevens' documentary iceberg, but perhaps in the future others who did not understand the magnitude of the collection will expose more.

Without M. James Stevens the present work would have been impossible, and to him this book is dedicated with thanks.

ACKNOWLEDGMENTS

The Mississippi Coast Historical and Genealogical Society sponsored this book, but two institutions—the Mississippi Gulf Coast Junior College and the Biloxi Public Library—made it possible. The tremendous resources of both institutions were available throughout the project.

As chairman of the Social Studies Department of the Perkinston Campus of the Mississippi Gulf Coast Junior College, the author wishes to thank the faculty, staff, administration, and students for their support. Dr. and Mrs. J.J. Hayden offered much needed and appreciated aid, encouragement, information, and advice from beginning to end. Vice-President Clyde Strickland, Public Information Director Winfred Moncrief, Media Director Richard Marlowe, and Diane Sekul, who proofed and typed the original manuscript, are particularly deserving of gratitude as are the scores of students who braved the fauna, flora, topography, and climate of the district in search of "stories on stones."

As local history and genealogy librarian of the Biloxi Public Library, the picture researcher wishes to thank her director, Charlene Longino, and past director, Marcia Mohn, for their encouragement and for allowing her not only to use the existing library holdings but to add to the collection materials uncovered during research. She thanks the Library Board, the entire staff, and the book's patrons for their support, encouragement, and understanding throughout the duration of this work. She wishes to express particular gratitude to Assistant Director Jamie Lynn Hengen.

Numerous institutions and historical societies aided both the author and the picture researcher in the preparation of this book. Every library in the south Mississippi counties helped at some point, but we wish to express special appreciation to Josephine Megehee of the Margaret Reed Crosby Memorial Library; Cathy Kanady and Mary Ann Louviere of the Ocean Springs Library; Norman Graham, director of the Harrison County Library System; and Coleen Byrd of the Gulfport-Harrison County Library for allowing us to use books and photographs in their collections. Members of every historical society in the six counties responded to inquiries regarding little-known facts about their particular areas and towns, and we wish to tender special thanks to Dottie Cooper of Pass Christian, Margaret Gibbens of Bay St. Louis, and Tommy Wixon of Pascagoula. Dr. Lionel Eleuterius of Gulf Coast Marine Research Laboratory in Ocean Springs, throughout this project, furnished information running from Civil War history to regional topography. Robert Bradley deserves special thanks for making available to us the entire historical collection of the Gulf Islands National Seashore and also for his sincere enthusiasm. We are particularly grateful to Edwin C. Bearss (chief historian of the National Park Service), Grady Howell, and Roger Hansen for sharing their expertise concerning the Civil War on the Gulf Coast. And of course, we would like to thank the officers of the Mississippi Coast Historical and Genealogical Society for their assistance with all stages of this project.

So many families, individuals, and organizations aided us that a mere listing of them would resemble the coast phone book, so we single out only a few—the Mallet-Tydall and allied families who took us aboard their "time machine" at New Prospect Camp Meeting and arranged those unforgettable interviews with Emile Bonham and Celeste Havens; Gulfport architect Bill Guild who taught us about coast historical architecture; Ann and Julius Lopez for allowing the use of their personal collection; all the families of the Lieutenant Colonel John Bond Reunion; and all members of Stanford's Mississippi Battery, the Seven Stars Artillery, and Jefferson Davis Camp 786, Sons of Confederate Veterans at Beauvoir. We remember with special appreciation Blanche Saucier, who first told us about families of the Piney Woods; Nollie W. Hickman, who so graciously allowed use of his work; Lieutenant Colonel John H. Napier III, who provided information about Pearl River County; and Walter Fountain, who shared his knowledge of the seafood industry. We also thank Madel Morgan and Martha McBee of the Mississippi Department of Archives and History; Michele Wykoff of the Historic New Orleans Collection; Liz May of Coast Consultants; Colonel Newton Carr of Beauvoir; and Detective Louie Atchison of the Biloxi Police Department, who went beyond the call of duty to help us.

Charles Sullivan
Murella Powell

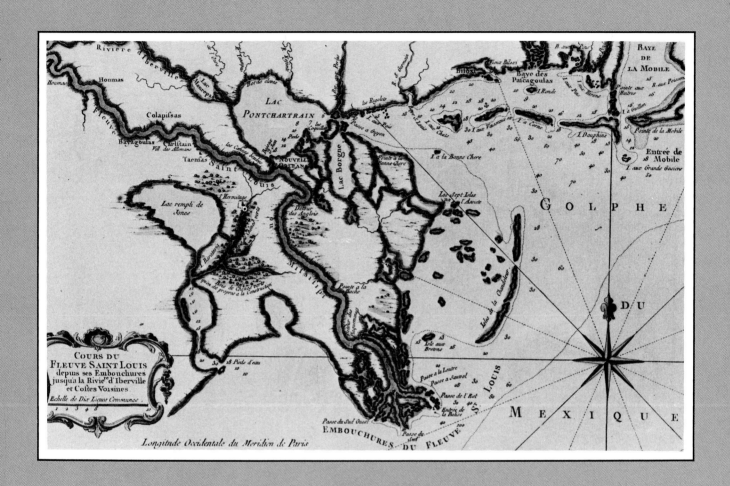

Chapter One

FROM WILDERNESS TO THE FLEUR-DE-LIS

This map of the late French Dominion period shows many place names that have endured. Courtesy, The Historic New Orleans Collection (HNOC)

The retreat of the North American continental glacier at the close of the most recent ice age set in motion the complex chain of events that created the present topography of the Gulf Coast. Alluvium-laden meltwaters cascading from the edge of the dying ice sheet between 10,000 and 15,000 years ago created the Mississippi River, which debouched its muddy floodwaters into the Gulf of Mexico to form a vast bird's-foot shaped delta. The attendant rise in sea levels accompanying worldwide glacial melt inundated the Gulf Shore, drowning the lower courses of preexisting river valleys and forming numerous bays and estuaries. Among these are Mobile Bay, Pascagoula Bay, the Bay of St. Louis, and Lake Pontchartrain.

In the shallows 12 miles offshore, current and wave action built a chain of barrier islands arrayed like dreadnoughts in battle formation. From east to west these are: Dauphin, Petit Bois, Horn, Ship (since sundered by Hurricane Camille), and Cat. This island chain protects an 81-mile-long lagoon known as Mississippi Sound, which merges imperceptibly in the west with Lake Borgne, which in turn is connected to Lake Pontchartrain via a narrow strait called the Rigolets. Mississippi Sound, with an average depth of only 10 feet, contains two notable islands. One of them, Round Island, is a deltaic mud lump at the mouth of the Pascagoula River, and the other, Deer Island, is an elongated bar at the mouth of Biloxi Bay.

The only natural deep-water harbor along the entire length of the shallow Mississippi Sound is in the lee of the northwest end of Ship Island. This anchorage, large and deep enough to shelter an armada, cast that island in its role as both the roadstead and the Gibraltar of the coast until recent times. Ninety-five miles south of Ship Island lies the mouth of the Mississippi River. For most of that distance the longbow barrier of the Chandeleurs provides a sheltered passage via the sound by that same name. Thus Ship Island held the key to the water passages of the entire area.

A trellis of streams originating high in the pine hills enters the Mississippi Sound. The greatest of these are the Pearl and the Pascagoula. Between these two flanking rivers are two large bays, each served by small dual river systems. The Wolf-Jourdan empties into the Bay of St. Louis, while the Biloxi-Tchoutacabouffa serves Biloxi Bay. The courses of all these rivers and their tributary creeks and bayous once were marked by forests of oak, gum, and cypress.

Except for the actual stream courses, the coastal marsh, and the beach fringe, the land between and beyond the Pearl and the Pascagoula and for 150 miles inland supported a vast primeval stand of magnificent longleaf yellow pine. The giant trees stood widely and evenly spaced, shafting 90 feet and then blossoming a needle-leaf crown of 20 feet or more. Their canopies shaded out underbrush and carpeted the earth with pine straw, creating the

Fur trader and adventurer René Robert Cavelier, Sieur de La Salle, descended the Mississippi River to its mouth on the Gulf in 1682 and claimed it and all the vast territory it drained for France. La Salle named the territory Louisiana in honor of Louis XIV. Courtesy, Louisiana State Museum (LSM)

Hernando De Soto gazes upon the Mississippi River for the first time in this painting by Alexander Aleau. Credited with its discovery, De Soto was actually not the first white man to see the river, and the spot from where he "discovered" it is not certain. Courtesy, Mississippi Department of Archives and History (MDAH)

appearance of a park. Early travelers remarked upon their ability to ride through these woods at full gallop in perfect safety. Others, awed and perhaps a bit frightened, compared these forests, unbroken by streams sometimes for 20 miles, to the barren wastes of the Sahara—hence the descriptive term "pine barrens."

Climatically the region has the potential to be one of great seasonal contrast. Its Gulf location at the narrow end of the funnel created by the Rockies and the Appalachians places it squarely in the middle of a battleground for air masses. The balmy south winds of summer may give way to icy northers in years when the jet stream convolutes to push a Siberian express down the funnel to the sea.

Despite the violence of the climate, the fertility of the bottomlands and access to the resources of the sea attracted the first aboriginal inhabitants some 4,000 years ago. By early Columbian times at least three small tribes (300-500 persons each) lived on the Mississippi Gulf Coast. Each tribe maintained a riverine central village composed of palmetto-thatched mud huts enclosed inside cane palisades. Both the Biloxis and the Pascagoulas lived on the Pascagoula River, while the Acolopissas lived on the Pearl.

These Indians were subsistence farmers and hunter-gatherers. They planted corn and ate it roasted, as porridge, grits, gruel, hominy, and bread. Each family sowed its corn patch also with pumpkins, melons, beans, peas, sunflowers, and tobacco. The Indians supplemented their diet with nuts and berries gathered in the forest, fish from the streams, and Gulf shrimp and oysters. During the growing season and in winter, hunting parties ranged the entire Gulf region in search of deer, bear, buffalo, and other game. The Bayogoulas, a tribe whose village lay on the Mississippi, maintained close ties with the coast Indians and hunted with them.

The eventual demise of these Indians' simple existence became a certainty with Spain's 1492 landfall in the West Indies. In ensuing years the Spanish overran the West Indian islands, converting them into bases for the grand assault on the New World, spearheaded by their conquistadors. One of them, Juan Ponce de León, sailed from Cuba in 1513 in search of a mythical "Fountain of Youth." Instead he discovered the North American continent and named its entire southern half "Florida." Six years later the Spanish followed up with a naval expedition commanded by Alonso Álvares de Piñeda that charted the Mississippi Sound under the name Mar Pequeñe ("Small Sea") and discovered the mouth of the Mississippi.

These peripheral probes sparked two full-fledged expeditions in search of El Dorado. In May 1528 Pánfilo de Narváez, Spain's most inept conquistador, led a party of 300 Spanish soldiers on an east-west trek along the rim of the Gulf Coast. The four survivors who reached Mexico managed to interest another captain of conquistadors, Hernando de Soto, in a virtual repeat performance of the Narváez catastrophe. In 1539 de Soto plunged into the Florida wilderness at the head of 600 soldiers. Their long march from the Carolinas to Texas yielded a great deal of blood but no treasure. Following these twin disasters, the Spanish abandoned the northern rim of their Caribbean-Gulf Mare Nostrum for a century and a half and concentrated on exploiting their richer holdings in Latin America.

The rise of France and England as imperial powers ended Spanish complacency. By the last quarter of the 17th century westward-moving settlers from England's Atlantic seaboard colonies were infiltrating Spanish Florida, while the French, operating out of Canada, were probing southward down the Mississippi River.

The French stole the march on both the Spanish and English in a daring downriver thrust from Canada to the Gulf that split Spanish Florida in half. René Robert Cavelier, Sieur de La Salle, the famed French explorer of the Great Lakes, commanded this expedition. With him was his chief lieutenant, Italian-born Henri de Tonti, better known as "Iron Hand." The La Salle party reached the mouth of the Mississippi on April 9, 1682, and claimed for Louis XIV all the coastal lands between the Mobile River and River of Palms in Mexico and all interior lands between the Rockies and the Appalachians. This territory he named Louisiana in honor of his sovereign. After the customary musket volleys and hurrahs, La Salle returned to Canada and, leaving Tonti behind, sailed thence to France to report to the king.

Two years later La Salle departed France with four shiploads of soldiers and colonists bound for the mouth of the Mississippi under royal orders to fortify it against the Spanish and English. Unfortunately, on the approach from the Gulf, the expedition missed the swampy river mouth and landed on the Texas coast. There members of the crew, demoralized by hardship and unable to convince La Salle to withdraw, turned mutinous and murdered him.

Meanwhile Tonti descended the river in 1685 for a rendezvous with La Salle. Unable to find his captain and unaware of his fate, Tonti left a letter for La Salle in the hands of an Indian chief and returned upriver to Canada. The chief never forgot Iron Hand, and he kept the letter for 14 years. After learning of La Salle's death, Tonti and other prominent Canadians continued to press the king to protect French claims to Louisiana by the establishment of a river-mouth fortification. All such plans had to be shelved when Louis XIV detonated a world war in 1688.

Henri de Tonti wore a hook to replace his left hand, which was blown off in the Sicilian wars. Tonti, the Canadian connection to the Gulf Coast colony, became a victim of yellow fever at the Mobile settlement in 1704. Courtesy, Museum of the City of Mobile (MCM)

Above: Jean Baptiste LeMoyne, Sieur de Bienville, was the younger brother of Pierre LeMoyne, Sieur d'Iberville. Bienville became governor of Louisiana at age 22. He held the infant colony together in its struggle for survival, earning the title "Father of Louisiana." MDAH

Top: Iberville's fierce hatred of the British spurred him on to a brilliant military career. Ultimately Iberville founded at Biloxi the first European settlement in the lower Mississippi Valley. MDAH

Although the War of the League of Augsburg (1688-1697) delayed French settlement of the Gulf Coast, it produced the tall, blue-eyed, yellow-haired Canadian hero who would plant the first colony there: Pierre LeMoyne, Sieur d'Iberville, one of 11 sons of the wealthy Charles LeMoyne of Montreal. By war's end Iberville's bravery had won for him the Cross of the Order of St. Louis and the king's commission to fortify the mouth of the Mississippi. Under the direct orders of the powerful French minister of marine, Jerome Phélypeaux de Maurepas, Comte de Pontchartrain, the 37-year-old warrior departed Brest, France, on October 24, 1698, in command of two armed frigates—the *Badine* and the *Marin*. Iberville's 20-year-old brother, Jean Baptiste LeMoyne, Sieur de Bienville, served as midshipman aboard his flagship, *Badine*.

The two ships, laden with colonists, many of whom were Canadians, picked up a contingent of buccaneers in the French West Indies, bringing the total complement to 200 men. After a rendezvous with a warship escort, the expedition sailed for the Mississippi.

England and Spain, informed by their spies of Iberville's mission, moved to checkmate him, and the three-way chess match for control of the northern Gulf littoral and the mouth of the Mississippi began. Spanish governor Andreas de Arriola hastened from Veracruz to fortify Pensacola Bay, the finest deep-water harbor of the Gulf Coast, solely to deny it to the French. English authorities dispatched a ship from the Carolinas under orders to reach and fortify the mouth of the Mississippi before the arrival of Iberville.

On January 26, 1699, while hugging the coast Iberville spied two vessels riding at anchor in Pensacola Bay. Nearby on the shore 300 Spaniards were busily erecting fortifications. Iberville, in need of fresh water and supplies, requested permission to enter the bay. Governor Arriola, fearing treachery, refused the request, but he did send out wood and water.

Pushing westward the Frenchmen probed the indented coastline in search of another deep-water roadstead. Iberville, determined not to repeat La Salle's mistake, intended to shelter his ships in a protected anchorage and search for the swampy river mouth in small craft. Due to faulty sounding techniques, the Frenchmen missed the Dauphin Island passage into Mobile Bay, but they found the channel between Ship and Cat. The tiny fleet dropped anchor in Ship Island harbor on the morning of February 10.

Three days later Iberville and Bienville with 13 men in two small boats rowed across Mississippi Sound and landed at a spot where they found "some rather good oysters." At dawn the next morning Iberville awoke to find two Indians watching from afar. After leaving some presents for them at the campsite, Iberville and one man strolled eastward along the shore, while the other Frenchmen trailed them in the small boats. Still the Indians refused contact.

When he saw six canoes full of Indians flee Deer Island bound for the eastern shore of Biloxi Bay, Iberville hailed his small boats and gave chase. The Indians beached their craft and ran for the woods, abandoning everything, including one sick old man who soon died. In the course of the next three days the Frenchmen gradually made contact with a few of the Indians whose tribal name they rendered as "Biloxi" and found that they lived 27 miles to the east near another tribe called the "Pascagoula" on a river and bay by that name.

On the afternoon of February 16, Iberville left his brother and two other

Frenchmen as hostages to entice three of the Biloxis aboard the French ships at Ship Island. There he awed them with presents and cannon fire. Upon his return at dusk the following day, Iberville found that his booming guns had attracted a hunting party of Bayogoulas who lived to the west on the banks of the river he sought.

The Bayogoula chief approached Iberville, passed his hands over his own face and breast and then over those of the Frenchman, whom he then embraced. Iberville mimicked those amenities, and then, as if by signal, the ritual spread among all the Bayogoulas, Biloxis, and Frenchmen who were present.

As night fell on February 17, 1699, the French broke out the brandy. Indian chants mingled with French sea ditties around the bonfire as Iberville presented to the Bayogoula chief a three-foot-long iron calumet (peace pipe), the bowl of which resembled a ship flying a fleur-de-lis flag. While the tobacco-filled calumet made the rounds, the Bayogoula chief declared as allies of France four Indian nations west of the Mississippi and six east of it, including his own, the Biloxis, the Pascagoulas, and the Acolopissas on the Pearl River. The chief sealed the union with a gift of three muskrat blankets. Iberville was pleased and relieved—pleased with the alliance, and relieved because he hated to smoke. This first Mississippi Gulf Coast beach party broke up at midnight. The alliance that was concluded that night with the four coastal tribes would last, with few breaches on either side, for the entire 64-year period of the French dominion.

Acting on intelligence gleaned from the Bayogoulas, Iberville moved quickly to fulfill his mission. He and Bienville together with Lieutenant M. de Sauvole and 48 men sailed southward from Ship Island in four small boats. They threaded the Chandeleurs and entered the Mississippi on March 2, but the river, being in spring flood, revealed no proper settlement site for 200 miles inland. Disappointed, Iberville sent Bienville and Sauvole back downriver with most of the men while he led a few men in two canoes east through an alligator-infested bayou bound for two lakes which the Indians said opened to the sea. The first of these he named Maurepas and the second Pontchartrain in honor of the French minister of marine, his immediate superior.

Exiting Lake Pontchartrain via the Rigolets, Iberville entered the Gulf and sighted the mouth of the Pearl River. On March 30 he camped on the shore of the Bay of St. Louis and built a huge bonfire to alert the ships of his impending arrival. The day after he reached the ships, Bienville and Sauvole arrived with a piece of "talking bark" given to them by an old chief in their trek downriver. This was Iron Hand's letter to La Salle written 14 years before, and it proved beyond all doubt that they had indeed found the Mississippi. Now, with supplies running low, a fortification had to be built as quickly as possible, and the site had to be close enough to the ships to use their crews for labor. With the Mississippi in flood, the nearby Pascagoula closed by oyster banks, and the Mississippi Sound too shallow to admit approach to the mouth of the Pearl or to Lake Pontchartrain, Iberville decided to leave the ships where they were and build a fort on the east side of Biloxi Bay. From this temporary site, exploration for a permanent one could be launched at leisure.

On April 24, 1699, Iberville mounted 12 guns on a sturdy fort composed of palisades and block bastions. He left 81 men at the fort under command

In his journal Iberville noted that Indian men wore a loin flap made of woven bark, or they wore nothing at all. Indian girls wore a red and white apron consisting of an eight-inch belt from which long tassels were suspended. "The women are sufficiently concealed" noted Iberville "as the tassels are in constant agitation, giving their bodies a sinuous appearance." He added, "I have not seen a single pretty one." He changed his mind, however, when 15 of "the prettiest young girls"—wearing tattoos, body paint, and feathers in their hair—performed for him to the beat of drums and rattling gourds. Drawing by Ginger Kirkpatrick

Above: This is the first phase in the construction of a replica of Fort Maurepas, located on Ocean Springs Beach Drive. Construction of the original fort began on April 8, 1699. While work was in progress, Iberville took one man and explored Back Bay. According to Iberville's journals, the two men landed on the north shore and walked inland for 12 miles to find abundant pine woods and deer. Photo by Charles Sullivan and Murella Powell

of Sauvole with his brother as deputy commandant and returned to France. In his report to the minister of marine, Iberville referred to the fort as Maurepas in honor of that official. But in most documents of the period, the fort is designated simply as Biloxi.

The French suffered greatly in the first long hot summer at Fort Maurepas. A combination of blistering sun and drought killed the food crops planted beside the fort. Even drinking water was at a premium until Sauvole, on a hunting trip, accidentally discovered the springs for which modern Ocean Springs is named. The men, attacked by hordes of insects (particularly mosquitoes) and stricken by fever, dysentery, and crushing boredom, hoarded their daily liquor ration until they had enough to tie one on, thus presenting Sauvole with disciplinary problems. Alligators and snakes contributed to the general misery. Sauvole's dog died 15 minutes after stepping on a rattler.

While Sauvole minded the fort, Bienville reconnoitered the coastline from Mobile Bay to the Mississippi River. At Mobile he found the deep-water channel missed previously. He then sounded Lake Pontchartrain and portaged from the lake to the Mississippi across the future site of New Orleans. Heading south from that point on September 15, 1699, with five men in two canoes, he encountered a warship in a large bend in the river. This was the English vessel sent from the Carolinas to claim the river for England, having arrived months late due to contrary winds and difficulty in locating the river. Bienville boldly boarded the frigate and ordered the captain to withdraw or be sunk by the guns of the French forts upstream. The bluff worked. That river bend is still known as "English Turn."

Iberville returned to Fort Maurepas on January 8, 1700, with two ships bringing 60 more men to add to the garrison at Biloxi. When he heard the news of the English ship, he ordered the immediate construction of tiny Fort Mississippi 54 miles up the east bank of the river as a deterrent to those who might challenge French claims. Tonti's surprise arrival from Canada at the head of a party of French *coureurs de bois* occasioned a great uproar among the workers engaged in the construction of this new bastion. Thereafter riverine contact with Canada was fairly secure.

While Iberville busied himself on the Mississippi, a Spanish strike force from Pensacola slipped into Ship Island harbor bent on the destruction of Fort Maurepas. Spanish Governor Arriola, unaware that two French warships lay at anchor there, hastily revised his plan for an attack in the face of so much firepower. Instead he assuaged his honor by sending an imperious note to Sauvole demanding surrender.

Following the expected polite refusal, Arriola sailed proudly out into the Gulf headlong into a storm that smashed all three of his ships on the Chandeleur Islands. Several days later the haughty governor, hungry and half naked, floated into Biloxi Bay in a dinghy. The Frenchmen wined him and dined him, collected his surviving men on the island, and took all of them home to Pensacola.

Iberville, after a severe bout with fever on the Mississippi, returned to Biloxi. Anxious to take something of value to France from the colony, he ordered Sauvole to seek pearls on the river by that name while he investigated the villages on the Pascagoula. Sauvole found no pearls and Iberville found the Biloxi and Pascagoula villages decimated by white man's diseases, particularly smallpox, to which the Indians had no immunity.

Following Iberville's departure for France on May 28, Sauvole continued his duties as commandant of the garrison at Fort Maurepas, now composed of 120 men. He often entertained delegations of Indians, ensuring their loyalty with gifts of guns, powder, axes, and trinkets. The Indian tribes were true to the French, but they fought among themselves, constantly casting Sauvole in the role of peacemaker.

In return for European goods, the Indians supplied the French with some food and taught them the ways of the wilderness. Sauvole augmented his tiny fleet of longboats by constructing 12 pirogues in the Indian manner. In an attempt to put the colony on a paying basis, Sauvole stockpiled deer and bear skins, beaver pelts, and buffalo robes in preparation for Iberville's return, but he never found the rumored pearls of the Acolopissas. The refusal of his men, especially the Canadians, to farm thwarted all his agricultural endeavors.

The chronic food shortage at Fort Maurepas and Fort Mississippi worsened as a steady stream of Canadians came down the river. Sauvole considered them a lazy lot and complained that they had to be roused out of bed and watched or they did not work at all. Even though they refused to obey his orders in the fort, he found them "strong, swift, and alert for expeditions." When he refused to feed them, they went out to live with the Indians, an arrangement that suited everyone but the Jesuit fathers and, incidentally, spawned a number of half-breed children.

Summer heat brought a resurgence of yellow fever, which had claimed several lives the previous year. On August 22, 1701, Sauvole joined the victims of that nemesis and was laid to rest in the cemetery behind the fort. Bienville succeeded him as commandant.

Iberville learned of the death of Sauvole on December 5, 1701, when he sailed into Pensacola from France to be greeted with open arms by the Spanish. This ironic turn of events resulted from yet another world war touched off by Louis XIV. Through marriage diplomacy Louis had assured the eventual ascension of his grandson to the Spanish throne and, in effect, a practical union of the two nations. The English, objecting to this blatant upset of the balance of power in Europe, promptly declared war on both France and Spain when the long-awaited event occurred in 1701. Thus, Iberville arrived on the Gulf Coast with orders to move the exposed Biloxi colony to Mobile Bay to be near France's new Spanish ally before the inevitable outbreak of colonial hostilities attending this War of Spanish Succession (1701-1713).

Iberville ordered the immediate stripping of Fort Maurepas and the transport of munitions and supplies to newly constructed warehouses on Dauphin Island. He further ordered that 20 men remain at the fort until the transfer could be completed and the old fort burned to deny it to enemies. Fort Mississippi, because of its strategic value in guarding the river, was to be held.

By March 1702 a new French citadel stood on a bluff overlooking the Mobile River a few miles above Mobile Bay. Iberville, his task completed, left Bienville in charge and sailed back to France never to return. Shortly after a brilliant assault on the British West Indies, Iberville died of yellow fever in Havana.

The French government practically abandoned the Gulf Coast colonies for the duration of the war, reducing the 140 Frenchmen strung out from Mobile to Fort Mississippi to a virtual hand-to-mouth existence. Through the

The Indians taught the French how to make a pirogue. A 30- to 35- foot bed of glowing charcoal was laid out along the shaft of a cypress log and allowed to burn to a predetermined depth. The charcoal was then extinguished and the hollow scraped to produce a serviceable and hardy craft. Such boats were still being constructed on the coast in the same manner as late as the 1930s. Photo by Charles Sullivan and Murella Powell

force of his personality and remarkable resourcefulness, Bienville shepherded the colony through this starving time. But by early 1704 famine forced him to alleviate the food scarcity by allowing half his men to go out to live among friendly Indians.

André Joseph Penicaut, a young ship's carpenter, volunteered for this duty and enjoyed it immensely. He and his comrades ranged the entire coastal region, joining first one friendly tribe and then another for hunting and for attacks against enemy Indians that yielded slaves for the work force at Mobile. André and a friend who played the violin taught the minuet to the Indian girls, who responded in kind with their sensual dances.

The Jesuit fathers, of course, frowned on what they viewed as libertine intermingling on the part of French men and Indian women and constantly railed against it. In a combined church-state effort, the one and only boatload of French women to enter the colony during the war years sailed into Mobile aboard the *Pelican* in 1704. Twenty-four city-bred Parisian *mademoiselles* with visions of a Garden of Eden stepped ashore into a humid, insect-ridden land of rude huts and ruder inhabitants who subsisted mainly on corn gruel. In the end all the women, save one, married. That one, despite Bienville's wrath, refused on the grounds that she was superior to all the eligible men in the godforsaken colony. Her attitude did not ruffle the majority of the Frenchmen who, much to the chagrin of the holy fathers, still preferred the Indian women. Bienville flatly informed the government that only farm girls would be welcome in the future. The *Pelican* brought more than women. The yellow fever that boarded it in the West Indies killed 40 people at Mobile, including the redoubtable Tonti.

The climate collaborated with the colonists' natural aversion to farming. Spring floods and summer sun destroyed the wheat and barley. Winter cold killed the sugar cane, banana plants, and citrus cuttings imported from the West Indies. Only the cattle and pigs did relatively well. Time after time Bienville billeted his men among the Indians.

Above: With the selection of Biloxi as the new capital of Louisiana, the French Colonial Council ordered the construction of Fort Louis on the beachfront of the Biloxi peninsula. This plan for the fort was executed circa 1721. However, Fort Louis was never completed because New Orleans replaced Biloxi as the capital of Louisiana in 1722. MDAH

Above left: To establish Biloxi solidly, marriageable women were needed. Therefore, women were sent from France, called "femmes de casquette" because they carried chests with a trousseau. Eighty such women arrived at Ship Island on January 1, 1721. This particular group, orphans reared and educated in Paris, were guarded by Ursulin nuns until married. Many coast residents claim descent from these "casquette girls." HNOC

Because it lacked a seaworthy craft, the Mobile colony could no longer maintain contact with Fort Mississippi and abandoned it in 1707. British corsairs attacked and pillaged the Dauphin Island port in 1708 and again in 1710. The next year severe floods destroyed even the Indian crops. Only the fortuitous arrival of a supply ship, the first in years, saved the colony that time. Desertion and death combined to offset the gains registered by immigration and natural increase during the war years to produce at war's end in 1713 almost exactly the population of 1702.

With the coming of peace, the impending bankruptcy of France led Louis XIV to divest himself of the ailing coast colony by granting it to financier Antoine Crozat for a period of 15 years. Crozat, through his Company of Louisiana, intended to put the colony on a paying basis and extract a profit.

In August 1717, after four years of mismanagement, a Camille-grade hurricane delivered the *coup de grace* to Crozat's dreams. Crozat went broke, and the colony reverted to the crown. The Duc d'Orléans, regent for young Louis XV who replaced the dead Sun King in 1715, unloaded Louisiana on John Law, another get-rich-quick schemer. Law, touting Louisiana as a paradise, set up the Mississippi Company with a 25-year charter empowering him to sell stock and send thousands of Europeans and slaves to the colony.

The 1717 hurricane had choked Dauphin Island harbor with sand and had split the island, the western fragment becoming Petit Bois Island. This event forced Bienville to seek a new capital and port of entry for Louisiana. He selected a site on the old portage route from Lake Pontchartrain to the Mississippi and in March 1718 began construction for a settlement he christened New Orleans in honor of the prince regent.

The superior council of the colony vetoed Bienville's choice and, citing the importance of the Ship Island anchorage, returned the capital instead from Mobile to the vicinity of old Fort Maurepas on the east side of Biloxi Bay in November 1719. One year later the council ordered the relocation of the capital across the bay to New Biloxi and authorized the construction of Fort

At the corner of Highway 90 and Elmer Street, Biloxi, stand cannons that were found in a sunken ship in Biloxi Bay. The ship, discovered by an oyster tonger in 1892, probably was French and went down in a hurricane in either 1717 or 1723. (Windsor)

Louis near the shore facing Mississippi Sound.

The Biloxi port of entry consisted of Ship Island and the unfinished Fort Louis. Into this Ellis Island without a metropolis, Law's Mississippi Company poured a human avalanche between 1719 and 1721. At one point 2,500 French, German, and Swiss colonists and black slaves lay immobilized on the sands of Ship Island. Shiploads of women, called *femmes de casquette* because they carried company-furnished chests containing marriage outfits, also arrived. Lacking food, water, and even the boats to transport them to far-off concessions in upper Louisiana, hundreds died as Bienville stood by helplessly.

The more fortunate settlers were those whose concessions lay within walking distance of Biloxi. Those assigned to the concession of Madame de Mezieres on the Bay of St. Louis and those bound for the concession of Madame de Chaumont on the Pascagoula were dispatched to them overland. Little is known of the history of the Mezieres concession, but that of the Chaumont settlement is well documented and both likely shared the same fate.

Two Canadians, who had arrived at Fort Maurepas on Iberville's second voyage in 1700, had already obtained land grants at the mouth of the Pascagoula as early as 1715. The plantation of Jean Baptiste Baudreau de la Graveline occupied the west bank of the river from the present site of Gautier northward for several miles. Joseph Simon de la Pointe's holdings included much of the site of the present city of Pascagoula on the east side of the bay.

Approximately 60 persons, 20 of them black slaves, settled the Chaumont claim in 1721 one mile south of the present Wade bridge bordering Graveline's plantation. Though they produced a wheat crop that first year, the yield was small in a top-heavy system in which 40 whites oversaw the work of 20 slaves. The French never sent white farmers to Louisiana in any appreciable numbers.

Even as Bienville and his officers strove to overcome the monumental problems of supply and logistics involved in transporting the 4,400 whites and 600 slaves already dumped in the colony by the company, Law's Mississippi bubble burst. The schemer escaped the financial rubble of France one step ahead of an irate lynch mob composed of fleeced stockholders. When the news reached Louisiana in 1721, many of the colonists already dispatched to distant concessions on the Red, Arkansas, and Yazoo rivers abandoned their lands and returned to Biloxi.

In 1722 Bienville at last prevailed upon the colonial council to transfer the capital to the fledgling city of New Orleans. The following year the defunct Mississippi Company yielded to the Company of the Indies, which divided Louisiana into nine civil and military districts, each under a commandant. Three of these districts were New Orleans, Biloxi, and Mobile.

In September 1723 a violent hurricane swept over the coast, destroying 32 buildings in New Orleans and flattening the crops on the Pearl, Pascagoula, and Mobile rivers. The Chaumont settlers, already demoralized by financial difficulties and hardships, abandoned their concessions and fled to Mobile or New Orleans. Many settlers at Biloxi and on the Bay of St. Louis followed their example. This hurricane delivered the final blow to the Mississippi Gulf Coast settlements already fatally injured by the transfer of the capital to New Orleans. In 1727 the few troops left at Fort Louis of Biloxi departed, and the coastal place names formerly so prominent in previous dispatches disappeared altogether.

Lumbering was one of the Gulf Coast's first industries. French colonials exported lumber and naval stores to France and the West Indies. A sawyer stood atop a squared log and pulled the saw upward, while the pitman stood underneath and pulled the saw downward. (The saw cut only on the way down.) HNOC

Official French records of the period after the removal of the capital to New Orleans note happenings between that city and Mobile primarily in regard to disasters. Two fierce hurricanes one week apart, September 11 and September 18, 1740, wreaked havoc among the settlers at Mobile and Pascagoula and destroyed hundreds of cattle. Six years later yet another hurricane so thoroughly destroyed the coastal food supply that aid had to be rendered by the French of the Illinois country.

French Louisiana, spawned in the crucible of two Anglo-French world wars, died at the close of a third. This war, larger than any in previous Western European history, had the unique distinction of beginning in America as the French and Indian War and expanding to Europe as the Seven Years War. In the peace treaty signed in Paris in 1763, defeated France split Louisiana between its British rival and its Spanish ally. Spain received all French holdings west of the Mississippi plus the city of New Orleans. Great Britain received everything east of the river, which of course included the Mississippi Gulf Coast.

The 1763 population of all Louisiana totaled a mere 7,500, of whom 4,500 were black slaves. The legacy of 64 years of French dominion on the Mississippi Gulf Coast consisted of only a few families scattered between the small town of New Orleans and the feeble post of Mobile. In the final analysis, the French failed in their attempt to colonize the Gulf Coast because they did not begin by cultivating the soil. Two French companies bankrupted themselves and the French government lost additional millions in the futile attempt to build a commercial house upon agricultural sand.

Chapter Two

A STRUGGLE
FOR SUPREMACY

The Battle of New Orleans ranks as one of history's most decisive engagements. In the words of historian Samuel Eliot Morison, this contest "wiped out all previous American defeats, ending the Second War of Independence in a blaze of glory." Furthermore, it settled once and for all the centuries-long dispute over ownership of the Mississippi Valley. LSM

The remnants of the Biloxi and Pascagoula Indians and some settlers of the French period, preferring Spanish to British rule, moved west of the Mississippi with the change of regimes, but most of the established coast families remained. A list of 25 citizens who journeyed to newly formed British West Florida's capital of Pensacola to take the oath of allegiance to their new masters contains many names familiar today. Among those names were Carriere, Dupont, Farve, Gollott, Krebs, Meaut, Necaise, and Ladner.

As stipulated in the Treaty of Paris of 1763, the boundaries of British West Florida were on the north the 31st parallel, on the south a line in the Gulf inclusive of the barrier islands, on the east the line formed by the Apalachicola and its Chattahoochee tributary, and on the west the line formed by the Rigolets, Lakes Pontchartrain and Maurepas, Pass Manchac, and the Mississippi River. The following year, discovering that the Natchez District had been excluded from its new possession, the British arbitrarily moved the northern border up to a straight line running from the mouth of the Yazoo River to the Apalachicola-Chattahoochee. The southern section of that huge rectangular tract was designated as the County of Charlotte and included the Mississippi Gulf Coast.

British long-range plans for protection of the new colony included a chain of forts along its western and southern rim as a bulwark against Spanish Louisiana and its capital of New Orleans. British troops occupied the French fort at Mobile and established posts on the Mississippi at Pass Manchac, Baton Rouge, and Natchez. Major Robert Farmar of the 34th Regiment reconnoitered Biloxi Bay and urged the establishment of a principal fort on that site with Ship Island as its anchorage. Satellite fortifications on the lakes between the proposed Biloxi fort and the post at Pass Manchac would, he argued, effectively block all trade between the Gulf Coast and Spanish New Orleans. The British authorities, due to lack of ships and troops, never carried out Farmar's sound plan.

The evident weakness of the British occupation forces proved to be both a boon and a bane to the 500 mostly French coastians strung out from the Pascagoula to the Pearl. On the one hand, it enabled them to pursue with impunity the only lucrative vocation now open to them—smuggling. Alienated from the British by the twin barriers of language and Roman Catholicism and unable to sell all their products in the tiny garrison village of Mobile, they retained their cultural and illegal economic ties to the larger town of New Orleans. On the other hand, isolated as the coastal people were in a few allied family groupings along the bays and rivers, they could expect little or no protection from Indian depredations and no government aid in times of natural disaster.

The classic account of the commerce of the people of British West Florida

Above: This seal was attached to land grants given by the British government when the Gulf Coast became part of the province of British West Florida. The area came under British rule in 1763 as a result of French defeat by England in the Seven Years War. MDAH

Above right: A British map shows the Gulf Coast portion of West Florida at the time of Bernard Romans' journeys. HNOC

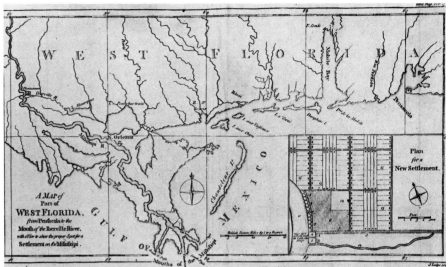

came from the pen of Captain Bernard Romans, Dutch-born cartographer and botanist who journeyed through that colony during the years 1771-1773 in the service of "His Britannick Majesty." "The amazing plenty of the country," wrote Romans, allowed the plainly dressed inhabitants to "keep princely tables at small expense." In the gardens every vegetable known in Europe plus those indigenous to America grew year round, "all beyond description perfect." Oranges, grapes, plums, pears, and other fruits matched the vegetables in quality and quantity. Wild game and seafood abounded to grace the table alongside the pork and beef provided by the large herds of pigs and "black cattle." One must keep in mind that Romans, in addition to his other duties, had been hired by the king as a one-man booster club to attract colonists to the region.

Cash crops observed by Romans included tobacco, cotton, and indigo, items that comprised much of the smuggling trade. Mindful of the burgeoning textile mills of the English midlands, Romans waxed especially lyrical about the production of cotton in the valleys of the Pearl and the Pascagoula. He displayed particular interest, possibly too much, in the workings of the peculiar machine he encountered on the Krebs plantation at Pascagoula. At a time when a prime field hand in the Carolinas spent an entire day separating by hand one pound of cotton lint from the seeds, his interest was quite understandable. The power of one slave turning a wheel on this engine spat seed from the lint at a rate requiring the hard labor of two other slaves to shovel the seeds out of the way. Krebs, to protect his invention, partially dismantled the contraption before allowing Romans to examine it and steadfastly refused to answer questions about it.

The industries for which the coast would become so famous were in embryo form in the early 1770s. At Biloxi Romans observed the French inhabitants producing lumber, pitch, tar, and charcoal from the pine forests. Another contemporary traveler who stopped at the Farve residence on the lower Pearl reported regular shipments of tar from that place across Lake Pontchartrain to New Orleans. Indeed, three schooners were constantly employed in that business. Romans and other British authorities deplored this "scandalous and illicit trade," but they lacked the requisite vessels to mount an effective blockade.

At Pascagoula Romans noted the construction of a ship of "30 Tons Burthen" for the purpose of trading for corn and deerskins with the Choctaw towns far upstream. That may have been the first sizable ship built in what later became the industrial heart of the Gulf Coast.

But life on the coast was not quite the idyll portrayed by Romans. No semblance of intellectual life existed, and the usual amenities of civilization were absent. There were no newspapers, few books, and fewer people who could read them since no schools existed. Marriages usually existed in fact until an itinerant priest passed through to render them retroactively *de jure*. The alternative to the infrequent coming of the priest was an arduous pirogue journey to the church in either New Orleans or Mobile.

The isolation under British dominion resulted in a precarious existence for coastians at the mercy of the Indians of the forest and the hurricanes of the Gulf. The Choctaws, staunch allies of the French, bore no love for the British, who for decades had armed their constantly attacking enemies, the Chickasaws and the Creeks. The large herds of black cattle on the coast thus became fair game to marauding bands of vengeful Choctaws who struck from the Pascagoula to the Pearl. By 1767 these Indians had driven the few families on the Bay of St. Louis out to Cat Island for safety. Other families moved to the other barrier islands.

In the year 1772 what Romans had called the "blessed climate" of the coast displayed its every possible vagarity and freakish extreme. It began with a Siberian winter that killed all the orange, apple, and pear trees. Iced limbs of oak and pine cracked and broke, echoing through the forests with reports like those of musket and cannon fire. Summer struck back with tropical intensity, capped on August 31 by a powerful hurricane. Mountainous waves overwhelmed the barrier islands and blasted the Chandeleurs off the map for a time. A British troop ship floated completely over Cat Island. But the storm directed its greatest violence at Pascagoula, where it destroyed all crops and most of the buildings of the Krebs plantation. From Mobile to the Pearl the storm surge rolled in as far as five miles in places. Ships and logs crashed into the flooded houses of Mobile. For 30 miles inland the raging winds, in the words of historian Charles Gayarre, did "the work of a million intoxicated demons." The limbs were twisted off the few trees that remained standing in the whole area of devastation. Ironically, New Orleans, untouched, enjoyed a serene day with a balmy wind from the east. Following this catastrophe the survivors on the barrier islands abandoned them for a time. The remnants of the 10 families on Cat Island removed to Deer Island and Old Biloxi.

After 1775 coastal life was further complicated by international events destined to put an end to Britain's presence on the Gulf. In that year the British crown designated West Florida a refuge for Tories or "those who refused to participate in the unnatural rebellion which has broken out in many parts of North America." Accordingly, the crown ordered the West Florida colonial administration to grant land on liberal terms to those refugees. Most of those taking advantage of this decree settled in the Old Natchez District, but a few did emigrate to the coastal region.

The revolt of 13 English-speaking colonies against their mother country meant little at first to the French-speaking inhabitants of the Gulf Coast. But then France joined the contest on the side of the fledgling American nation.

Crude cotton gins existed on many Southern plantations in the late 18th century, but Hugo Krebs' obviously superior machine would have qualified him for the title "inventor" of that device. Instead, his refusal to tell Romans how his machine worked left the way open for Eli Whitney, a Yankee tutor on a Georgia plantation, to claim that accolade in 1794. From Franklin L. Riley, School History of Mississippi, 1915. Courtesy, Gulfport Library

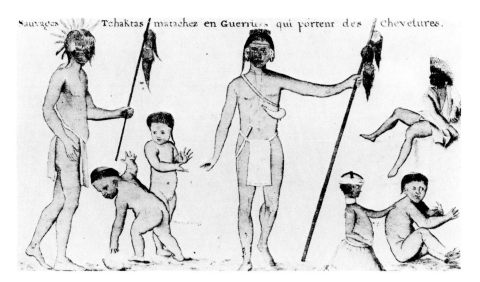

Sauvages Tchaktas matachez en Guerriés qui portent des chevelures.

In this illustration Choctaw Indians are seen dressed for war and carrying scalps. Because the Indians allowed him to move with impunity among their villages to carry out his surveying, Bernard Romans penetrated the pine woods to Bogue Homma (Red Creek), the boundary between Florida and the Choctaw lands, where he saw grisly evidence of strife among the tribes—an Indian head on a pole. From the Anthropological Archives. Courtesy, Smithsonian Institution

On the heels of this news came the revelation that the French were using the bouquet of ownership of West Florida to woo the Spanish into an anti-British alliance. Under these circumstances British toleration of the coast dwellers' smuggling activities with New Orleans ceased. In 1777 a heavily armed British ship aptly named the *West Florida* blockaded the lakes and confiscated the goods of those who chose to ignore warnings.

In that same year, with the extension of the Franco-American alliance to include Spain, American agent Oliver Pollock joined forces with newly installed popular and energetic Spanish governor Bernardo Gálvez in New Orleans. Gálvez and Pollock organized their Spanish-American troops and awaited an opportunity to "twist the British lion's tail."

In February 1778 Captain James Willing, at the head of a contingent of mounted American partisans, raided and plundered the English settlements in the Natchez District. The warm welcome and consequent protection from British retribution extended to Willing and his band by Gálvez brought swift retaliation. The British poured 1,200 troops into West Florida and beefed up their defenses at Pensacola, Mobile, Baton Rouge, and Natchez.

Spain declared war on Britain in June 1779, and Spanish-American forces operating in tandem under Gálvez and Pollock assaulted and captured Natchez, Baton Rouge, and all other posts on the Mississippi. West Florida's west wall crumbled by September. Using Ship Island as a staging area, Gálvez bombarded Mobile into submission in 1780 and the next year the capital of Pensacola as well. By the terms of the Treaty of Paris of 1783, British West Florida became Spanish West Florida.

Following the conquest, Gálvez and his successors displayed remarkable restraint in dealing with the defeated inhabitants of West Florida. In return for an oath of allegiance to the Spanish crown and the Catholic Church, Gálvez confirmed all the holdings of persons engaged in real occupancy and improvement of lands granted in the previous British and French dominions. In addition, the Spanish freely granted new tracts.

With the stipulation that he clear ground and build a road within one year and construct a residence and commence farming within three, Spanish authorities granted Philip Saucier's July 6, 1794, request for "a tract of vacant land situated on Bay Saint Louis on a Bayou called de Lisle, having a front

THE EIGHT FLAGS TO FLY OVER THE MISSISSIPPI GULF COAST

TOP ROW Left: The Bourbon flag of France, the fleur-de-lis, was carried by La Salle in 1682 when he came down the Mississippi River to its mouth and by Iberville when he established the first French colony on the Gulf Coast. The "golden lilies" waved over French territory until 1763. Right: The British Red Ensign was hoisted on the Gulf Coast in 1763 when English forces occupied the newly created province of British West Florida. SECOND ROW Left: Bernardo Gálvez pushed the British off the Gulf Coast in 1779-1780 and unfurled the Spanish Lions and Castles. (In 1785 the Province of Aragon became the dominating influence in Spain and the flag was changed to the Bars of Aragon, which waved over Spanish West Florida until 1810.) Right: After a successful rebellion by American planters around St. Francisville, the Lone Star of the Republic of West Florida was raised at the captured Spanish fort at Pascagoula on December 4, 1810. (The flag predates the Texas Lone Star by 26 years.) In 1861 the Lone Star appeared again at the Mississippi Secession Convention and inspired the song "The Bonnie Blue Flag," which became the second-best-loved song of the Confederacy after "Dixie." THIRD ROW Left: On January 9, 1811, the American flag was unfurled on the Gulf Coast for the first time. This flag with 15 stars and 15 stripes, one for each state at that time, was the flag when Mississippi became a state in 1817. It soon became apparent that stripes could not continue to be added as the Union grew, and in 1818 the stripes reverted to 13 with only a star added for each new state. Right: On January 26, 1861, the State of Mississippi adopted as the official state flag a banner of white with a magnolia tree in the center and the Lone Star in the upper left corner. BOTTOM ROW Left: the original official Confederate flag, the Stars and Bars, resembled the Stars and Stripes so closely that in the Battle of Manassas the Confederates fired on their own men. This flag, designed not to be confused with the U.S. flag, became the accepted Confederate battle flag but was not made official until after the war. Right: The Mississippi State Legislature adopted the present-day state flag in February 1894, replacing the Magnolia flag. This flag has a replica of the Confederate battle flag in the canton corner. Photos by Coast Consultants. All flags courtesy, Gulf Coast Carnival Association

Above: Thousands of people, mainly German and Swiss, responded to this propaganda poster that John Law circulated throughout Europe, misrepresenting Louisiana as a land of riches, a virtual paradise. The unfortunates sailed on overcrowded "pest ships" to Ship Island and disillusionment or death. HNOC

Left: The first printed map of the Gulf Coast was based on the 1584 de Soto map and other sources. It remained the basis for charts and maps of the Gulf Coast for more than a century. LSM

Right: Roman Neumaier of the Gulf Coast Chapter of the Mississippi Archaeological Association inspects salvaged parts of the Pelican, an 1847 sidewheel steamboat that burned and sank in Biloxi Harbor. Dredging for the establishment of the Biloxi Commercial Docking Facility in 1980 uncovered the remains of the Pelican, which became the subject of a subsequent research operation. Courtesy, Mr. and Mrs. Roman Neumaier

Above: In the Battle of Lake Borgne, depicted in this oil painting, Lieutenant Thomas Ap Catesby Jones fought the last naval engagement against a foreign enemy in American territorial waters. HNOC

Below: Painted by Charles Giroux circa 1853, The Sylph at Biloxi reflects a time before the Civil War when the Mississippi Gulf Coast was the playground for upstate cotton planters and the wealthy of New Orleans. Grand houses lined the beachfront, each with its own wharf. The Sylph was one of the many yachts that dotted the Gulf waters and took part in the summertime regattas. The Sylph was owned by J.G. Robinson, whose "Long Eight Cottage," now known as the Dantzler house, is shown. To the left is the Biloxi Lighthouse. Courtesy, New Orleans Museum of Art

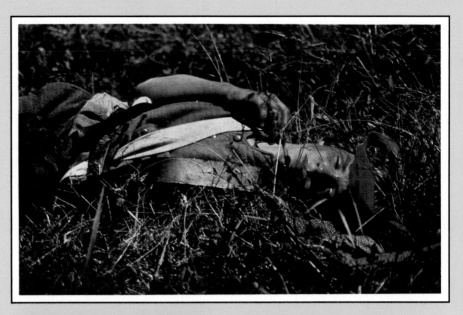

Left: General George H. Nixon's grave is located at Pearlington (formerly Farve's Farm) in Hancock County. General Nixon led the coast troops in the two-year campaign associated with the War of 1812, which culminated in the Battle of New Orleans. Photo by Charles Sullivan

Above: As the Federals bombarded Confederate forces on the Mississippi River, a soldier 90 miles away on Ship Island recorded in his diary on April 24, 1862: "About 2:00 the most fearful cannonading ever heard on this continent broke loose. Ship Island shook as with an earthquake from the terrific explosions which continued until daylight." This painting of the bombardment was executed by J. Joffray. Courtesy, Chicago Historical Society

Top right: During the Civil War the Mississippi Coast lost a generation in what might have been called the "Boys' War." More than one-third of the soldiers on both sides were 18 or under, approximately 150,000 were 15 or under, and several hundred were 13 and under. This photograph of Pascagoula youth Brian Conner was taken at the 119th-anniversary reenactment of the Battle of Champion Hill. Photo by Chris Geotes

Right: Earlier in the 20th century the "gully boat," a small vessel that shrimped the shallow waters near the shore and islands, was a common sight in the Gulf. Fishermen went overboard and dragged the huge seines by hand. Oil painting by Joe Moran

Above: An oil painting by William Woodward depicts now-world-famous George Ohr, the "mad potter of Biloxi," at his wheel. Ohr's outrageous work was outdone only by his eccentric personality. Known also as the "father of the visual-verbal in American ceramics," Ohr never duplicated a design because "God never made nothing the same." Courtesy, Biloxi Public Library (BPL)

Left: Logs were branded much in the same way as cattle were branded. Each owner registered his individual mark, which was cut deep into the shaft of the log. Photo by Dave Davis, DeSilver

Opposite page, center: The firm composed of L. Lopez, Sr., and W.K.M. Dukate was at one time the largest individual packer of oysters, shrimp, and figs in the United States. According to a reporter for the Biloxi Daily Herald in 1904, "the head of the firm, Mr. Lopez Sr., is one of the most progressive men in the state, while his partner, Mr. Dukate, keeps an even pace in that line." Courtesy, Mr. and Mrs. Julius Lopez

Opposite page, bottom: Martin Fountain opened his seafood company at the foot of Myrtle Street, Biloxi, about 1922. Fountain's labor camps stood on pilings in about eight feet of water by the factory; the houses were former shipyard housing that were brought by barge from Pascagoula. Pictured is a label from a Fountain seafood can. HNOC

31

of twenty arpents on said Bayou, bounded in the South West by land belonging to Bartholemis Grelot, and on the North East by Vacant land." Although the Spanish sent few settlers to the coast themselves, their enlightened land policies resulted in the retention of most of the French and British settlers already there and even enticed a few Americans.

In the wake of victory over their common British foe, the Spanish-American alliance dissolved in bickering over boundaries. The new American nation, intent upon fulfilling the "manifest destiny" implicit in its westward movement, favored the 31st parallel as Spanish West Florida's northern border. The Spanish, for their part, hewed to the line running eastward from the mouth of the Yazoo River. This dispute, involving primarily the ownership of the Natchez District, continued until the Spanish accepted the 31st parallel in the Treaty of San Lorenzo (1795).

Even after they signed the treaty, the Spanish refused to evacuate the disputed area for three years. When they finally did pull out, the American Congress, on April 7, 1798, established the Mississippi Territory. This huge area, bounded on the south by the 31st parallel, on the north by the Tennessee border, on the west by the Mississippi River, and on the east by the Apalachicola-Chattahoochee line, comprised the modern states of Alabama and Mississippi with the exception of their coastal panhandles.

This legislative action opened the Old Southwest to American settlement on an unprecedented scale. The trickle of traders, trappers, and a few farmers prior to this time gave way to a steadily mounting demographic flood of 20 years' duration, which would bear the appellation "The Great Migration." The first wave of American pioneers began penetrating the pine barrens of the coastal area at the turn of the 19th century. Ignoring both Indian claims and Spanish borders as they trekked westward, these hard-bitten Southern frontiersmen were unlikely to accept for long a situation in which the mouth of every single south-flowing river east of the Mississippi lay in the hands of a foreign power. Resentment reached the boiling point when Spanish authorities, backed by Spanish guns, levied a 12-percent tariff (both ways) on the cargoes of all commercial craft penetrating the 31st parallel on the Pearl, the Pascagoula, and all the rivers entering Mobile Bay.

A peaceful solution to the problem seemed in the offing in 1803 when Napoleon Bonaparte, having forced his Spanish vassal to retrocede Louisiana to France, sold the huge area to the United States. President Thomas Jefferson, on the basis of the borders originally claimed by La Salle, considered Spanish West Florida to be part of the Louisiana Purchase and prepared to occupy the Mississippi Gulf Coast. The Spanish, however, refused to budge and placed their West Florida garrisons on alert. Unwilling to fight, the United States merely registered its claims to the territory between the Mississippi and the Perdido, a small river flowing into the gulf between Mobile and Pensacola.

In 1804 the American government organized the southern portion of the Louisiana Purchase into the Territory of Orleans, an area corresponding to the present Louisiana boot minus the toe. Even as territorial governor W.C.C. Claiborne took office in New Orleans unrest broke out in Spanish West Florida. The Americans there, already angered by their exclusion from the Mississippi Territory six years earlier, staged a minor revolt in the vicinity of St. Francisville and Baton Rouge when they learned they had been left out of the Territory of Orleans as well. Although the Spanish quelled the

Above: Spanish soldier Bernardo Gálvez was made governor of Louisiana and captain-general of the lands of West Florida in 1784. For his brilliant and courageous campaign that drove the British out of the Gulf area, he was given the right to bear the heraldic motto "I Alone." MDAH

Opposite page: "You are cordially invited to be present at the Grand Ball of Her Majesty Ixolib," read the invitation to the Mardi Gras Ball of 1925. "Ixolib"—"Biloxi" spelled backwards—has always been and still is the name given to the year's reigning Mardi Gras queen. BPL

revolt quickly and bloodlessly, it proved to be a harbinger of things to come. The Kemper brothers—Samuel, Nathan, and Reuben—who emerged as leaders in this early revolt, awaited the opportunity to present Spain with a real revolution.

In the period following the Louisiana Purchase, the interest of the American government in the Mississippi Gulf Coast reached the highest levels. President Jefferson sent a detailed list of questions to Ephraim Kirby, the American magistrate at Fort Stoddard (located above Mobile on the Tombigbee) requesting information regarding coastal settlement.

The Kirby Report, dated May 1, 1804, contained the following information: "From the town of Mobile to the Pascagoula there are about 18 families settled along the shores of the Bay and at the mouth of the river; and from thence to Pearl River, and upon the same are about 30 families."

As to the character of the people, Kirby deemed the original French as "few in number but generally honest, well disposed citizens." The next most ancient group, Tories and others who had fled Georgia and the Carolinas during the American Revolution, he dismissed as treasonable and "felons of the first magnitude." Since territorial status, however, American emigrants of a more "meritorious class" had arrived. He concluded by informing Jefferson that only the establishment of American rule could end the economic depression of the area wrought by Spanish control.

The extension of American postal service to New Orleans in 1804 prompted Jefferson to inquire about possible overland post routes designed to connect that city with the principal southwest-tending trunk out of Washington, D.C. Judging from the 1805 report sent to the President by post rider Issac Briggs, roads were almost nonexistent. The 200-mile journey on horseback from Fort Stoddard through Mobile across the coast to New Orleans required 25 days of hard traveling. Briggs crossed the Pascagoula approximately 20 miles above its mouth by borrowing a canoe and swimming his horse alongside. From that point he rode in a generally southwesterly direction to the Farve Farm on the Pearl and there, to avoid the virtually impassable Pearl River swamps, boarded a schooner for New Orleans. American authorities approved this route for use, but due to the certainty of its closure in the event of trouble with the Spanish, they also decreed the blazing of an alternate route. This Federal Road, authorized in 1806, ran the length of the 31st parallel from Fort Stoddard to the Mississippi River but at Ford's Fort on the Pearl a fork ran south from it to the north shore of Lake Pontchartrain.

By the portentous year of 1810 the new roads and trails penetrating the pine barrens had opened the region to an ever increasing number of settlers moving overland from Georgia and the Carolinas. These people, of primarily Anglo-Saxon and Celtic stock, were herdsmen and hunters-gatherers who grew a few subsistence food crops on the fertile lands of the creek bottoms. They and their descendants raised huge herds of cattle and swine, which fed on the grasses and pine mast of the forests. They were crack shots hunting the deer of the forests and the bear of the canebrakes. They were content with, and indeed sought, a life of unrestrained freedom bereft of the amenities of civilization, and they were not fond of Indians or Spaniards.

A traveler's account of that same year gave a more complete situation report of coastal families than that of Kirby six years before. This account listed 18 families on the lower Pascagoula and more upstream, 12 families at

Biloxi, 10 to 15 French families at the Bay of St. Louis, and just under 20 families on the east bank of the Pearl. At the village of Pass Christian "4 or 5 French free Negroes and Mulattoes" were in residence and owned land. Moreover, a number of wealthy New Orleanians had established summer homes at that place. Even at this early date the trend of escaping the summer heat and yellow fever of the city in the salubrious climate of the coast had begun.

In 1810 the population of the city of New Orleans and its suburbs reached 24,550, having trebled in the seven years of American control. Mobile, on the other hand, had withered to the status of a village of 300 souls due to the ruinous Spanish tariffs that had virtually shut off its riverine trade.

On September 23, 1810, the Spanish West Florida pressure cooker exploded. American rebels stormed the fort at Baton Rouge, brought down the Spanish flag, and replaced it with one bearing a lone white star centered in a field of blue. At St. Francisville the leaders of the revolution proclaimed the independent Republic of West Florida and organized a government, which appealed to American President James Madison for admission as a state.

After gauging the political winds for a bit over a month, Madison, in accordance with American claims previously advanced, issued a proclamation dated October 27, 1810, annexing West Florida to the Louisiana Purchase. Spain simply ignored the proclamation while the rebels refuted it since it did not give their new republic statehood status.

The West Florida Rebellion reached the Gulf Coast when Reuben Kemper contacted Sterling Dupree, a self-styled rebel leader residing on the Pascagoula River near the 31st parallel. As captain of a locally recruited force of West Florida troops, Dupree descended the Pascagoula and captured the Spanish fort at its mouth, plundering the homes of area citizens in the process. According to eyewitness accounts, Dupree raised the Lone Star flag at Pascagoula on December 4, 1810, and the next day stole three ships from the Krebs and other families. These ships he loaded with slaves, liquor, and all manner of plunder including even the door locks from the plantation houses. When a posse of 13 irate citizens showed opposition, the raiders shot one of them dead and then sailed upriver to the 31st parallel with their booty.

Meanwhile United States troops under orders from Governor Claiborne of the Orleans Territory occupied all Republic of West Florida posts on the Mississippi. On December 10 the Stars and Stripes replaced the Lone Star, ending the life of the Republic it represented after only 74 days.

The establishment of American hegemony on the Gulf Coast required another month. On January 4, 1811, Claiborne issued a proclamation declaring that portion of former West Florida from the Mississippi to the Perdido to be annexed to the Territory of Orleans as the county of Feliciana. Of the six parishes that made up this new county, two encompassed the Gulf Coast.

The area between the Pearl and Biloxi Bay became the Parish of Biloxi. The area between Biloxi Bay and the Perdido became the Parish of Pascagoula, but as the Spanish retained a dogged hold on Mobile, the real occupancy of this last parish extended only slightly east of its namesake river.

Following the issuance of his proclamation, Claiborne instructed Dr. William "Fat Doctor" Flood, a prominent New Orleans area planter and physician, to proceed to the coast and raise the American flag at each inhabited spot. The governor further ordered Flood to appoint justices of the

William C.C. Claiborne was appointed the second governor of the Mississippi Territory in 1801 at the age of 26. He went on to become governor of the Territory of Orleans and first governor of American Louisiana. MDAH

In 1836 Hiram Roberts of Port Gibson built Grasslawn at Mississippi City. It still stands as a relic of the era and has been restored by the Spanish Trail Historical Foundation. Courtesy, Esther Barrett

peace at those places and to present to them copies of the United States Constitution and copies of the territorial law code.

On January 9, 1811, Flood docked the sloop *Alligator* at the Simeon Farve Farm on the east bank of the Pearl, raised the flag, and appointed Farve as a justice of the peace of Biloxi Parish. Flood repeated this ritual later that same day at the Bay of St. Louis and Pass Christian, appointing Philip Saucier as justice of the peace. At Flood's next stop on Biloxi Bay, Jacques Ladner received the American documents and assumed office.

On the morning of January 13, Flood reached the Pascagoula where he named Benjamin Goodin, Fortesque Coming, and United States Navy Sailing Master George Farragut as justices of the peace for Pascagoula Parish. A half century later this last man's son David would command the Federal Civil War fleet that would conquer New Orleans, the Mobile forts, and the Gulf Coast. Descendants of this family still reside in the Pascagoula area.

The anarchy attending the rebellion in the Pascagoula area ended with the establishment of American control. Flood, unable to proceed to Mobile because of the Spanish presence there, returned to New Orleans. In his report to Claiborne, he estimated the population of Biloxi Parish at 420 and that of Pascagoula Parish at 350. Although most of the residents were of French ancestry, Flood deemed them pleased to be attached to the United

States.

On April 12, 1812, the Territory of Orleans became the State of Louisiana. A few days later Congress enlarged its boundaries to include the area between the Mississippi and the Pearl. On May 14 the area from the Pearl to the Perdido entered by statute the Mississippi Territory. In September that entire vast tract was christened Mobile County. Three months later, on December 14, the Mississippi Territorial Legislature chopped that one county into three. Hancock County, honoring Declaration of Independence signatory John Hancock, included the area from the Pearl to Biloxi Bay (encompassing the modern counties of Hancock, Pearl River, Harrison, and Stone). Jackson County, honoring frontier politician and military commander Andrew Jackson, included the area from Biloxi Bay to a point east of the Pascagoula (encompassing the present counties of Jackson and George). A special problem attended the formation of the third county, extending from the Jackson County boundary to the Perdido, which retained the original name of Mobile. Its namesake bay and town still lay in Spanish hands. Contemporary international events rendered that situation intolerable.

In June 1812 the United States declared war on the Empire of Great Britain, sparking a conflict that would bear two designations—the War of 1812 and America's Second War of Independence. Spain, then allied with Britain against Napoleon in Europe, threw open its American ports to British fleets wishing to attack the cities of the United States. This meant in particular that the ports of Havana, Pensacola, and Mobile might soon host British fleets and armies.

In response, American General James Wilkinson sailed from New Orleans and advanced on Mobile. The city surrendered in April 1813, and its Spanish garrison retired to Pensacola. From Pensacola the Spanish continued a long-standing policy of inciting their Creek Indian allies against Americans moving overland from Georgia and the Carolinas. In August that policy resulted in the massacre of 500 settlers at Fort Mims on the Alabama River above Mobile.

Governor David Holmes, alarmed and angered by the slaughter, mobilized the Mississippi Territorial Militia and ordered an immediate assault on the Creeks. Among the coast units responding to the call were those commanded by Colonel George H. Nixon and Captain John Bond of the Pearl River area, and the Pascagoula River contingent under Lieutenant Colonel Sterling Dupree. These officers and their men joined approximately 700 other Mississippians of all ranks who would serve with unsurpassed courage and fortitude in a two-year military campaign that began as a local Indian War and culminated in a battle that shook the world. Their fiery supreme commander was destined to be a Tennessee backwoods military genius possessed of an iron will and blessed with either the devilish luck ascribed by his detractors or the divine guidance attributed by his admirers.

When the news of the Fort Mims Massacre reached Nashville, General Andrew Jackson lay in bed recovering from two bullet wounds suffered in a tavern brawl with political opponents. Swearing vengeance against the Indians and their Anglo-Spanish incendiaries, he rose from his bed, called up the Tennessee Militia, and headed south. On March 27, 1814, Jackson personally led the charge against the Creek stronghold at Horseshoe Bend that wiped out 900 braves. In a single stroke he ended the Indian menace and catapulted himself into national prominence. Following the Battle of

The descendants of Lieutenant Colonel John Bond—pictured circa 1815—gather annually at the Bond Cemetery near Howison in Stone County. Of the numerous family reunions held every year in the panhandle, this reunion, which features flag raisings and speeches, may be the only event in all of Mississippi commemorating the War of 1812. Courtesy, David Cunningham

Horseshoe Bend, he was the only logical choice for defender of the Gulf Coast against a possible British invasion.

At the behest of the American high command, Jackson assumed control of the Seventh Military District (Louisiana, Tennessee, and the Mississippi Territory). Only a few thousand regular army troops and federalized militia existed in this huge district to defend the Mississippi River and a lengthy coastline from the greatest naval power on earth. And, too, the Spanish still held Pensacola and had made its fine harbor available to the British enemy.

From the outbreak of the war until mid-1814, the British had contented themselves with a strangling blockade of the American coastline and with the constant threat of invasion across the Great Lakes from British Canada. This cat-and-mouse game ended in April when Britain and its allies toppled Napoleon after 11 years of war and sent him into exile. The pacification of Europe enabled the British lion to exert its full force against the upstart colonials in the form of amphibious assaults on vital points. The redcoats burned Washington, D.C., in August. President Madison and the high command, having virtually ignored the southern front throughout the war and now on the run, had little time and less patience for Jackson's requests for men and matériel for the defense of the Gulf Coast. Moreover, the British, having upheld their honor by humiliating the United States, seemed ready to talk peace, and American peace commissioners met with their British counterparts in Ghent, Belgium.

Even as they held out the olive branch, the British sent forth a massive strike force bound for the Gulf Coast to split the United States in half by taking the Mississippi and linking up with British forces in Canada. The struggle for the key river city of New Orleans would decide the victor in this war. The British commander bore orders to continue the attack even if a peace pact were signed. Thus, a British success at New Orleans would result in a stillborn treaty; an American victory would end the war.

Jackson expected the British to establish a beachhead either at Mobile or Pascagoula and use it as a base to strike overland to a point on the Mississippi north of New Orleans, ending with a descent on the city. The problems inherent in an opposed ascent of the Mississippi under sail and the obstacles posed by the shallow lakes and marshes from all other quarters bore out this conclusion.

Jackson's army feverishly built up the defenses of Mobile as the Spanish welcomed the advance British naval and marine contingents at Pensacola. The British moved against Mobile on September 16, 1814, and suffered a stunning repulse. Always one to take the initiative, Jackson struck back, driving the British out of Pensacola and neutralizing the Spanish. These victories heartened the defenders of the Gulf Coast and simultaneously forced the British to make a frontal assault on New Orleans by denying them a deep-water port as a base for overland operations. In the wake of these twin victories, "Old Hickory" rode out of Mobile along the Federal Road on the 31st parallel, a mere wagon rut through the piney woods. One of his staff officers, Major Howell Tatum, noted in his *Journal* the particulars of his journey. Using fords and ferries, they crossed the Pascagoula, Black Creek, Red Creek, Wolf River, and the Pearl. At Ford's Fort the party turned south to the north shore of Lake Pontchartrain, arriving by boat in New Orleans on December 1, affording Jackson precious little time to prepare his defenses.

Various contingents of the American army moved along the Federal Road with some units, especially those with artillery, turning south to follow the Pearl to Gainesville where small boats took them on into New Orleans. Some of the soldiers, struck by the aspect of the valley, would return as settlers after the war.

On December 12 the mightiest armada ever to approach the shores of America loomed off the Mississippi Gulf Coast. Boasting the firepower of 1,000 guns and manned by 20,000 veteran sailors, soldiers, and marines, the British fleet anchored at the north end of the Chandeleurs and in the lee of Cat and Ship islands. To oppose this, Jackson could count two warships in New Orleans, five small schooner-rigged gunboats on the lakes, one steamboat, and 4,500 mostly inexperienced troops.

The struggle for New Orleans began on December 13, 1814, in Mississippi Sound. Youthful Lieutenant Thomas Ap Catesby ("Tac") Jones commanded the five American gunboats and two tenders stationed at Fort St. Louis, really only a small battery on the shore of the Bay of St. Louis. His orders were to intercept the British fleet at Pass Christian, fall back to the Rigolets, and "sink or be sunk." The relative power of his mosquito fleet rendered only the latter possible.

Forty-five shallow draft barges, each mounting a bow cannon and filled with British sailors and marines, moved to the attack. Jones, in accordance with his orders, fell back before them. At the Bay of St. Louis seven barges detached to shell the shore battery and its protecting tender, *Sea Horse*. The Americans fought for half an hour, blew up the ship and battery to deny the ordnance to the British, and fled overland to New Orleans.

Jones retreated all night before the on-rowing barges. The next day, with his gunboats stuck in the muddy shallows off the Rigolets, Jones stood and fought. After two hours of gore, grapeshot, and flashing blades, the wounded Jones surrendered in defeat. He had followed his orders, preserved his honor, and gained precious time for Jackson.

On Christmas Eve in Ghent the American and British peace commissioners signed the treaty ending the War of 1812. Two weeks later, on January 8, 1815, Andrew Jackson's ragtag army of free blacks and pirates, Creoles and Kaintucks, Mississippians, Georgians, and Tennesseeans ratified it with musket butts, bullets, and cannonballs. At battle's end 2,036 redcoats, many of them crack veterans of the Napoleonic Wars, littered the field in front of a rampart of Mississippi mud on the Plain of Chalmette.

In the euphoria following the battle, a proud new spirit swept the ranks of the defenders. The polyglot inhabitants of the Gulf Coast now saw themselves as Americans, and that spirit of nationalism swept the country. Sectionalism vanished, at least for a time, as the nation embarked on its common goal, "manifest destiny."

The Great Migration, temporarily checked by the war, resumed with the defeat of the Indians and the British. By 1817 sufficient population existed to warrant congressional sundering of the huge Mississippi Territory into the State of Mississippi and the Territory of Alabama (which in turn achieved statehood status two years later). The new Mississippi-Alabama line, which followed the water divide between the valley of the Pascagoula and Mobile Bay, closed the fourth side of the rectangle already bounded by the barrier islands, the Pearl River, and the 31st parallel to create the Mississippi Gulf Coast Panhandle.

Chapter Three

STEAMBOATS, YELLOW JACK, AND THE SIX SISTERS

In 1854 a lighthouse was erected on Spanish Point, on the west bank of the Pascagoula River. Since the river was already marked by the Round Island Lighthouse, the entrance lighthouse was small. Courtesy, Tommy Wixon

The growth of towns and trade on the Mississippi Gulf Coast in the antebellum period (1815-1861) resulted from a process, an invention, and a disease. The urbanization process of the two flanking metropolitan areas of New Orleans and Mobile, the advent of steam power, and the terror of yellow fever combined to produce a string of six "watering places" (resort spas with curative waters) on the Mississippi littoral and simultaneously spawned commercial-industrial villages at bay heads and river mouths. The watering places, known as the "Six Sisters," were Shieldsboro (Bay St. Louis), Pass Christian, Mississippi City, Biloxi, Ocean Springs, and the Pascagoulas (East and West). The major commercial-industrial village was Handsboro on Back Bay Biloxi, but others of importance were Pearlington, Gainesville, Napoleon, and Logtown on the Pearl, Elder's Ferry (Moss Point) on the Pascagoula, and Wolftown (Delisle) at the head of the Bay of St. Louis.

Shieldsboro and Pass Christian shared a common origin as watering places in the late colonial period. Creole Catholics tended to favor the first, while Protestant Anglos congregated in the latter. Because of their proximity to New Orleans and the early establishment of sailing sloop service between the two villages and that city, Shieldsboro and Pass Christian were the fastest growing of the Six Sisters in the pre-steamboat era.

In 1789 Thomas Shields secured a Spanish land grant on the west side of the Bay of St. Louis. The village that grew on a portion of that grant became known by two interchangeable names, Bay St. Louis and Shieldsboro, but the latter was the official legal designation until 1875.

In 1820 seven hundred men of the Eighth Regiment, U.S. Infantry, commanded by Lieutenant Colonel Zachary Taylor, built a road from the Pearl River to the western shore of the Bay of St. Louis. The medical officer attached to the troop cantonment at the road's terminus described a bayside strip of homes and summer cottages three or four miles in length with "the little village of Shieldsborough" in the middle. He characterized the area as a long-established summer retreat for the Creole population of New Orleans and the planters of the Natchez District. The small permanent population consisted primarily of descendants of original French and Spanish settlers.

By 1842 Shieldsboro boasted a first-class hotel in addition to a number of boardinghouses. In that same year the hotel owners, in league with a number of public-spirited citizens, raised the funds necessary to extend the town wharf 80 feet farther into the bay so that boats could land in all seasons without any danger of running aground.

All the places of accommodation constructed bathhouses in the water off

Architectural studies date the old Spanish "customs house" to around 1790-1800. The designation "customs house" has always been given to the structure, but there is no documented evidence that it was built or used for that purpose. Photo by Bob Hubbard

the beach for the use of guests. These rectangular affairs consisted of palm posts enclosed in wooden lattice. The palm posts, imported from Florida and known as "cabbagewood" in local parlance, resisted sea worms in that pre-creosote age. The bathhouses, called bathing boxes when attached to wharves and piers, enjoyed their greatest popularity at high tide.

Through eyewitness accounts and documents of the period it is possible to reconstruct the village of Shieldsboro and capture a bit of its flavor in the summer of 1851. From Grand Bend (Waveland) in the southwest, the beach road followed the steadily rising ground, which peaked into bluffs at Main Street and diminished back to sea level at Cedar Point in the northeast. Beginning at Grand Bend with two cotton plantations, 60 residences—divided into two groups by Main Street—faced the bay on the five-mile front to Cedar Point. At the intersection of Main Street and the beach road stood a cluster of businesses composed of two bakeries, a drugstore, a saddler, a cigar store, a blacksmith shop, a general store, a barroom, a combination barroom-grocery, and a soda shop owned by a well-to-do free black woman who sold excellent sarsaparilla in gallon jugs. The calaboose and a schoolhouse stood on the south side of Main. Across the street on June 24, 1851, the Masons laid the cornerstone on the newly completed Lodge Number 147, described as superior to any in the Crescent City. Washington and Union streets counted only one residence each.

Two large hotels, each with a long wharf, served the bay that summer. One stood near the Catholic church some distance south of the main intersection. The proprietor of the other hotel, which faced the bay several squares north of Main, engaged Ordell's Band for the summer of 1851, but the grand soiree of Saturday, August 3, was washed out by a thunderstorm that prevented the arrival of enough guests to form a cotillion. Each day at sunset an array of feminine fashion graced the wharves and the beach road. A cavalcade of side-saddled beauties attired in long gray skirts and wide-brimmed straw hats rode by young misses *"à la bloomer"* accompanied by nurses fussing about with toddlers *"en pantalette."*

The aldermanic elections of August 11, which involved a spirited progressive challenge to the conservative old guard, commanded unusual interest

ROADS AND SETTLEMENT IN THE ANTEBELLUM PINEY WOODS

In the antebellum period only a few roads wandered through the pine barrens, and they were more properly wagon ruts used by a handful of farmers. Thousands of settlers had poured into the piney woods on the heels of Andrew Jackson's victories over the British and Indians. When they found the lands ill suited to agriculture beyond the level of subsistence farming, most of them moved northward after the Choctaw cessions of 1820 and 1830 opened the rich prairie lands in the midsection of the state. Those who remained became small farmers, hunter-gatherers, and large-scale cattle and sheep herders. Overgrazing and forest fires depleted the open range, driving many of the forest dwellers into the growing timber industry by the 1850s. Settlement was extremely sparse and scattered, but a few backwoods hamlets did spring up, most notably Hobolochitto (Picayune), Coalville (Woolmarket), Flint Creek Post Office (near present Wiggins), and Jackson County Courthouse (near present Wade).

The Federal Road along the 31st parallel rapidly fell into disuse after its artificial reason for existence ended with the annexation of West Florida to the American domain. A more direct route from Mobile east to Jackson County Courthouse near the Pascagoula, thence southwestward to Farve Farm (Pearlington), became the new primary east-west artery. In 1848 the first telegraph line to link Mobile and New Orleans was affixed to the trees along this route, giving it the name Wire Road.

The best description of the antebellum road system of the Mississippi Panhandle comes from the field notes of Benjamin L.C. Wailes, assistant professor of geology at the University of Mississippi, who made a journey through the area in the late summer of 1852 conducting research for his agricultural and geological survey of the state. Leaving the Ford House near the 31st parallel on Friday, August 13, Wailes drove his carriage through Hobolochitto to the Hancock County seat of Gainesville in two days. Continuing on this Gainesville Trace through Napoleon to Pearlington, he turned west to Shieldsboro. There, to avoid the arduous two-day circuit of the Bay of St. Louis, he loaded his carriage aboard a mail steamer and crossed over to Pass Christian.

Two roads led out of this town. The Red Creek Road ran northward following the ridge dividing the Wolf from the Red Creek-Biloxi River system. An early farm-to-market trace, the Red Creek Road brought in produce from as far north as Black Creek for sale in the Pass Christian farmer's market. Today its lower reach is called Menge Avenue.

The other road, named for the town, had begun as an Indian path following the first coastal terrace inland from Mississippi Sound. This Pass Christian Road traversed Harrison County all the way to Biloxi, a distance of 25 miles. The earliest official road of the county, Pass Road, still exists by that name and a variety of others along various sections of its course pass through the modern cities of the coast.

Wailes traveled east on Pass Road to Biloxi. After spending several days there, Wailes doubled back to Handsboro and turned right on the Augusta Road, the coast panhandle's main north-south artery, still preserved in its lower course as Lorraine Road. He made overnight stops at the Saucier farm—five miles east of the present town—and at Flint Creek Post Office before leaving the region west of Augusta, seat of Perry County and site of the area's

On the eve of his execution, James Copeland wrote a letter to his mother, laying the blame for his life of crime and violence on her. Pictured is an illustration of his 1857 hanging. From J.R.S. Pitts, Life and Confessions of James Copeland, *1909*

federal land office, 10 miles above the 31st parallel.

On his tour of the Mississippi Panhandle, Wailes noted few ferries or bridges, and settlement was so sparse that houses often stood 10 miles apart. Since another hundred tortured miles separated Augusta from the state capital, few people used the Augusta Road as a highway.

The piney woods remained a barrier for a reason other than unimproved roads and paucity of habitation. An antebellum Dixie Mafia known as the Copeland Gang used the area as a base of operations. James Copeland began his notorious career in 1835 at age 14 by stealing pigs and then burning Jackson County Courthouse to squelch the indictment. Four years later his gang burned and pillaged downtown Mobile. In the 1840s this mob engaged in far-flung enterprises, including slave stealing, cattle rustling, and murder, culminating in a gangland shoot-out on Red Creek. That action led to Copeland's arrest in 1849 and his abrupt departure from this life by hanging at Augusta in 1857, but the legend remained and so did many of the gang members.

Sisters of the Order of St. Joseph stroll on the grounds of St. Joseph's Academy for Young Ladies. The boarding academy was founded in 1855 in Bay St. Louis and operated until 1964. It reopened in 1971 as Our Lady's Academy for junior and senior high school girls in consortium with St. Stanislaus College for boys. MDAH

among townsfolk and guests. The conservatives, having presided over the 15-year evolution of Shieldsboro from village to town, fully expected the citizenry to buy another round, but:

Their opponents, on the contrary, entered earnestly into a fight, and determined to oust a clique, whom they accuse of having neglected the interest of their constituents for their own benefit, and imposed exorbitant taxes for objects quite distant from the improvement of the place—the roads, which have the first call upon their attention, being neglected to such an extent that they are fast becoming impassable, and exposing the place to premature abandonment and ruin.

To the amazement of the inhabitants, the outs went in with cheers three times three, and an impromptu fife-and-drum parade, spirited in every sense, advertised the victory until an advanced hour of the night.

In 1858 the Board of Aldermen completed the paving of the beach road with shells, and lots sold at a brisk rate as property values climbed. That same year the city fathers adopted a new charter of incorporation to replace the first one adopted in 1838. The estimated permanent population of the thriving little town stood at 400 in 1860.

Antebellum Pass Christian was not a town that possessed a hotel but rather a hotel that possessed a town. The opening of the Pass Christian Hotel circa 1836 put the village on the map, and two years later the state legislature granted Pass Christian a charter of incorporation. At its zenith this hotel became the epitome of the term "watering place." During the pre-Civil War period few coast hotels equaled, none surpassed, and all mimicked it. On May 18, 1838, an announcement for the opening of the Pass Christian Hotel for that year's season appeared in the *New Orleans Daily Picayune:*

This Establishment will be opened by the subscribers on the first day of June next [1838].

A wharf has been erected directly in front of the hotel sufficiently wide for Carriages to be landed with facility.

The West wing of the Hotel has been finished and considerable improvements have been made in various ways to render this not only the largest but one of the most desirable watering places on the Lake.

The certainty of a passage to and from the city every day, the opportunity of getting over regular supplies of ice and marketing from town, are advantages not available to any other establishment on the Lake.

Regular fishermen have been hired who will draw the seine before the hotel every morning, and oysters will be constantly supplied.

The Bar, which is detached from the house, will be furnished with the best of Wines and Liquors.

The west wing will be exclusively appropriated to families. Attentive servants have been engaged, and every attention will be paid to the convenience and comfort of visitors.

Those wishing to engage rooms will please apply at the Bar of the St. Charles Exchange Hotel.

In the *New Orleans Commercial Bulletin* article announcing the opening of the 1838 summer season, the reporter described the Pass Christian Hotel

The Pass Christian Hotel building added a dome circa 1866, after it had become Christian Brothers College. Yellow fever practically wiped out both students and faculty during the epidemic of 1867. The structure was destroyed in a fire in 1877. Courtesy, Dottie Cooper

as "one of the best situated and best appointed houses in Louisiana" being "delightfully situated on Lake Pontchartrain." It seems that many New Orleanians considered the Gulf Coast to be part of their state and Mississippi Sound to be a mere extension of Lake Pontchartrain. Furthermore, the New Orleans newspapers reflected the interests of the city fathers in developing the villages of the Gulf Coast as summer places for the elite of the city. In a public notice for the June 1838 auction of Pass Christian beach cottages and lots, the *Commercial Bulletin* boosted the sale and concluded, "We feel some interest in those sales for we are glad to see our citizens building country seats in our individual neighborhoods sooner than absent themselves by going North."

Throughout the antebellum period the Fourth of July was the liveliest and most festive holiday of the year on the Gulf Coast. In 1838 the Pass Christian mayor and Board of Selectmen met at the hotel in convocation with the guests and numerous inhabitants of the town to celebrate the "Glorious Fourth." Thirteen toasts were proffered, each accompanied by a song sung to screeching fiddle and twanging Jew's harp. Among the toasts, "washed down by bountiful libations of potent drinks, suited to the occasion and cooled with ice," was a song dedicated to abolitionists entitled "Your way is dark and leads to death, why will ye persevere?" The white celebrants sang the pro-slavery ballad while black residents reportedly watched through the windows. Following the 13th toast a few celebrants, unable to navigate home,

ANTEBELLUM ECONOMICS AND POPULATION

Between 1830 and 1860 the population of Mobile leapt from 3,000 to 30,000. In that same period New Orleans rocketed from 50,000 to 168,000 to become the largest city in the South and fourth largest in the nation. Contemporaneously, the population of the Mississippi Gulf Coast Panhandle grew to 12,000. But these figures alone ignore the seasonal nature of habitation in all three entities.

Every summer affluent citizens exchanged the heat, dust, insects, and open sewers of New Orleans and Mobile for resorts near and far. Even in normal times the cities lost a quarter of their inhabitants, but in yellow fever years eyewitnesses often described them as ghost towns. Beginning about 1836 the coast attracted an increasing number of these seasonal visitors. After 1840 the populations of the Six Sisters doubled or even tripled in normal summers and swelled to bursting at the first appearance of yellow jack.

The population figures are skewed still further by a situation that prevails to this day. Many wealthy families who built palatial permanent residences on the coast held what amounted to a dual citizenship not recorded by census takers. Furthermore, by the late 1840s, rapid, reliable, and increasingly inexpensive steamboat connections between New Orleans and the near resorts of Shieldsboro and Pass Christian permitted year-round commuter service, which proved particularly advantageous for those able to compress the work week and extend the weekends. Those same improvements in transportation allowed the less leisurely thousands in the flanking cities to enjoy an occasional holiday at the beach.

New Orleans always had a far greater impact upon every aspect of coastal life than did Mobile simply

Some good-natured haggling seems to be going on in this print Mississippi Coast Peddler. *Transportation was mainly by boat in the 1850s, so peddlers went from pier to pier along the coast selling their wares. From the Antique Print Collection, BPL*

because of the size differential. Even in 1860 the population of New Orleans remained more than five times that of Mobile. Essentially the cities were much alike, with Mobile playing New Orleans' role on a smaller stage. The Mississippi bore a trade of continental proportions, while the Alabama River served a far smaller hinterland. King Cotton reigned in both and, in the words of a wag, both were cities

where the people live in cotton houses and ride in cotton carriages. They buy cotton, think cotton, and dream cotton. They marry cotton wives and unto them are born cotton children.

Cotton culture contributed very little directly to the economy of the Mississippi Gulf Coast. Only a few rather small plantations existed in the creek bottoms and in the deltas

of the Pearl and Pascagoula. All told, probably a million bales of the white gold produced in the headwaters of those two rivers cleared the tiny ports of Pearlington and Pascagoula during the entire antebellum half-century. New Orleans and Mobile together often cleared more than that in a single season, but that is precisely the point. The coastal economy, dependent as it was upon those two cities, rested ultimately upon a base of cotton. Cotton money paid for the champagne at Montgomery's Pass Christian Hotel, bought Gainesville's lumber, commissioned Handsboro's wrought iron, and built the cotton villas all along the coast.

Cotton, of course, meant slaves, and both cities had plenty of those. The black population of Mobile stood at 8,404 in 1860. Since only 817 were free, slaves accounted for a quarter of the city's inhabitants. The black population of New Orleans that year amounted to 25,000, but 14,000 were free, leaving a surprisingly small six percent of the city in bondage. However, neither the numbers nor the percentages of slaves in the two cities mean much in themselves, since both cities served primarily as ports for upriver areas containing huge slave plantations. Thus, the economic life of New Orleans and Mobile remained firmly rooted in the South's "peculiar institution," an integral feature of the region's culture from early colonial times.

The aggregate estimated population of the three counties stood at 12,000 in 1860. Harrison's was the largest with nearly 5,000 and Hancock the smallest with just over 3,000. Since each county estimated 1,000 slaves, Hancock rated the highest percentage, Harrison the lowest, and Jackson fell in between them at 25 percent. Harrison reported 53 free blacks, Jackson reported 80, and Hancock simply failed to report, although it had some.

All three coast counties came in well under the 55-percent statewide slave average because they produced so little cotton. Hancock, which produced the most, had the largest percentage. J.F.H. Claiborne's Laurel Hill Plantation, probably the coast's largest single producer, located near the mouth of the Pearl, worked about 100 slaves.

Slaves did work in the mills, boat yards, and hotels, but few coast families owned slaves, and those that did seldom had more than three or four. George Kendall, the largest slaveholder in Harrison County and perhaps of the entire coast, employed 151 slaves (116 men and 35 women) in his Back Bay Biloxi brickworks in 1850. In the timber industry whites generally cut and delivered the logs, while slaves did the heavy work in the mills.

After 1850 hotel keepers increasingly replaced slaves with cheap immigrant labor, particular the Irish, who entered through the port of New Orleans. Moreover, by that time, many of the grand hotels of the coast were being leased by hotel corporations in New Orleans that closed their doors at the end of

Laurel Hill—the home of J.F.H. Claiborne built about 1800 of timber hewn on the site and bricks made by slave labor—stood derelict for many years until it finally was demolished. From Nola Nance Oliver, The Gulf Coast of Mississippi, *1941*

winter and moved their entire staffs to the coast for the summer season.

tacked to the beach, and "midnight found some of them reclining quietly in the sand."

By the opening of the 1839 season a number of additional buildings had been added to the hotel complex. Among these were a dining room, ballroom, billiard room, a nine-pin alley, stables, and bathing houses. Accommodations existed in the hotel proper for 50 families and the "texas" in the rear of the property could bunk 300 single men. The term "texas" as an appellation for this 300-foot-long, two-story, barracks-like bachelor's quarters stemmed from a wag's remark drawing upon the reputation of the Lone Star Republic as a haven for hard-drinking desperadoes addicted to all-night card games and general loudness and scuffling. In time all the watering places built texases.

The prices for that year were (and these were general in first-class watering places) board, including lodging, $2 per day and $50 per month; and horse, $1.50 per day and $30 per month. Children and servants paid half the stated price. These prices remained more or less constant throughout the antebellum period.

By 1845 laudatory guests were calling the Pass Christian Hotel the "Saratoga of the South." That summer two companies of the Seventh U.S. Infantry Regiment, awaiting orders to join the attack on Mexico, encamped near the hotel. The guests attended morning and evening parades, and the excellent army band played for the hotel soiree every Monday night until the men sailed off to war in mid-August.

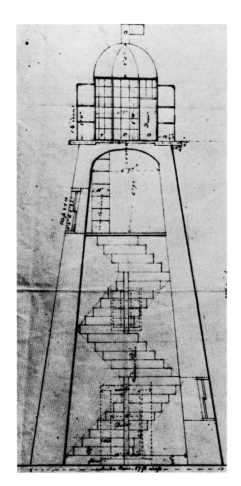

In 1831 the government began erecting "traffic lights of the sea" along the New Orleans-to-Mobile run. The first two, built that year and probably identical, were stubby, 30-foot towers of white-painted brick, whose lanterns cast rays for 14 miles. One stood on Cat Island and the other in the center of the village of Pass Christian. Together they marked the strait which lent its name to the town. Shown here is the plan of the Pass Christian Lighthouse. Courtesy, United States Coast Guard

R.H. Montgomery took over as manager of the hotel at the opening of the 1847 season. Conscious of his position as the prince of innkeepers charged with the stewardship of the largest and finest watering place, he spared no effort to improve his domain and reputation. During his eight-year tenure the Pass Christian Hotel reached its zenith and became known simply as "Montgomery's."

On a hot August Saturday night in 1848, one New Orleans visitor to this establishment, carpetbag in hand, hailed a public carriage on the corner of Canal and St. Charles for a drive to the glorified horse shed called a depot by the Pontchartrain Railroad Company. There he boarded a car with rock-hard seats to be ricketed and jolted five miles to Milneburg by a "one thousand mosquito power" locomotive. Jostling through the hot, dusty crowd at the lakefront, he secured passage on a Mobile-bound steamboat for the 60-mile voyage to Pass Christian. After five hours the puffing steamer, packed with men, followed the rays of the lighthouse seeking the long wharf in the darkness. The intrepid traveler fell to the rear as the arriving men crowded near the gangplanks to glimpse the women who came to meet them:

Such a collection of white and colored bonnets! Such a waving of delicately perfumed cambric! ... Husbands, brothers, and lovers for the past week have been in the tiresome, heated city, and Saturday night at Pass Christian (as in the sailor's legend and the olden farce) is a blessed night for sweethearts and wives.

The lines were thrown and the scattering commenced. Our correspondent followed the donkey cart laden with luggage across the slippery planks of the pier and clambered up the steep hill of ankle-deep sand, picking his way by the glimmering of the lighthouse to "Montgomery's."

The hotel buildings are drawn for your approach in true Military style— forming a hollow square, with a reserve of apartments attached that stretch out in solid lines—and look out with formidable aspect over the waters ... towards Ship Island, which, in the hazy distance, impertinently obstructs a gulf view for levelled telescopes, and keeps off any matter of surf that seaward gales might beget. The buildings are formed of a numerous collection of doors, windows, and piazzas.

At "Montgomery's," from early June until late October, there is eating and drinking; bowling and flirting; billiards and snoozing; gossip and toilette; driving and novel readings; sailing and yawning; bathing and mosquito scratching; dancing and music. ... boat excursions, lovely storms, snow-capped billows, boats capsized, bold swimming, sharks pursuing.

If all this failed to hold ennui at bay, one could join a hunting party into the pine barrens of the interior, blaze away in the pistol galleries, or engage in an "uninterrupted bombardment" of balls, soirees, and serenades.

The Pass Christian Hotel closed its 1848 season with the greatest social event in its history—a reception for General Zachary Taylor, hero of the Mexican War. The steamer *Oregon* departed Pascagoula with the general aboard, arriving off Pass Christian at 8:30 p.m. on Monday, September 11. In response to a salute rocket arcing into the heavens from the steamboat, three batteries of New Orleans' famed Washington Artillery placed at strategic points near Pass Christian boomed a greeting. Simultaneously, torchmen ignited huge bonfires lining the coast for a distance of seven miles. In the words of an eyewitness, "The light in the old lighthouse was completely eclipsed, and the moon, floating in the clear blue ether, paled as she looked down upon the glaring fires."

The *crème de la crème* of New Orleans, Mobile, Natchez, and all the towns of the Gulf Coast attended the Wednesday evening grand ball prepared by Montgomery for the distinguished guest. A gold medal authorized by Congress and sent to Pass Christian for the occasion was presented to the general, and the guests danced in the light of 3,000 lamps until 3 a.m.

On Saturday thousands attended the public barbeque given by the town in honor of "Old Rough and Ready." The general and his staff officers sat under a canopy of flags at a table atop an Indian mound in the live oak grove near the hotel. Following an address by John Henderson, nationally known lawyer and developer of the point of land that now bears his name, the feasting and dancing commenced on the sawdust apron laid around the mound. Less than two months later the people of the United States elected Taylor as their 12th president.

The 1849 season kicked off at the hotel with a most embarrassing incident. One of Montgomery's Irish waiters stabbed another one to death with a bread knife in the dining room. The fatal affair ended with the culprit being delivered to the proper authorities.

On July 11, 1849, Montgomery placed an advertisement in the *New Orleans Daily Picayune* destined to affect the entire Gulf Coast to the present day. He announced a sailboat race for 10 a.m., Saturday, July 21, to be held in conjunction with the formation of a sailing club. The prize was to be a $75 silver pitcher donated by himself. A dozen sleek craft representing almost as many towns and cities held their prescribed position at the appointed hour. At 10:15 a cannon's roar and the cheers of hundreds of spectators sent them off on a triangular course of 25 miles. Despite a gale that capsized some of the yachts, the *Flirt* of Biloxi crossed the finish line at 2:45 to capture the prize. The *Anna* of Pass Christian crossed nine minutes later, and the *Eliza Riddle* of New Orleans finished at 3 p.m. sharp.

The *New Orleans Crescent* hailed the race as a *tour de force*.

It was a novel experiment, but it was decidedly a successful one. Who had ever heard of a thing of the kind in the waters of the Gulf? The only thing curious about it now is that it never had been suggested before, for a more beautiful sheet of water for the handling of boats, or a finer location to view the sport could not be found on our coast from the Aroostook to the Rio Grande.

And the *Daily Picayune* asserted: "A new era in our sports has suddenly arrived and too much praise cannot be given to those gentlemen who have done so much to bring about a consummation so desirable."

The evening of the race the boating enthusiasts met in the hotel and formally organized the Southern Regatta Club, electing James W. Behan of Pass Christian as president. The organization subsequently changed its name to the Pass Christian Yacht Club, the name it still bears. The PCYC today holds the distinction of being the second oldest in North America, the New

LAKE SHORE PACKET, Steamer CREOLE—Winter arrangement, for New Orleans and all intermediate places—the splendid Low Pressure Packet Steamer CREOLE, Reuben Post, master, built expressly for the lake trade, with superior accommodations will leave Ocean Springs as follows:

OCEAN SPRINGS.	NEW ORLEANS.
Weds'day ev'n 5 P M	Tuesday ev'n 4 P M
Friday morning 5 A M	Thursday 9 A M
Sunday evening 5 P M	Saturday 4 P M

Passage. Cabin $3, Deck $1.25. Children and servants half price. The free list to all coast places is suspended. Jan 6th·1f

The Creole *served the Gulf Coast for nearly a quarter of a century. The Federals captured the steamboat at the outbreak of the Civil War, armed it, and rechristened it the* General Banks. *After the hostilities the boat assumed its original name and returned to packet service. This advertisement for the boat's service appeared circa 1850. Courtesy, C.E. Schmidt*

Ossian Hall, erected in 1849 by Seth Guion, later became known as the Miltenberger place. This "Greek Palace on the Gulf" burned in the 1950s. Courtesy, Chauncey Hinman

York Yacht Club having preceded it by a mere five years.

In the second regatta on August 6, twenty-two craft contended for three silver pitchers designated in descending order by value. The town filled to bursting for the race, which saw the *Undine* of Mobile place first. The judges disqualified the second boat to cross the line because of an improper sail, so the *Eliza Riddle* of New Orleans took second and the *Coralie* of Biloxi third.

The racing craze spread quickly to all the towns and cities of the Gulf Coast. Every summer thereafter throughout the balance of the antebellum period, yacht racing was an integral part of sporting life.

Not content with birthing one sport that summer, Montgomery inaugurated pistol matches in his shooting gallery with a silver cup as the prize. The aptly named Cuthbert Bullitt of New Orleans won the initial goblet, which he promptly baptized in the hotel bar. The hotel record, though, belonged to Colonel F.A. Lumsden, who twice placed six shots at 11 paces in a pattern measuring 5/16 of an inch. The pistol matches spread as far and wide as yacht racing and were often held in conjunction with it.

Women who summered at the Pass, circumscribed as they were by the Victorian strictures of the age, had little choice but to drift into the "Lydia Languish" life-style. Not even the idea of sunbathing existed, and the material of a single suit of women's bathing attire could make the stock of today's string bikini vendor for a month. In the words of Eliza Ripley, who spent many an antebellum summer at the Pass, "We walked the pier to the bath-houses in muslin dresses. Bathing suits were hideous, unsightly garments, high neck, long sleeves, long skirts, intended for water only." Riding, picnicking, boating, and shooting provided the main daytime activities for women, and many displayed deadly accuracy in Montgomery's pistol gallery.

In 1850 a mile of summer homes and magnificent villas flanked the Pass

Christian Hotel on either side. The hotel served as the nucleus of the settlement containing the post office, amusement arcade, business exchange, grocery, two-doctor clinic, and apothecary shop. Northwest of the hotel in a grove of live oaks stood year-old Trinity Episcopal Church. Many families who owned summer homes in the Pass signalized their dual citizenship by burying their dead in its cemetery.

Although essentially Protestant in character, the Pass counted a Catholic population sufficient to lay a cornerstone for a church in August. This church, to be constructed of brick, faced the sea three blocks down from Montgomery's or two blocks down from the San Souci, a rival hotel that opened in the summer of 1850. Preachers of other denominations were in-

Below: Michael Cuddy, 42 years of age when he met his opponent on the dueling field, is buried in the Live Oak Cemetery at Pass Christian. His grave is marked with a broken column, symbolizing a life tragically and prematurely ended. Photo by Charles Sullivan

vited to use the town hall for their services.

By 1853 Montgomery's remained open year round and entertained patrons from all sections of the country. The band played every night except Sunday, and apparently with gusto:

In the corner of the room, rather conspicuous, was ensconced four or five moustachioed musicians, at the head of which, one more ferocious moustachioed than the others, set violently gesticulating with his fiddle bow, whipping the rebellious air for not breathing melliferous sounds, while his men were blowing out their very brains.

But the celebratory pastimes of 1853 were marred by the arrival of "yellow jack." Exactly how many people died in the yellow fever epidemic that year in Pass Christian will never be known, but the numbers were considerable. The Trinity Church records specify 11, but there were many others, including

Above left: Dr. Thomas S. Savage, rector of Trinity Episcopal since its inception in 1849, established an academy and boarding school for young ladies. In 1857 Professor Ashbel Green established his Mississippi Military Institute. Thereafter "the Green boys and the Savage girls" figured prominently in the academic and social life of the community. Pictured is Trinity Episcopal Church circa 1849. Courtesy, Billy Bourdin

After Kentucky-born John Johnston McCaughan married Susan Tegarden, daughter of Dr. William H. Tegarden, in 1834, McCaughan, his father-in-law, and other promoters founded Mississippi City and Handsboro. McCaughan spoke forcefully, sometimes punctuating his remarks quite physically with his gold-headed cane. He died of Dengue fever in November 1860 aboard the steamer Matagorda and is buried in Berwick, Louisiana. Courtesy, John J. McCaughan, Jr.

the brother of Major (later General) P.G.T. Beauregard. In mid-September Montgomery finally admitted in the newspapers that guests at the hotel were dying, but he admitted to a total of only five victims and categorically denied that any of them had contracted the disease at the Pass.

In the words of a visitor in the summer of 1855, Montgomery possessed the courage and perseverence to "take Sebastopol," but apparently he could not take the September hurricane of that year. The Pass Christian Hotel, following extensive repairs, opened under new management the following season.

Shortly after dawn on Wednesday, May 21, 1856, Pass Christianians learned that all that target practice in the pistol gallery could have a serious side. Michael Cuddy, Esquire, a member of the firm of Cuddy, Brown & Company of Camp Street, considering himself offended regarding a "matter of business" by an equally prominent New Orleans merchant, E.W. Estlin, Esquire, of Estlin, Lee & Company, met his antagonist on the field of honor. Under the oaks behind the Pass Christian Hotel, at 10 paces, upon first fire Cuddy wounded Estlin in the right arm. Upon the second exchange Estlin's pistol ball entered Cuddy's groin on the right side, passed through the abdomen, severing two arteries, and lodged in his left hand. Cuddy preserved his honor at the price of his life.

Pass Christian underwent a building boom in the late 1850s, and by the end of the decade one observer described it as an "embryo city." According to another, "The life which formerly stagnated in the vicinity of the Hotel and wharf is now distributed for many miles on either side." A road paved with sawdust and shells extended east from Henderson Point for a distance of four miles. Beautiful cottages and villas lined the drive for its entire length, and more were under construction. The central business district east of the hotel contained a number of shops, among them a hardware store, a drugstore, a bakery, a combination billiard hall/cafe, and a tavern. Many shopkeepers and particularly the tavern owners still groused about the 1855 ordinance passed by the Board of Selectmen forbidding the sale of liquor or the operation of any business except the farmer's market on Sundays.

Sunday evenings were a special time for the black residents of Pass Christian. Dressed in their best clothes, "they turn out in great numbers for Sunday evening devotion, and that over, they crowd the sidewalk," said one observer.

Soon after his arrival Dr. Thomas S. Savage, rector of Trinity Episcopal since its inception, established an Academy and Boarding School for Young Ladies. In 1857 Professor Ashbel Green established his Mississippi Military Institute. Thereafter "the Green Boys and the Savage girls" figured prominently in the academic and social life of the community.

Because the post-Montgomery manager of the hotel belonged to one of the New Orleans units, militia companies from New Orleans and Mobile particularly favored Pass Christian as the site for their Fourth of July celebrations. In the 1859 celebration the Washington Artillery and the Continental Guards of the Crescent City met the Alabama State Artillery at the Pass for a stupendous display of cannonade and musketry. The artillerists fired at a 10-foot-square canvas located 600 yards offshore, while the riflemen set up a range in the woods behind the hotel. In the latter contest the Louisianans bested the Alabama shooters by one shot to claim the prize—a silver inlaid musket that had been carried by the original owner to his death in a

Mexican War battle.

On the eve of a much more terrible conflict, *The Southern Monitor*, published every Saturday morning in the growing town of 2,000, declared itself "bound to no theory or party, but seeking the highest good of all; advocating whatever tends to promote the intellectual, physical and moral good of man, but exposing evils and their causes."

In 1837 three promoters, John J. McCaughan, James McLauren, and Colin McRae formed the Mississippi City Company. On May 11 the state legislature authorized the company to sell lots, issue stock, and build roads and wharves. Simultaneously, the solons granted a charter of incorporation to nonexistent Mississippi City, making it the oldest official town on the coast.

The embryo metropolis, envisioned as a rival to New Orleans, was to be the southern terminus of the proposed Gulf & Ship Island Railroad, which would deliver the resources of the virgin pine forest to the Gulf Shore for dispersal to the world via Ship Island harbor. The optimistic view of the promoters was that Mississippi City would be

Postmaster and storekeeper Steven W. Callen (bottom) and his wife Ann (below left) ran the general store and post office at Mississippi City during the 1870s. The building (below) was located on Railroad Street. Courtesy, M. James Stevens

the sea-beaten rock on which the eagle of Mississippi shall whet his talons, and from which he shall dart his keen eyes over the waters of the dark blue sea, the home of the storm—but also the highway of national glory and individual wealth.

The New Orleans newspapers maintained a thunderous silence regarding the proposed establishment of their city's rival until January 9, 1838, when the *Daily Picayune* quoted a Mississippi state legislator as stating that the new port would free Mississippi "from an odious vassalage to New Orleans." That put a tin hat on New Orleanians who for years afterward delighted in pointing out from passing steamboats that "great invisible town destined to eclipse our own Crescent City."

The Mississippi City eagle never broke out of its shell because of the financial chaos engendered by the national monetary panic and depression of 1837-1839, which destroyed all chances for a railroad. In the words of

McCaughan, treasurer for the enterprise, "The whole project was a total failure and abandoned by all parties interested so far as building a City was concerned."

Still McCaughan and the others, determined to salvage what they could, used their remaining clout in the legislature to create a new county in February 1841. Named for William Henry Harrison, hero of the Battle of Tippecanoe and soon to be President of the United States, the boundaries of the new political unit ran from the head of the bays of St. Louis and Biloxi to the 31st parallel. Most of the territory thus encompassed had been a part of Hancock, but small areas formerly in Jackson were also included. Most notably the geometric line entering the head of Biloxi Bay was made to follow the channel of the bay out to sea, thus including Deer Island and the village of Biloxi in the new county. Mississippi City, more centrally located than the flanking towns of Biloxi and Pass Christian, became the county seat, and a log courthouse stood at the foot of the Courthouse Road before the end of the year.

In the same year McCaughan, in his capacity as a state senator, entered Mississippi City as a site in the race for the proposed University of Mississippi. When he lost by one vote to Oxford, the 280-pound, fiery Scotch-Irishman used a different kind of clout—his gold-headed cane over the skull of an opposing voter. Loose talk concerning the secession of the coast counties from Mississippi in favor of a union with Louisiana followed but came to nothing.

Mississippi City failed as a seaport, but it did become a watering place. As

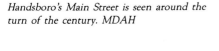
Handsboro's Main Street is seen around the turn of the century. MDAH

early as 1842 the Mississippi City Hotel advertised for boarders in the New Orleans papers. By 1850 advertisements appeared for Dr. William Tegarden's Hotel. Tegarden, father-in-law of McCaughan, located his hostelry at the foot of the thoroughfare that now bears his name and built an 800-yard wharf out into the Sound. When the government declined to honor his request for a lighthouse, he erected a private one on the shore to guide steamboats to the landing.

In a letter penned from Tegarden's, a *New Orleans Daily Delta* reporter wrote in 1851:

Above: A good woodcutter wielding a five-pound single-bit ax could fell 10 to 15 giant yellow pines per day (earning 10 cents apiece for his labor). The woodcutter would then deliver logs by caralog to the mills where slaves, working dawn to dark, processed them. Usan Vaughan, a remarkable slave belonging to Nezan Favre of Pearlington, invented a large, wide-tread wheel for caralogs that revolutionized the delivery of logs across marshlands. Pictured is an example of Vaughan's caralog system. Courtesy, Mrs. Truman Flurry

Left: In 1848 the brothers Miles and Sheldon Hand built identical homes just east of Cowan Road on the north side of Bayou Bernard. Of the two, this is the only surviving Hand home, currently owned and preserved by Margaret Kremer Bond. Courtesy, Margaret Kremer Bond

I will say this much for old man Tegarden, that the Western continent affords no finer bathing spot than his. Why, there is not a pebble or so much as a shell, on the clear, sandy bottom. The old fellow, though, must repair the steps that conduct to the water from the gentlemen's bathing house, as an obese friend of mine came near breaking his neck in making the descent.

In 1855 another long wharf projected into the Sound from the foot of

Texas Street, site of the newly completed William Barnes Hotel, a block west of the courthouse. The hurricane of September 15-16 destroyed both wharves and collapsed Tegarden's "texas," killing two and injuring seven. Undeterred, both proprietors repaired the damage.

In July 1857 a guest at the Barnes Hotel met ex-Secretary of War and then United States Senator Jefferson Davis. "He has," said the guest, "the eye of an eagle with the mildness of a lamb in his countenance. . . . He may well be regarded as a leader of the forlorn hope in the approaching struggle with the fanatics and Black Republicans of the North, and which is fast approaching the crisis."

The same correspondent pointed out the symbiotic relationship that existed between Mississippi City and the "flourishing manufacturing and business village" of Handsboro, "where are several of the best stores I have ever seen in a country town of such recent origin." Horse-drawn omnibuses daily plied sawdust-paved Courthouse and Tegarden roads, providing easy access between the two towns.

Originally called Buena Vista, the village was renamed Handsboro in the mid-1850s in recognition of the contributions of Miles and Sheldon Hand. These brothers, experienced metallurgists and machinists, removed from New York to Buena Vista circa 1846 in response to a trade journal advertisement placed by John J. McCaughan. Selecting a site on the north shore of Bayou Bernard, the Hands unloaded three prefabricated sawmills and all the materials necessary for the establishment of a foundry and a machine shop, including the technicians to man them. One of these, James N. Bradford, later set up his own foundry. Another, Jacob Knight, became a gunpowder manufacturer.

Handsboro's steam-powered mills, brickworks, and foundries forged the town's reputation as the "Antebellum Industrial Heart of the Gulf Coast." Steam engines produced there ran the saws in nearly a score of local lumber mills and those of the lower Pearl, Pascagoula-Moss Point, and elsewhere. The McBean boat yard produced schooners and steamboats to transport the coast's output of construction materials, naval stores, and household fuel (charcoal) to New Orleans and Mobile and to other points all along the Gulf rim.

The town even partially fulfilled the dreams of international trade envisioned by the Mississippi City Company. In 1852 the state legislature moved the customshouse from Shieldsboro to Biloxi to better serve foreign ships anchored in Ship Island roadstead awaiting literage of cargoes from the Back Bay Mills.

Handsboro's location near the mouth of Bayou Bernard at the extreme west end of Back Bay Biloxi enabled the lumbermen to exploit the timber resources of the Biloxi-Tchoutacabouffa River basin. Unfortunately, by the end of the antebellum period the Handsboro Mills had virtually exhausted the prime timber standing within the three-mile economic strike zone of a caralog throughout its water transport system.

In addition to its sheltered maritime location, which protected it from hurricanes and allowed access to the open sea via the mouth of Biloxi Bay, Handsboro also served as the road hub of the coast. The Pass Christian Road bisected the town on an east-west axis, the Augusta Road bisected it north-south, and a spur of the Red Creek Road entered it from the northwest.

In addition to the mills, factories, and six large mercantile establishments

Masonic Lodge Number 154, built in Handsboro in 1852, served as a meetinghouse for people in the surrounding countryside. Schools and religious congregations used the lodge until they could construct their own buildings, and the grounds were the site of a farmers' market. This antebellum cultural center still stands on Pass Road today. Photo by Charles Sullivan and Murella Powell

that earned for it industrial-commercial preeminence, Handsboro also deserved its reputation as the cultural and religious center of the coast. By the close of the period, the town boasted two newspapers, several churches, a seminary, and a number of girls' and boys' schools. And, according to the Reverend Henry T. Lewis, Methodist minister and editor of the *Handsboro Weekly Reformer:*

It has the negative merit of not having now, nor never having had within its borders one of those pestilential evils ... a grogshop. Our wives and daughters ears are not shocked with the ribald roarings of rum maniacs, nor our children taught to look upon drunkenness as an error to be endured, instead of a crime, as it is, against the law of God and man!

The population of Handsboro on the eve of war numbered nearly 1,000. Many of those, certainly the town leaders, were Northern born and bred, but that they had become "Southernized" with amazing rapidity is revealed in a letter written by James V. Lee to his brother in Maine on December 14, 1856:

Dear Brother,
I suppose you think me dead again but thank God I never enjoyed better health .... There is a fine little village here—we have two foundries and five saw mills also an academy .... If you think it worth spending time... you can write and let me know who of the family yet lives if they are not abolitionists.

To the east of Handsboro, Biloxi held the distinction of being one of the oldest sites of continuous settlement on the Mississippi Gulf Coast at the

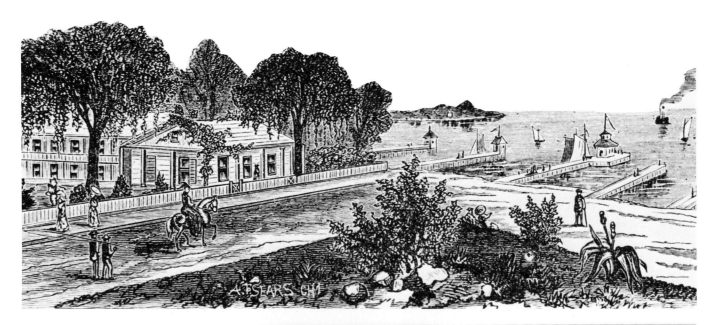

Above: An illustration of the resort village of Biloxi was published circa 1850. According to a description in the New Orleans Daily Delta, *"the town is right on the sea. There is no long beach to traverse before you can reach the sea." BPL*

Right: Saved by the City of Biloxi after it had stood derelict for years, the Magnolia Hotel is now restored and serves as an art gallery and museum. Established by John Hahn in 1847, it is the only surviving antebellum hotel building on the coast. Because of its location near the steamboat dock, the Magnolia was one of the most popular hotels. Courtesy, City of Biloxi

opening of the antebellum period, but since its brief reign as French colonial capital, its population had never exceeded more than a few score. The hurricane of August 25-28, 1819, dealt the village a severe blow, inundating it to a depth sufficient to loft a schooner completely over it into Back Bay and destroying a great deal of property and many lives in the process. In addition, the location of the village, near the midpoint of the arc of coastline connecting New Orleans and Mobile, retarded its growth until the late 1830s, when steamboats and navigational improvements made it more accessible. Chartered as a town on February 8, 1838, Biloxi rose rapidly to the fore as a watering place, to finish the period as the largest of the Six Sisters.

Biloxi entered the roll of watering places in the early 1840s. The New Orleans papers carried a card for the American Hotel in 1843, and thereafter

Founded in 1854 by Father Stanislaus Buteaux and operated by the teaching Brothers of the Sacred Heart, Stanislaus College (left) began as a boys' boarding school. Buteaux founded St. Joseph's Academy (below left), the girls' counterpart to St. Stanislaus, one year later. The Civil War, yellow fever epidemics, fires, and hurricanes have threatened the schools over the decades. Today the two schools, though separate, share some classes and activities and offer classes on the high-school and junior-college level. Courtesy, Tommy Wixon

many more advertisements for hotels, boardinghouses, and summer cottages appeared. Nixon's Hotel and Bachelor's Hall opened in 1845 followed by Pradat's Hotel and the Shady Grove Hotel the next year. By 1847 Biloxi had surpassed all the other seaside resorts, counting 600 permanent inhabitants with an average seasonal population more than double that number. Half a dozen hotels graced the beach that summer, including the newly completed Magnolia.

In the summer of 1848 the Biloxi Lighthouse began its role as the coast's most famous landmark. In that same summer the Biloxi Hotel, in obeisance to the town's French heritage, announced its first grand ball of the season for Bastille Day. A correspondent for the *New Orleans Daily Delta,* unable to attend the July 14 French gala, wrote, "We have seen some of the Biloxi girls dance—they wear no curls nor corsets, and throw their entire souls into their substantial heels."

The decade of the 1840s also marked a turning point in the religious life of the community. After more than a century of service by itinerant priests, in 1842 Biloxi received from Natchez a missionary with orders to establish a permanent parish and construct a church edifice. The Methodists organized in the same year as the Catholics, the Baptists in 1845, and the Episcopalians in 1849, but none of these Protestant denominations built structures before the Civil War.

The cornucopia of building materials pouring from the Biloxi Back Bay

YELLOW JACK

Iberville on his maiden voyage to the Gulf Coast called them "dreadful little beasts to men who need sleep." Later a Jesuit missionary set down an even more eloquent assessment of the mosquito: "Since the French have been on the Mississippi this little beast has caused more cursing than had been done in the rest of the world up to that time." One species of the "little beasts" did more than just annoy tired men, as the French in general and Iberville in particular sadly discovered.

An incubation period of several days' duration follows the bite of an infected *aedes aegypti* mosquito as the virus spreads throughout the body, attacking the liver in particular. Thereafter the symptoms appear in rapid succession—jaundice of the skin and eyes, rising fever,

Below: The aedes aegypti, *the only mosquito that carries yellow fever, breeds only in man-made containers—gutters, cement-contained ditches, and birdbaths, for example—but does not breed in marshes and ditches with walls of soil. Today, although the mosquito still exists, the disease is under control. An intensive mosquito control program has been in effect on the Gulf Coast since 1964. Courtesy, Gulf Coast Mosquito Control Commission*

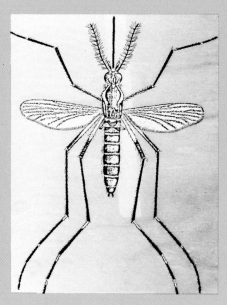

Above: A Frank Leslie's Illustrated Newspaper *illustration called "An Incident of the Shotgun Quarantine in Mississippi" shows yellow-fever refugees slipping by the guards at the quarantine station. BPL*

nausea, internal hemorrhaging resulting in the vomiting of black blood—often followed by death. This disease known variously as the "saffron scourge," "bronze john," "black vomit," and "yellow jack," was more commonly called yellow fever.

From colonial times yellow jack appeared along the Gulf Coast coincidentally with the warm-weather arrival of ships from Caribbean ports. Laden with the sick and carrying *aedes aegypti* larvae in their water barrels, these biological time bombs detonated upon entry into New Orleans and Mobile. Infected mosquitoes flew from their decks into the cities to spread the saffron scourge. For this reason strict quarantine of the plague-carrying

ships far away from the ports would have worked, but on the few occasions when zealous health officials attempted to impose such measures, commercial interests overruled them.

An astute doctor in Mobile as early as 1848 postulated a possible connection between mosquitoes and yellow fever, but most physicians continued to regard bronze john as a contagion produced by noxious air drifting in from miasmal swamps which spread from person to person. A New Orleans doctor disproved the contagion theory by immersing himself without ill effect in the putrid blood, black vomit, and effluvial matter issuing from the dead and dying. Ignoring the evidence, the populace of the coast cities and towns continued to battle the pestilence by firing cannons and burning tar barrels in the streets to dispel night vapors, and by fumigating clothing, furniture, and even letters by punching holes in them. Only the tar-burning accidentally helped by driving the real culprits away.

To the Mississippi Gulf Coast, yellow jack proved to be a blessing as well as a curse—a blessing when it filled the hotels at the watering places, a curse when the refugees brought the disease with them. A newspaper reporter wrote of Biloxi's 1851 season,

the town is not so well filled as last year, owing principally to the distressing healthy state of the city [New Orleans], an epidemic there being as much of a blessing to our sea-side resort as a ship wreck to Key West.

The reporter's sardonic humor revealed a great deal of truth: the "season" at the coast watering places extended from late May to early November, exactly paralleling the period of fever danger, which began with the inception of warm weather and ended with the first killing frost.

Fever-free years were rare, but mortality rates were usually low. Not so in 1853, when the worst epidemic on record earned New Orleans the epithet "Necropolis of the South." That year bronze john infected 30,000 and killed 10,000 of its inhabitants. In scenes resembling the Medieval Black Death, citizens responding to cries of "bring out your dead!" loaded bodies on wagons which trundled them to shallow graveyard trenches dug by chain gangs. The incessant summer rains repeatedly uncovered the cadavers, and the stench of rotting corpses hung over the city like a pall.

Persons fleeing the dying city spread the fever to every river port on the Mississippi and to all the towns on the Mississippi Gulf Coast. As the epidemic spread to the watering places, the hotel owners, motivated by the desire to avoid a general panic with its attendant loss of trade, placed advertisements in the New Orleans and Mobile papers denying its existence. The New Orleans papers were particularly willing to publish such ads since they, bowing to the city's political and entrepreneurial powers, declined to admit the presence of the disease in their city until July 24, by which time the death rate had reached 160 per day.

The yellow fever epidemic of 1853 became the yardstick by which all others were measured. The two other worst years were 1858 and 1878, but both of those epidemics together did not claim as many victims as did the 1853 visitation.

In a paper delivered in Havana in 1881, Dr. Carlos Finlay hypothesized that the mosquito was the carrier of the disease, but his thesis did not win acceptance until 1900, when the Walter Reed Army Medical Commission, conducting experiments in Cuba in the wake of the Spanish-American War, proved it to be true.

The last epidemic occurred in 1905. Thereafter, mosquito eradication programs snuffed out bronze john, ending New Orleans' reputation as "a great warehouse and a great cemetery," and freed the Mississippi Gulf Coast and the nation from the saffron scourge.

sawmills and brickworks in the decade of the 1850s sparked a building boom. In 1851 the Biloxi town corporation completed an eight-foot-wide plank sidewalk running the entire front of the downtown area. This promenade, unique on the coast, ended the annoyance of sandy shoes and resulted in an unrivaled daily parade of fashion. Another highlight of that season was the opening of the Jenny Lind Coffee House on Lameuse, which offered billiards by day and dancing at night. In August Nixon's Hotel hosted a Ladies Fair, the proceeds of which went to the building fund of the Catholic church. The ladies sold large amounts of gumbo, punch, and cake, while the fair-goers danced the waltz and other numbers "a trifle too Turkish" as the night progressed. The *Daily Delta's* correspondent regretted his inability to relate the ending of the festivities as his "last recollection" came "shortly after the witching time of night."

On June 29, 1853, a refugee from New Orleans, stricken with yellow jack, arrived in Biloxi. Commencing with the man's death five days later, Dr. Andreas Byrenheidt, a prominent Biloxi physician, kept careful accounts of what then happened. New cases appeared within two weeks. By late October he had recorded 533 cases and 111 deaths.

That summer the town's population swelled to 6,000, the highest ever, as New Orleans fell victim to bronze john's most terrible onslaught. In the midst of the epidemic, nature dealt Biloxi a novel blow. At 5 p.m. on Sunday, September 11, a severe earthquake shook trees and houses and created a great commotion in the waters. Then all was quiet.

On July 4, 1858, the steam packet *Virginia* advertised a patriotic excursion to Ship Island to view progress on the installation "for which purpose $100,000 was appropriated one year ago by Congress." Not much could be seen, but the foundation was being laid for the long-proposed fort needed to

Washington Avenue in Ocean Springs has the same historic flavor today that it had when this photograph was taken in 1905. Some of the buildings pictured are still standing, and the same oak trees still form a canopy over the avenue. Courtesy, Tommy Wixon

guard the Ship Island anchorage.

In August 1858 a visitor said of Biloxi:

This is too much of a town to be very pleasant as a summer resort. About the wharf it has a perfect fish market—inhabited by a class of people who are anything but quiet. Nevertheless, it is a place of great resort.... The hotels are full nearly all the time. The fishing is good—and they know how to serve them up. Biloxi is universally celebrated as the place to get a good fish dinner. The roads are good in the immediate neighborhood of the town, and it is very shady. It is a great place for children. I have seen more here for the number of adults around than I ever saw at any other place.

Until 1851 the scattered settlement opposite Biloxi on the other side of the bay simply bore the name East Biloxi. But that year on the south bank of Fort Bayou a sawmill operator surnamed Lynch discovered springs, soon christened Lynchburg Springs. A sample of water sent to Dr. J. Lawrence Smith of the University of Louisiana in New Orleans yielded these findings:

The medicinal virtue of these waters is to be looked for more particularly in the oxide of iron and sulphurated hydrogen, both of which exist in notable quantities; and it is therefore apparent that many chronic diseases might be cured, or receive important alleviation from these waters. As a bath, it would be applied with much advantage.

By 1852 improvement at the site included bathing rooms with marble seats and a nearby boardinghouse for accommodations.

In June 1853, just in time for the season, Enoch Everitt hastily completed a new grand hotel in a "forest where the axe had not been heard for more than a century." Simultaneously, the government established the Lynchburg Springs post office, which shortly changed its name to that of the hotel—Ocean Springs.

The advertisements for the Ocean Springs Hotel offered all the advantages and inducements of other watering places with the added attraction of medicinal waters. Everitt built the hotel on the sea, leased the springs, and ran horse-drawn omnibuses between the two.

This "Lourdes of the South" boasted two principal springs—"one a chalybeate, the other sulphur." To one or the other or both, sufferers ascribed many miraculous cures. Everitt naturally collected and published these unsolicited testimonials with alacrity. One of these, obviously tongue-in-cheek, hailed the springs to be "the fabled waters sought for with so much diligence by Ponce de León." One satisfied customer who partook of the chalybeate elixir found himself "rejuvenated and refreshed by his stay."

The medicinal properties of the water are wonderful. Chronic cases of the most direful diseases have been speedily cured.... Among the most remarkable instances of cure were Scrofula, Dropsy, Hepatalgia, Paralysis and Rheumatism. These had eluded every specific for years, but soon yielded to the healing properties of the simple "spring."

Apparently the waters cured neuralgia, too, as an assault of that affliction felled Everitt himself for two months following his grand opening. By Au-

George Washington Andrews, a Biloxi carpenter working on Fort Massachusetts on Ship Island, laid down these tools in 1861 to join the Biloxi Rifles and fight the Yankees. Andrews was captured, returned to the island as a prisoner of war, and put back to work on the fort. The tools have remained in the Andrews family to the present day. Courtesy, the Dudley Andrews family

gust he was entirely recovered and doing battle with the New Orleans newspapers over the existence of yellow fever at his hotel. In September the disease did strike, but its duration was short and only a few died.

On September 10, 1853, the village's first newspaper, *The Ocean Springs Naiad,* in its premiere issue published a letter to the editor from a "John Smith" to beat all testimonials:

For several years, owing to having been run over on a railroad, my only medium of locomotion was a pair of wooden legs. About one month ago, I commenced taking the water of the springs; about a fortnight since my pedals began to extend, the feet to form, and now, thanks to the medicinal virtues of the springs, my understanding was never better.

CAPTAIN JOHN GRANT:
FATHER OF GULF COAST TRANSPORTATION

Above: Captain John Grant died in 1887, about 10 years after this photograph was taken. He is buried in Pascagoula, in the family cemetery on the site of his former home on Grant's Lake. Courtesy, Tommy Wixon

Above right: Captain John Grant maintained and collected tolls at Grant's Pass, a direct steamboat connection between the Mississippi Sound and Mobile Bay, until the packet trade was diminished by the railroad. MCM

In the antebellum period, water—both fresh and salt—served as the main avenue of commerce and travel. The coast had plenty of both in the form of rivers and lakes. In antebellum parlance the term "lakes" included Lake Pontchartrain, Lake Borgne, Mississippi Sound, and Mobile Bay. Hence advertisements in the New Orleans and Mobile papers for boats engaged in the lakes trade included stops at every village from Shieldsboro to Pascagoula. The steamboat, which first appeared in New Orleans in the opening years of the century, revolutionized area transportation by eventually establishing rapid connections between that city and Mobile.

The first regularly scheduled steamboat entered service on the New Orleans-to-Mobile run in 1827 carrying freight, passengers, and mail between the two cities, but the first voyages exposed three obstacles that rendered any regular schedule impossible to keep. In the first place, New Orleans needed to develop some type of rapid transit to move passengers five miles north through the swamps to the steamboat landing at Milneburg on Lake Pontchartrain. In the second place, the reefs between Dauphin Island and mainland Alabama blocked direct entry between Mississippi Sound and Mobile Bay. This situation forced boats into the open Gulf at Ship Island Pass and left them prey to sudden storms as they ran the gauntlet to the mouth of Mobile Bay. Thirdly, the shallow depth of Mobile Bay required 30 miles of lighterage for freight and passengers from the east end of Dauphin Island to the city proper. The man destined to solve all three of the problems, John Grant, who bore the honorary title "Captain," arrived on the Gulf Coast at the age of 36 to begin a

55-year career that would earn him the title "Father of Gulf Coast Transportation." As the inventor of the Baltimore Harbor Dredge, Grant was hired by the federal government to dredge Mobile Bay. Beginning work in 1827, Grant cut a channel from Dauphin Island to a point only five miles from the city, ending the costly and time-consuming lighterage problem and greatly enhancing Mobile's value as a port.

In 1829 the city of New Orleans called upon Grant to help build a railroad from downtown to the steamboat docks at Milneburg. Two years later he completed the Lake Pontchartrain Railway, probably the third line in the entire nation. After the first year of operation, a tiny steam locomotive replaced the horse-drawn cars. In 1839 Captain Grant cut a six-foot-deep pass through the Dauphin Island reefs,

providing a shorter and sheltered direct steamboat connection between Mississippi Sound and Mobile Bay. Grant's Pass halved the freight rates between New Orleans and Mobile, cut insurance costs by two-thirds, saved uncounted lives, and made the port of Pascagoula possible.

During his long career Captain Grant held what amounted to triple citizenship in Alabama, Mississippi, and Louisiana, and he served in the legislatures of all three. He owned houses in New Orleans, Mobile, and Pascagoula, but he put his roots down in the last, where he built the town's first church and made his home on the tidal lake that now bears his name. His son married a Krebs, and his daughter married a Delmas, uniting his family with two of the most prominent in town.

Below left: The steamboat New Orleans, *whose reconstructed plan is shown here, inaugurated steamboat service on the Mississippi River in 1812. Three years later in preparation for the Battle of New Orleans, the steamboat* Enterprise *was pressed into service, becoming the first steamboat used for warfare. By 1827 steamboats began the New Orleans to Mobile run. HNOC*

Bottom left: The first steam locomotive south of the Ohio River, "Smoky Mary" began service in 1832. For decades the tiny engine jolted passengers along the five-mile Pontchartrain Railroad from downtown New Orleans to the Milneburg steamboat docks for departure to the Mississippi Gulf Coast. HNOC

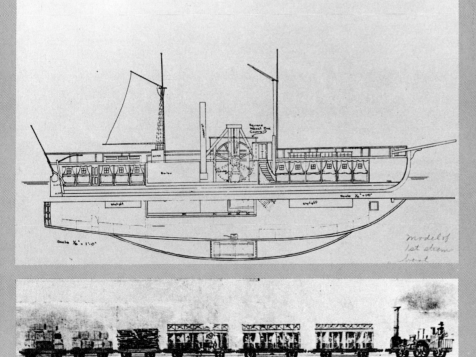

Above: John J. McRae, governor of Mississippi from 1854 to 1857, helped in the removal of Indians to the West. McRae represented Mississippi in the first congress of the Confederate States. He died in 1868 while on a visit to Belize, British Honduras. MDAH

Right: According to local legend, Henry Wadsworth Longfellow visited and wrote poetry at Pascagoula's famous "Longfellow House." Built in 1854 of native pine and cypress, the house, originally called "Bellvue," has been beautifully preserved and is now a restaurant and inn. MDAH

By 1855 the village had a principal street, Jackson, and in 1859 a guest at the hotel described Ocean Springs as a "quiet, respectable, and healthy watering place."

The key to the growth of the last Mississippi Gulf Coast watering place was the Pascagoula River. Born at the confluence of the Chickasawhay and the Leaf just south of the 31st parallel, the Pascagoula meanders southward 109 miles before dividing into two principal distributaries as it enters its estuarine delta. These two branches flow a farther 13 miles on either side of a marshy mesopotamia to debouch into Mississippi Sound three miles apart.

The colonial settlements on the firm, wooded slopes flanking the mouths of the twin rivers grew during the antebellum period into the villages of East Pascagoula and West Pascagoula, though often in the literature of the period the directional designations were dropped in favor of the single common appellation. Today the former is known as Pascagoula-Moss Point and the latter as Gautier.

In a letter dated July 13, 1813, a female relation of Governor W.C.C. Claiborne visited the area and described it thusly:

The village of Pascagoula is three miles in length and contains about twenty families, each family having a little farm. They are not ... wealthy ... but are independent ... and accommodating. The situation of this place is elegant, a most beautiful bay in view affording always a sea breeze and abounding in fish and oysters. We are plentifully supplied with butter, fish, fowls of various kinds, vegetables, melons, peaches, grapes, figs, and in fact, everything the heart could wish.

Pascagoula's birth as a watering place and as a port was principally the work of a Scottish family by the name of McRae. The patriarch of the clan, John J. McRae, removed in 1817 from North Carolina to Winchester, the head of navigation for riverboats on the Chickasawhay. Recognizing the importance of the Chickasawhay-Pascagoula system as a trade artery, McRae became the first to barge cotton downriver to the Gulf. By 1819 he set up a depot at West Pascagoula and seven years later established his permanent residence there. John's wife, Elizabeth, bore him four sons—Malcolm J., Colin J., John J., and James, all of whom made distinguished contributions to the growth of Pascagoula and the coast.

The McRae sons attended a school in East Pascagoula established in 1820 by Louis Fredric, a former engineer in the army of Napoleon Bonaparte decorated for valor in the Russian campaign. After the fall of Napoleon, Fredric had emigrated and married the daughter of Valentine Delmas. Together the two men, using Fredric's engineering ability, laid out the streets of the village of East Pascagoula in 1829, naming the two principal ones for themselves. In that same year Fredric became the community's first postmaster.

In 1836 the East Pascagoula House opened for the reception of visitors, advertising the usual surf bathing and seafood. Within a year a rivalry commenced with the opening of the West Pascagoula House, which advertised a capacity for 300 guests. On February 9, 1838, the state legislature granted a charter to East Pascagoula (also known as Krebsville), despite the small permanent population of only 20 families. In that same year Ebenezer Clark opened Jackson County's first shipyard six miles above Elder's Ferry (Moss Point) at the confluence of the Pascagoula and Clark Creek. But the greatest early boost to the local economy came in 1839 with the opening of Grant's Pass.

By 1842 John J. McRae was running a regular steamboat route from New Orleans up the Pascagoula, and his mother, then a widow, held sway over the West Pascagoula House. Two years later the family achieved a virtual monopoly on the area's hotel business when Malcolm J. purchased the East Pascagoula House.

On September 15, 1846, John J. wrote a letter to the United States Coast Survey Department offering for sale and giving details regarding one of the earliest—possibly even the first—steamboats constructed in Pascagoula:

There is a St. Boat now being completed at Pascagoula to be called the Pascagoula, *built expressly for the carrying trade between Mobile and N. Orleans.... She is built of the most superior materials—Live Oak and Cypress. Length 135 ft. Breadth of Beam 21 ft. 5-1/2 feet hold—draft of water 22 to 26 inches when light, and may be loaded to 5 ft. to run the coast in safety.*

This Boat is built under the superintendence of Mr. James F. Bradford at his landing in East Pascagoula, who is one of the oldest and leading citizens of Jackson County, and has been twenty years engaged in building vessels. Mr. Bradford is the principal owner, and I have myself one fourth interest in this vessel. She is launched about this time and will be ready for service the 15th of October.

General David Emanuel Twiggs built a "princely mansion" in East Pascagoula. An ardent secessionist, he disobeyed President Zachary Taylor's orders to evict the Round Islanders in 1849. In February 1861 while still in the Federal uniform, he would deliver 19 Federal army posts to Texas authorities before the state's secession. Twiggs would later command the Gulf Coast Confederate forces. HNOC

During the Mexican War (1846-1848) the War Department pressed into service as troop carriers a number of steamboats serving the coast, and selected Greenwood Island and an adjacent strip of the mainland two miles east of the East Pascagoula Hotel as a permanent military installation site. Camp Jefferson Davis under General David Twiggs was to serve as a combination troop encampment area and veterans' hospital. At war's end in July 1848 nearly 3,000 soldiers poured into the camp.

The McRaes lavishly entertained Twiggs, his staff, and war hero Zachary Taylor, but the accommodations for the other soldiers were less elegant. "The greasy food and the water is the worst I have ever seen used by people," wrote one soldier, who further stated that "the duties and hardships we encountered in Mexico were nothing to compare to what we are subject to here." Hundreds of the men died or deserted, and others volunteered for yellow fever duty in New Orleans rather than live in such a place. The dispatch of most of the troops from the camp to Missouri and California finally alleviated the problem.

In the summer of 1849 General Twiggs, newly appointed commander of the Western Division of the army, once again made the East Pascagoula Hotel his headquarters, and the installation on Greenwood Island was re-christened Camp Twiggs in his honor. In early August another army appeared on another island in Pascagoula Bay. A Colonel George White assembled 500 unarmed mercenaries, termed "filibusters" in the language of the time, on Round Island. These soldiers of fortune, many of them veterans of the late unpleasantries with Mexico, drawn by circulars promising land and plunder in exchange for a year of service, were part of the attempt by Cuban exiles to liberate Cuba from Spanish control.

On August 11 President Zachary Taylor issued a proclamation declaring the proposed invasion to be a violation of American neutrality laws and called upon all civil and military authorities to arrest and prosecute the offenders. General Twiggs responded swiftly and inexplicably. He ordered all coast troops in garrison from New Orleans to Pensacola, including those at Pascagoula, aboard steamboats and took them to Tampa Bay to fight the Seminoles.

The United States Navy responded more directly. Commander Victor Randolph, senior officer afloat in the Gulf of Mexico, anchored three warships off Round Island and issued a proclamation declaring martial law and a blockade of the island effective August 28 for the express purpose of starving the filibusters into submission.

By late August the events at Round Island had attracted national attention, illuminating the widening chasm between the North and the South. The New Orleans and Mobile papers viewed the blockade as a violation of the civil rights of an assembly of unarmed citizens and as a violation of states' rights in that U.S. warships had invaded the territorial waters of Mississippi to enforce an illegal federal order. The *Chicago Tribune,* on the other hand, supported the actions of the President and the navy, reflecting the Northern suspicion that the liberation of Cuba was a Southern conspiracy to chop up Cuba into a number of slave states, thus heading off the impending upset of the North-South balance of power in the Senate.

In the end both sides backed down. Randolph, feeling the fury of the New Orleans and Mobile press and now the target of threats of legal action by the State of Mississippi, lifted the blockade on September 5. Three weeks later, with the knowledge that Randolph would sink him on the high seas,

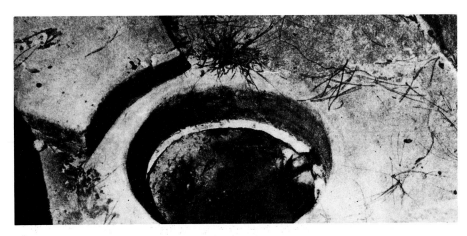

Colonel White ordered his men to disband and disperse. The navy, in the spirit of conciliation, then ferried the mercenaries to the mainland and even enlisted a few for a term of service.

The defenseless inhabitants of Pascagoula naturally took a dim view of the dumping of so many indigents in the midst of a family resort. Following a fracas at William Dobson's oyster bar, involving the proprietor on the one side and Round Islanders accompanied by naval personnel on the other, an armed vigilante group composed of inhabitants and guests formed to protect the community. With the departure of the mercenaries, the crisis ended.

In 1850 the filibusters did invade Cuba, resulting in an antebellum Bay of Pigs. The Spanish authorities shot the captured mercenaries and publicly garroted their Cuban exile leaders. The federal government indicted Mississippi's Governor John A. Quitman in connection with the debacle. Quitman, a pro-slavery fire-eater angered by the abolitionist tinge of the Compromise of 1850, which threatened the extension of slavery in the Mexican Cession Territory, was even then planning a Mississippi secession convention. Resigning his office to stand trial, his secession movement lost momentum and failed, but Quitman passed his political torch on to John J. McRae of Pascagoula. McRae, destined first for state prominence as governor from 1854 to 1857 and then for the national scene as a U.S. congressman, ranked as chief politician of the Mississippi Gulf Coast in the antebellum era.

In 1850 the McRae hotel monopoly at the Pascagoulas ended. Elizabeth, the clan matriarch, converted West Pascagoula House into a private residence and retired, while Malcolm J. sold out and moved to Mobile. Two summers later, on August 4, the new owner of the East Pascagoula Hotel became embroiled in a row with his servants, discharging several of them in the process. Later that same day a fire, originating mysteriously in the kitchen, gutted the entire structure. Twenty days later a hurricane destroyed the wharf, killing three guests and one slave who worked for Dobson's Boarding House and Ice Cream Parlor, which was located next to the burnt-out hulk. The same storm destroyed Elizabeth McRae's wharf along with several yachts and killed two of her slaves. The fire and storm of 1852 virtually ended Pascagoula's days as a watering place.

Despite the setbacks, the Pascagoulas continued to grow as a commercial-industrial center. The several sawmills and the boat yard in the area stepped up production, and upriver cotton continued to flow through the port. Government recognition of the town's growing importance as a port came with the construction of a lighthouse at the mouth of the East Pascagoula in 1854. The town even attempted a comeback as a watering place with the grand opening of a new first-class East Pascagoula Hotel in 1860, but the Civil War put a finish to that effort.

Above: Mississippi Governor and former Mexican War hero John A. Quitman sensed the ultimate separation of the states and believed in an expanding South. "By sternly standing by our principles," he said, "a time may come for us to strike with effort. We may succeed in securing an equality in the Union, or our independence out of it, or at least fall gloriously." MDAH

Above left: The springs and bathing holes that attracted tourists to the coast's watering places were bricked but left uncovered. This way bathers could fully benefit from sunshine and pine-scented air as they soaked. The water reached the bricked-in holes, pictured, through bamboo tubes in the springs. From Nola Nance Oliver, The Gulf Coast of Mississippi, *1941*

Chapter Four

WAR COMES TO THE GULF COAST

In 1859 Southern fire-eaters determined to preserve slavery at any price and Northern abolitionists bent on its eradication at any cost ran out of words and reached for their swords. The spirit of compromise over the issue of slavery, which had forged the Constitution in the first place and preserved the Union in 1820 and 1850, evaporated over the Kansas dispute. The last futile attempt to head off the irrepressible conflict dissolved on the prairies of Bleeding Kansas and birthed the Republican party as the abolitionist party of the North.

In early October 1859 the citizens of Mississippi elected Kemper County fire-eater John J. Pettus by a landslide. A few days later abolitionist John Brown raided the government arsenal at Harpers Ferry, Virginia, in an attempt to arm slaves for a revolt. Pettus, calling that ominous event "the beginning of the end," placed two bills before the state legislature, both of which passed almost unanimously. The first ordered all free blacks out of the state by July 1, 1860, on pain of re-enslavement. The second authorized the expenditure of $150,000 for arms to repel the "aggressions of the antislavery organization." Within a short time the state placed an order for 4,000 muskets and began raising four regiments of militia.

In 1860 the Republican party, sensing its impending victory over the hopelessly fragmented Democrats, announced its candidacy of Abraham Lincoln for the Presidency. South Carolina, long the Southern tinderbox, announced its intent to secede from the Union in the event of his election. Pettus announced Mississippi's similar intent.

On Wednesday, July 4, 1860, the trumpeter of Captain J.D. Howard's Biloxi Rifle Guard roused the sleeping populace to a bright, sunny day. The tourist trade was a bit off due to the disgustingly good health of New Orleans and Mobile, but even so nearly 1,500 guests were in town for the Independence Day festivities. Following drill at Armory Hall on Lameuse Street, the 44-member Guard treated the town to a fife-and-drum parade and a shooting match. Adjourning to the Sazerack Saloon to take the edge off the 96-degree temperature, the shooters claimed their awards. Private W.B. Param claimed the gold medal, and Lieutenant Frederick Prime, engineer officer in charge of constructing the fortifications on Ship Island, presented the silver medal to Lieutenant L.B. Holley. Sergeant G.W. Andrews won the leather medal for the worst showing. The patriotic day climaxed with a Grand Military Ball at Nixon's Hotel.

One month later the Guard turned out again in full regalia to welcome New Orleans' Jackson Fire Company Number 18, which arrived aboard Captain A.P. Boardman's steamer *Alabama* for its annual outing at Gus Richards' Gem Hotel. Richards, himself a former New Orleans fireman, kept the champagne flowing for a day and a night, and his compatriots departed in good cheer.

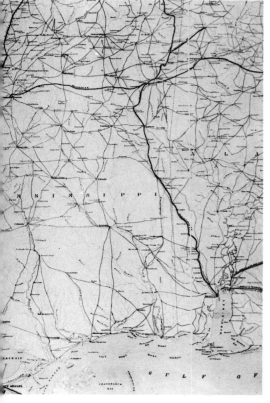

Three days later on Wednesday, August 8, the wind freshened from the south, kiting hats and umbrellas and billowing hoop skirts. The next day Captain Thomas Rhodes of the steamer *William C. Young*—bound from Pascagoula with a tow of square timber, rosin, and turpentine to finish the cargo of the British ship *Elizabeth Bibby* standing off Ship Island—was forced by the freshening wind to anchor near Round Island. Aboard the vessel along with 12 crewmen was James B. McRae, the owner of the cargo.

At 4 p.m. Friday the gale reached hurricane force, and Rhodes built up a head of steam nosing the boat into the wind to avoid dragging anchor. At noon on Saturday the tow began breaking up under the increasing wind velocity. At 6:30 p.m. the chimneys went. The next gust blew off the cabin, and the men grabbed planks and scattered in the blackness as the boat sank under them. Rhodes and a 15-year-old boy drifted outside Ship Island. Near dawn debris in the water broke the boy's arm, sweeping him away. Just after daybreak Rhodes drifted through Dog Key Pass back into the Sound. When he saw the first fin he pulled himself upon the plank, lashed himself to it, and lay broiling in the hot sun. Within an hour eight 10-foot sharks were escorting him. In Rhodes' words:

By this time the situation had become interesting, if not exciting. As they, evidently bent upon my amusement, pursued their gambols chasing each other back and forth, lashing the water at times into a perfect foam, I could not but wish they had chosen another locality, or waited until I could look upon them as a less interested spectator. They seemed, however, determined to stay by me which they did so long as I remained upon the plank.

A passing schooner rescued Rhodes and took him to Pensacola.

McRae and six other survivors of the *William C. Young* floated ashore near the works on Ship Island. Lieutenant Prime and his men rescued them and took them by schooner to Gus Richards' Gem Hotel in Biloxi. Except for the havoc wrought by the 10-foot storm surge among the yachts gathered there for a regatta, Biloxi had escaped practically unscathed. The same was true of all the watering places. Except for a visitation of huge black mosquitoes, the coast returned to normal within 10 days, as attested by the soiree given at the Tegarden Hotel on August 21.

At 5 p.m., Saturday, September 15, a blustery, blowy day in New Orleans, Captain Boardman loaded another company of firemen aboard the *Alabama* for a jaunt to Gus Richards' in Biloxi. In Boardman's words, the "night was dark and stormy" as he prepared to disembark passengers at Shieldsboro. Unable to find a wharf, he proceeded to Pass Christian and found no wharf there, either. Boardman plucked seven men from a wrecked schooner near Mississippi City and learned that another hurricane had struck the Gulf Coast. One eyewitness aboard the *Alabama* described Biloxi at dawn of September 16.

...the scene before us beggars description—not only are the wharves gone, but the houses unroofed, and some blown down and entirely destroyed.

Our friends the "boys" of Washington 20, were to have spent last night and today with their fellow fireman, Gus Richards—but, alas, Gus has no roof left, his house having been almost entirely demolished by the pitiless storm.

The whole beach, as far as the eye can reach, is one mass of wreck and ruin. A more desolate prospect I never beheld.

The same situation prevailed in every one of the Six Sisters. The timbers of every single wharf, bathhouse, and beach structure from Pascagoula to Shieldsboro had been rendered into missiles and hurled into the houses and businesses fronting the Sound. The telegraphers of the new line laid the previous year between Mobile and New Orleans would have informed those cities of the devastation if they could. But the telegraph line, which followed Pass Road on land, had been submerged under every river, bay, and strait. Boats dragging anchor in the storm had cut it in every water body from Pascagoula Bay to the Rigolets, isolating the Six Sisters from one another and from the flanking cities.

The storm had been tightly packed and fast moving. It struck unheralded by thunder and lightning at 2 a.m., Saturday, September 14, and 12 hours later the eye passed over Shieldsboro. In Shieldsboro and vicinity the winds destroyed the town's 97 public and private wharves and killed 300 cattle on Cat Island.

At Pascagoula the storm broke up the beach from Bayou Casotte to Captain John Grant's house and utterly wiped out the government barracks and veterans' hospital on Greenwood Island. General David Twiggs' residence, north of the beach on higher ground, became the refuge of the survivors. At the height of the gale a town resident was heard to cry out, "This is God's judgment. It is a token of his wrath and displeasure; for the people here drink too much whiskey, play cards too much, and never look out for them-

Above: In October 1859 the people of Mississippi elected extreme states'-rights candidate John Jones Pettus to be governor. The coast counties supported Pettus heavily in the election, and Jackson County cast not a single vote for his opponent. Pettus died of pneumonia in 1867 while attempting to elude Federal capture in the swamps of Arkansas. He is buried in an unmarked grave. MDAH

Opposite page, top: This map of a section of the Gulf was drawn in 1859. HNOC

Opposite page, bottom: On the eve of the Civil War, railway links did not exist from the coast panhandle to anywhere. By 1858 both New Orleans and Mobile had completed lines to Jackson, seen in this circa 1860 map. Thus, to travel to their state capital, coastians had to take a steamboat to either flanking city and then a train north. Courtesy, Library of Congress

Lieutenant Frederick E. Prime, posted to Ship Island in February 1859 as superintending engineer for the fort to be constructed there, fulfilled his duties until seizure of the island by Confederate forces. Promoted to captain, Prime was wounded, captured, and paroled near Mill Springs, Kentucky, in December 1861. Courtesy, Gulf Islands National Seashore

selves." The utterer of these pious remarks was later observed plunging into the waves to rescue a case of claret.

All up and down the coast boats were driven into the woods for sometimes as much as a mile. Though only about a dozen persons died, thousands of bloated cattle littered the shores and woods.

A sort of ennui settled over the population stunned by a second storm so soon after the first. Biloxi, hit hardest of all, lay virtually paralyzed. From Pradat's Hotel to the lighthouse, a distance of two miles, nearly every house had been damaged or destroyed. The lighthouse, its foundation undermined, leaned dangerously.

Miraculously, except for the death of a barber near Brown's Hotel and the two bodies floating near Deer Island, few lives had been lost in Biloxi, but the press of 1,500 tourists upon the inhabitants of the largely undamaged interior of the town occasioned much distress. These refugees from the collapsed beach hotels overwhelmed the remaining meager accommodations and rapidly depleted the isolated town's supplies of food and ice.

Little wonder that both the townspeople and the tourists rejoiced at the appearance of Captain Boardman's *Alabama* at dusk on the Tuesday following the storm. Having no wharf, the *Alabama* anchored offshore and sent a longboat ashore with mail and a few passengers. At the same time a number of small boats containing New Orleanians anxious to return home set off for the steamboat. Exactly what happened then will forever remain a matter of conjecture, but the frayed nerves of the refugees and Boardman's desire to proceed to Mobile to lay up the *Alabama* for repairs and return in the *Creole* certainly sparked the ensuing events. Boardman informed the men and women in the approaching craft that they could await his return in two or three days with the *Creole* or they could pay full fare to Mobile and return with him. He would let no one board without paying the fare. At that point a longtime female acquaintance of his in one of the boats smiled and said, "Captain, you'll allow me to come on board, won't you?" His reply was, "Madam, you can come on board if you have nine dollars to pay the clerk." Great consternation. The man seated next to the woman rose in the boat and vented his opinion of the matter in language liberally salted with graphic invective directed at the captain. Concluding with an oath of vengeance, the dissatisfied customer returned to the shore to harangue his fellow sufferers, who were already out of sorts because the *Alabama* was a day late and carried no food or ice. At the intelligence that the boat was bound the wrong way and, in their view, profiteering to boot, the crowd turned nasty.

Producing knives, rifles, and pistols, the mob hauled the *Alabama's* longboat ashore and detained its crew. Boardman sent another longboat ashore to rescue the first, and the irate people seized it as well, setting up a cry, accompanied by the distinct cocking of guns, for the captain to come ashore and get his men and boats. A member of the party on the beach later admitted to one gunshot in the air. Boardman attested to several whistling very near his steamer. Now fearful of a boarding party, the captain raised anchor, abandoned his stranded crew, and chugged across Biloxi Bay. In the darkness near Ocean Springs the *Alabama* ran aground atop a sunken vessel. Having no longboats to ketch it off, the steamer remained there until the morning tide raised it.

Returning in the *Creole* on Thursday, Boardman, acting under orders from his superiors, stopped at all the watering places except Biloxi. When news of the incident reached New Orleans, the *Daily Crescent* engaged in a veritable orgy of yellow journalism, proclaiming in banner headlines:

INTERESTING NEWS
FROM BILOXI AND THE GULF SHORE
ANOTHER OUTRAGE BY THE MONOPOLY
THE STEAMER ALABAMA MOBBED
NO BOAT TO TOUCH AT BILOXI
THE PEOPLE THERE TO GET HOME AS BEST THEY CAN
DISTRESS AND EXCITEMENT ALONG THE COAST
THE MAIL COMPANY LEAVES THE BILOXIANS TO LOOK OUT FOR
THEMSELVES

J.O. Nixon, the paper's editor, expressed his opinion that the New Orleans and Mobile Mail Line Company:

a powerful and heartless monopoly ... has perpetrated the most inexcusable, unmitigated, and dastardly outrage that ever any company inflicted upon white people during the whole history of steamboating. Our limits forbid us giving some other things we would like to state in this connection.

After a week of blockade, some of the Biloxi refugees booked steerage aboard New Orleans-bound lumber schooners, while others walked to Mississippi City or took skiffs to Ocean Springs.

Three hundred boarded the *Creole* at Ocean Springs on the morning of September 24, and hundreds more came out to board at Mississippi City later that day. There Boardman, fearing that the boat might founder, ordered the crew to admit no more passengers. As the crew moved to push the boat people away, a resolute New Orleanian, whose family still sat in one of the skiffs, pulled a pistol and "swore he would put a bullet through the head of the first man who tried." When other passengers backed the gunman, the crew relented. The day climaxed with another rumpus at Pass Christian, and Boardman finally arrived loaded to the gunwales at the Milneburg dock late that night. "Now," railed the *Daily Crescent,* "if the Mail Line Company blockaded Biloxi because of the difficulty there, they have an equal excuse for blockading Mississippi City."

That same night the Biloxi Board of Selectmen met at Armory Hall under the chairmanship of the Honorable John L. Henley and appointed a committee to draft a resolution. That document, copies of which were sent to all the New Orleans newspapers, condemned Boardman and the mail line. But J.O. Nixon, now realizing that he had cut his own throat by criticizing the mail line, his major source of news, hastily reorganized his loyalties and declined to publish it, predicting that the whole mess would blow over by Christmas.

It blew over only a few days later on October 1 when a third hurricane slammed into the coast. A Pass Christian correspondent to the *Daily Delta* put it succinctly:

Last night saw the end of storm no. 3, a final blowout of the season it is hoped.

As the hurricane of Sept. 15 had swept the coast clean of bath houses and wharves, there was not much for its successor to do; but some few unfortunates who had gallantly gone to work to repair damages, again saw their timber afloat and will have to begin anew.

Twenty days later a Pass Christianian, writing under the *nom de plume* "Patriarch Dismal," deplored the return of the mosquito pestilence in the wake of the last storm, but on the bright side reported full employment all along the coast among sawmill workers and mechanics engaged in the massive rebuilding efforts.

The coast, emerging from the devastation of three hurricanes, found itself embroiled in a political maelstrom of far greater consequences. Captain Boardman, now forgiven for his real or imagined sins, hosted a straw poll in the saloon of the *Alabama* as it plowed the waters of the Sound on the eve of the Presidential election. Thirty men and 13 women (enfranchised for the occasion) voted 40-3 for secession in the event of a Lincoln victory in the race. Even the three women who voted for union made that contingent upon the North giving the South "all her Constitutional rights." The *Alabama* vote reflected reality with amazing accuracy. Lincoln's election detonated a secessionist fever in the South that quickly steamrolled the tiny minority of Constitutional Unionists.

The legislature of South Carolina remained in crisis session on November 6 until the election results were known, and immediately called for a convention to meet in Columbia on December 20. At that meeting the representatives of the people of South Carolina unanimously declared that state's secession from the Union. That same day Mississippi chose its representatives for a similar convention to be held at Jackson. Every coast county elected men pledged to dissolution of the Union.

Pass Christian served as an excellent barometer of the gathering storm. The lately formed Vigilance Committee seized Tom Guy, the town abolitionist, and purchased tickets for him and his family aboard a northbound steamer, where it was hoped "he may become an ornament and a glory to the society of Negro worshippers." Colonel Ashbel Green, commander of the Mississippi Military Institute, put the town cannon in order and continued to drill his company of recently formed "Minute Men."

A duel reflecting the disparate political views of the antagonists added a note of chivalry to the proceedings. French Charley, appointed by President James Buchanan as keeper of the new iron lighthouse constructed the previous year at Pass Marianne, came ashore on one of his rare flights from the rigorous confines of his job. While in the state of great elation that marked all such occasions, he chanced to overhear one Armour refer to his lame-duck boss as a "damned rascal, coward and turncoat." Incensed, Charley challenged Armour, who accepted, and the pair squared off under the oaks behind the Pass Christian Hotel. Unknown to either, their seconds neglected to place balls in the pistols, hence Charley's consternation when his paper wadding only scratched the cheek of his opponent. But as the "lion ... having lapped blood," Charley demanded another shot. As his second made great show of ramming the ball down the muzzle, Charley's nerve broke and he expressed his willingness to stand the entire assemblage to a round of another kind, thus ending the crisis.

The impending duel between North and South did not end so amicably.

On January 9, 1861, the state of Mississippi became the second to leave the Union. In the five months between the election of Lincoln and his inauguration, state after state followed the lead of South Carolina. During this period, newly formed paramilitary units in the Southern states moved to take over forts, arsenals, and other U.S. government installations.

The brick walls of the unfinished and unnamed works rearing nine feet above the sand of Ship Island represented the only fort in the state of Mississippi. On January 13, 1861, elements of the Biloxi Rifles and the Handsboro Minute Men landed on the island and informed Lieutenant Frederick Prime's overseer that they were taking possession, but after a few hours they reboarded their boats and departed. That afternoon yet another armed party landed, claimed possession, raised a homemade flag, and, after billeting 10 men in a vacant building, the balance of the invaders returned to the mainland. Since it looked as though the occupation troops were planning no interference, the overseer continued construction until January 20 when a third armed party appeared and ordered him and his workmen off the island. Prime, who had been on leave at his New York home, learned of these events when he returned to Biloxi on January 26 and immediately notified his superior that as of January 20 he considered himself no longer responsible for the installation. The Rebel occupation force, informed by

The fort on Ship Island is seen in this 1861 engraving. The victorious Federals did not rename Fort Twiggs. Rather, by association with men of Massachusetts and with the ship of that name, the fortification acquired the sobriquet "Fort Massachusetts." Not until June 1884, however, did an official document refer to the Ship Island fortification by that title. Courtesy, Gulf Islands National Seashore

Right: The Reverend Father Henri Leduc, pastor of Bay St. Louis beginning in 1859, dedicated 38 years to developing the parish. In 1868 he founded the town's first private school for blacks. Courtesy, Bob Hubbard

Far right: Melancton Smith, commander of the U.S.S. Massachusetts, "captured" Biloxi on December 31, 1861. This circa 1863 portrait of Smith is an official Navy photograph. Courtesy, Department of the Navy

Governor Pettus that no armament could be provided for the fort, deserted the island as well.

Lincoln took office on March 4, and the uneasy *sitzkrieg* ended on April 12 with the bombardment of Fort Sumter. One week later Lincoln ordered a blockade of the Southern coastline. With enemy ships en route to the coast, each town stepped up military preparations, each forming two units—one of ages 21-35 for field duty and those above that age as home guards. Governor Pettus, unable to provide arms, urged all units to outfit themselves with guns by any means possible. Pass Christianians took him at his word and hijacked a load of rifles bound for the state arsenal at Jackson.

Despite the danger posed by the oncoming Federal fleet, the Six Sisters exhibited a holiday mood. On May 11 Captain Robert Eager's Shieldsboro Rifles hosted a barbecue for the Gainesville Volunteers and the Pass Christian Coast Guards. At high noon, with the companies assembled in an oak grove in the heart of Shieldsboro, Captain Eager stepped forward to receive a magnificent silken banner presented by a matron accompanied by a bevy of maidens clad in white muslin and scarlet ribbons. Charged to "conquer or die," the captain accepted the ensign as the Christian Brothers Band struck up the bewitching strains of "Dixie." Immediately thereafter the companies wheeled into columns and marched to the church where Father Henri Leduc consecrated the banner and delivered an address in French. A ball at Levis' Hotel climaxed the festivities.

As a squadron of Federal warships steamed into the Gulf to take up positions from Key West to the Mexican border, Confederate President Jefferson Davis named General David Twiggs of East Pascagoula as commander of Department Number 1, which included the state of Louisiana and the coasts of Mississippi and Alabama. Twiggs, aged 71 and ailing, reported to his headquarters in New Orleans specifically charged by Davis to preserve the communication line between that city and Mobile by the immediate occupation of Ship Island.

Despite the war the watering places announced the opening of the summer season, and one observer in Pass Christian predicted a fine one since few

Southerners would be resorting to the North in view of the circumstances. On June 9 four hundred gray-clad guests disembarked at Barnes' Wharf in Mississippi City. These four companies, the lead contingent of the 4th Louisiana Regiment, set up camp near the hotel.

The next day in Handsboro the populace gave a rousing sendoff to Captain Fleming Adams' "Adams Rifles." The men stood proudly in their butternut uniforms, sewn for them by the town matrons in the Masonic Lodge, while 11 little girls, each representing a seceded state, delivered a recitation. After the flag presentation many of the townspeople followed the troops down to Harrison's Wharf at the foot of Dubuy's Road, and they all boarded the steamer *Creole* for the ride down to Barnes' Wharf where relations made their last farewells. The 4th Louisiana, encamped on the beach, saluted as the coast troops, destined for far-off battlefields, headed for New Orleans and the northbound train.

The process of stripping the coast of its troops and replacing them with companies of the 4th Louisiana continued over the next several days. Pass Christian, Biloxi, and Pascagoula received two companies each. These 1,000 men, strung out on a 50-mile front with no earthworks and precious few cannon, constituted the entirety of the coast's defense.

On June 17 Commander Melancton Smith of the screw steamer U.S.S. *Massachusetts* took as the first prize of the blockading fleet the schooner

Among the Federal warships anchored at Ship Island in early 1862 were the twin "Terrors of the Sound." In this antique print of a view off Ship Island, Commander Melancton Smith's Boston-built iron steamer Massachusetts *is located on the extreme right, while Lieutenant Abner Read's shallow-draft steam gunboat* New London *occupies the left foreground. MCM*

In 1862 the 24-gun steamer Brooklyn *on the right, and her equally powerful sister ship* Powhatan *on the left, blockaded the mouth of the Mississippi River and the Mississippi Sound, capturing a number of Confederate steamboats and schooners as prizes. HNOC*

Achilles, bound for the Ship Island Lighthouse with a load of supplies. Using that shallow-draft vessel, Smith landed on the island, inspected the still-deserted works, and raised the American flag. Yachtsman J.G. Robinson of Biloxi spied the flag and reported the sighting to Mayor James Fewell. The next day Smith departed Ship Island to report to his superior lying off the mouth of the Mississippi, and on that same day Fewell ordered the lamp extinguished in the Biloxi Lighthouse. It would not be lit again for five-and-a-half years.

The following Sunday morning, June 23, Smith nosed the *Massachusetts* into Ship Island Pass and dispatched the now-armed *Achilles* to the center of Mississippi Sound, where it disgorged three launches of sailors who took up positions near the west end of Deer Island. Captain Abraham Myers, commanding the Mobile-bound mail packet *Oregon,* ran headlong into the trap. Amidst the plumes of bursting shells, Myers spun his boat about, raised the Stars and Bars, and, as he retreated, returned fire with the only armament aboard—a passenger's revolver. Five trading schooners were not so lucky. Smith captured them and hauled them off into the Gulf.

In the ensuing days the alarm spread up and down the coast as the *Massa-*

chusetts steamed outside the islands sending its schooner and launches into the Sound to harry boats and steal water and food. When the mail line suspended operations, the New Orleans papers howled for Twiggs to end the depredations.

Twiggs pressed the mail steamers into Confederate service on July 4 and ordered them to transport troops and war materiel to Ship Island. Captain Myers of the *Oregon,* delighted with the opportunity to settle the score with the *Massachusetts,* sandbagged his boilers, loaded up, and led the way.

By the following Monday night, July 8, nearly 400 Confederate soldiers and marines manned the works of the newly christened Fort Twiggs, and they extinguished the Ship Island light. Commander Smith, returning to the darkened island that night, deduced that a Rebel force had been landed during his absence and anchored the *Massachusetts* outside gun range. At daybreak Smith saw through his glass three Rebel flags and four batteries of

Left: John Walker fought with both blue and gray in the War between the States. He returned to Biloxi after the war to become a businessman, bank president, and mayor of the town. Courtesy, City of Biloxi

Far left: John L. Henley was elected mayor of Biloxi in 1866. In 1872 he became the third owner of a home on Back Bay. Known today as the "old brick house," it is one of Biloxi's earliest buildings. Courtesy, City of Biloxi

cannon. Calling his men to general quarters, the Yankee commander steamed toward the island and opened up with his deck guns. The Confederates chased the incoming Yankee shells around in the sand and gleefully loaded them up and fired them back. After 20 minutes the *Massachusetts* pulled out of range and the battle ended. Casualties: one Rebel slightly injured in the leg. The New Orleans newspapers hailed the victory and praised the brave defenders, and the coastal inhabitants breathed easier.

For its part, the *Massachusetts* simply remained anchored outside gun range. Four days later Myers, determined to get that Black Republican steamer, loaded a large, smoothbore cannon on his deck, ran up the American flag upside down, and, along with another mail packet similarly armed, charged.

When Smith saw them coming, he pumped up steam, raised anchor, and primed his guns. John L. Henley of Biloxi, a future mayor of that town, worked the gun on the deck of the *Oregon* as it plowed into battle. Aiding him was John Walker, steersman of the boat and also a future Biloxi mayor. Sixty shots later, with no hits scored by any boat involved, Myers spotted another Lincoln man-of-war on the horizon, and the "secesh" boats broke off

In this engraving the Confederate Stars and Bars flies from Cat Island Lighthouse. Rebel forces destroyed the tower—built in 1831—so that the Federal navy could not use it. HNOC

and ran for the cover of the Fort Twiggs batteries. The next day Henley put in a rush order to the Mississippi State Arsenal for a rifled cannon, and Smith requested one from the U.S. War Department.

Over the next two months the Confederates strengthened the fortifications on Ship Island. Occasionally the cannoneers traded shots with the *Massachusetts* to divert its attention from the privateers and blockade runners cruising the Sound seeking an opportunity to break for the open sea.

Offshore fishing boats continued to ply their trade, and some, lured by Yankee gold, supplied food, water, and the New Orleans newspapers, which contained an incredible amount of military information, to the *Massachusetts* and the other blockaders. On July 21 Lieutenant John V. Toulme and a detachment of the Shieldsboro Rifles boarded a schooner in the Jourdan River that contained a large cargo of onions, potatoes, cabbages, and oil. The two Italians aboard claimed to know neither one another nor the name of their captain. Toulme gave them plenty of time to remember in the local jail.

At the end of August, Brigadier General Charles Dahlgren of Natchez arrived in Pass Christian to take command of the various contingents mustering there to form his 3rd Brigade, Army of Mississippi. As units poured in by land and sea, Dahlgren settled the troops into a camp of instruction near the Indian Mound and proceeded to whip them into shape. Subordinates and superiors alike soon learned not to cross this hot-blooded commander, who carried as souvenirs of successful duels the tip of a bowie knife in his skull and two pistol balls in his ribs. He was especially sensitive about the fact that his brother John, inventor of the famous Dahlgren gun, was serving with the blockaders.

Upon completion of organization Dahlgren's Brigade was divided into two regiments—the 3rd Mississippi Regiment, commanded by Colonel John B. Deason, and the 7th Mississippi Regiment, under Colonel Enos J. Goode. Upstate men filled the ranks of the latter, but half of the 3rd Mississippi's 10 companies were composed of coast men: Company A—Live Oak Rifles of Ocean Springs; Company E—Biloxi Rifles; Company F—Shieldsboro Rifles; Company G—Gainesville Volunteers; and Company H—Dahlgren Guards of Pass Christian. Several of these companies, having departed for other commands in the first flush of war, had returned to join the coast brigade, much to the delight of coast residents.

As more and more men-of-war appeared on the horizon off Ship Island, Twiggs, under pressure from President Davis, ordered the evacuation of men and guns from that exposed position. Upon completion of this Dunkirk on the night of September 16, the final contingent of Rebel troops filled the

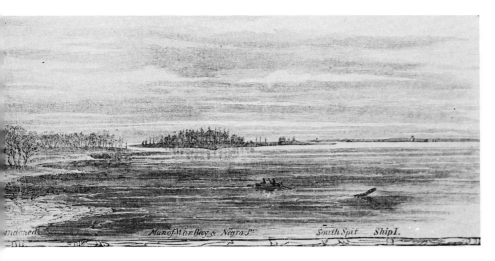

General Mansfield Lovell replaced aged General Twiggs as commander of the Confederate coast defenses on October 17, 1861. Rebel commanders' requisitions of men and materiél from his department left Lovell outnumbered six to one by his foe and rendered a successful defense of New Orleans impossible. LSM

brick lighthouse with pine lumber and torched it along with all the other buildings on the island. In the words of a soldier on the last boat out:

It was the prettiest sight I ever saw. The little huts were right on the beach, and the fire and smoke dripped down into the waves that were rolling up the beach, and seemingly trying to put the wicked fire out.

Alerted by the flames, the *Massachusetts* and the other Lincoln vessels approached cautiously. Smith fired one round from his new rifled cannon, delivered the previous day, at the dimly visible evacuating fleet.

On the fort's bulletin board the next day, Smith found a note addressed to "The Commander of the *Massachusetts*":

By order of my Government I have this day evacuated Ship Island. This my brave soldiers, under my command do with much reluctance and regret.

For three long months your good ship has been our constant companion. We have not exactly "lived and loved together" but we have been intimately acquainted...

In leaving you today we beg you to accept our best wishes for your health and happiness while sojourning on this pleasant hospitable shore.

That we may ... meet face to face in closer quarters is the urgent prayer of very truly, your obedient servant,

> *H.W. Allen*
> *Lieutenant-Colonel, 4th Louisiana*
> *Infantry, Commanding Ship Island*

One of Smith's junior officers actually accepted the challenge via a Mississippi City-bound fishing smack, but the duel set for shotguns on Cat Island never took place.

With the fall of Ship Island, the Confederate mosquito fleet fled into Lake Pontchartrain, severing the water connection between New Orleans and Mobile, thus leaving the rail link via Jackson as the only reliable avenue for the exchange of mail, passengers, and freight between the two cities. Coast guests and residents stampeded aboard the last boats out as the Mississippi Sound turned into a Federal pond. Almost immediately the Union forces cut the telegraph cable running under the Bay of St. Louis. Although the Confederate authorities restored the service quickly, they also rushed to put up a new line paralleling the interior rail connection between New Orleans and Mobile.

On September 24 four slaves from Handsboro appeared off Ship Island in a rowboat. Taken aboard a blockader they gave valuable information regarding troop dispositions on the shore, and they told of a powder mill running full blast at Red Bluff at Bayou Bernard.

In early October President Davis received a letter from concerned citizens in New Orleans suggesting that he replace aged and infirm General Twiggs. A few days later Twiggs himself wrote a letter seconding the motion. Forthwith, Brigadier General Mansfield Lovell, a younger, more vigorous officer, took command of the New Orleans defense.

In October and November 1861 the *Massachusetts,* together with Lieutenant Abner Read's U.S.S. *New London,* fought a series of sharp engagements with Confederate gunboats and privateers in the Sound and captured a number of prizes. Contemporaneously, Confederate Army commanders, charged with protecting a vast territory with too few men, played a game of musical regiments. The 4th Louisiana left the coast to take up duty stations in its home state, and Lovell ordered the 3rd Mississippi Regiment to Columbus, Kentucky, to parry a Union thrust from that quarter. When the dust settled, only the 7th Mississippi, then at Shieldsboro, supported by the Brookhaven Light Artillery and the Seven Stars Artillery, still remained. Except for home-guard units composed of old men and young boys, no other Confederate forces existed between Shieldsboro and Mobile.

On December 4 the U.S.S. *Constitution,* a huge troop transport, entered Ship Island harbor and landed two regiments as the vanguard of 18,000 Union soldiers headed for the island under the command of Major-General Benjamin F. Butler for the impending assault on New Orleans. One of these regiments, the 26th Massachusetts, promptly set to work upon the fort already unofficially renamed for their home state by Melancton Smith's crew.

Three days later Captain Myers of the *Oregon,* under orders from General Lovell, ran the gauntlet into Handsboro and took aboard the town's powder mill machinery. With the aid of the Brookhaven Light Artillery battery on his deck, Myers shot his way through a trap laid by the Yankee gunboats and delivered the precious machinery to New Orleans.

Cognizant of the weak coastal defenses, Smith struck at Biloxi on the morning of New Year's Eve. For weeks a formidable sand battery near the lighthouse had kept the Federals at bay. When his flotilla of three gunboats loaded with several hundred soldiers failed to draw fire from the guns on the beach, Smith went ashore under a flag of truce.

Upon close inspection all but two of the bristling guns turned out to be Quaker cannon—black logs. Of the two real cannon, only one was operable. With ill-concealed merriment, Smith asked to see the mayor. A short time later Fewell arrived, and Smith delivered him a one-hour ultimatum demanding the surrender of the battery, the town, and all Confederate vessels and military stores. At the expiration of the time limit, the mayor complied.

As the soldiers dismantled the battery, knots of Biloxi citizens gathered around to talk. Some offered to trade sugar and molasses for coffee and tea, commodities long since shut off by the blockade. A more rebellious lad, resentful of this invasion, admitted a shortage of luxuries but informed the

Yanks that they would "have to put a blockade on the mullet" to starve Biloxi into submission. Taking the guns and a lumber schooner, the Union force withdrew to Ship Island.

In view of the massive buildup of forces on Ship Island and the surrender of Biloxi, General Lovell and Governor Pettus each sent a number of frantic telegrams to Jefferson Davis requesting the return of the 3rd Mississippi Regiment. Their appeals bore fruit, and by the end of January 1862 the men of that regiment were distributed once again in the largely deserted coastal towns. Nearly all citizens with the funds to do so had fled inland to escape the Yankees and to prevent their slaves from escaping to Ship Island, as many had already done.

In mid-February Smith's *Massachusetts* returned to New York laden with prisoners and booty, passing the title "Terror of the Sound" to Read's *New London*. Late on February 19 the *New London,* disguised with a secesh flag, crept into an inlet on Cat Island. Read's objective was the capture of the coast's oystering fleet, which was gathering, in addition to bivalves, intelligence on Yankee movements. On the afternoon of the following day, with unsuspecting Rebel smacks all about him, Read replaced the Stars and Bars with the Stars and Stripes and sent forth manned launches to board the boats as prize crews.

Two of the sailors boarded the smack *Clide,* tied their launch aft, and ordered its captain to sail for the *New London.* The captain hospitably offered grog and biscuits to the boarders, which they readily accepted. As they relaxed and put down their muskets, the captain grabbed one of the guns, blew out the brains of one sailor, and placed the bayonet at the throat of the other, who quickly surrendered.

That evening, as Read towed his 11 prizes to Ship Island, the men of the 7th Mississippi Regiment gathered on the beach at Shieldsboro to view the body of the dead U.S. sailor and question the prisoner. They buried the body of the first-known fatality of the coast campaign in the camp cemetery.

The *Constitution* and other transports continued to land regiment after regiment on the white sands of Ship Island, which evoked images of Coney Island to the New York troops. Though certainly not a resort area, the beaches of Ship Island offered excellent recreational opportunities, and fresh water could be obtained by simply sinking a barrel in the sand. Lumber from captured schooners provided plank floors for the tents and the material for the construction of clapboard cabins, wharves, and storehouses.

With the enemy forces on Ship Island approaching 5,000, Captain Job M. Foxworth of the 7th Mississippi bemoaned the lack of gunboats or even coastal land defenses, but, he confided to his diary:

I am not the least surprised, knowing our governor. He never does anything until the occasion for it is past and gone, then he commences all in a blaze .... It appears that every solitary thing Pettus has done since the war broke out was a blunder—nothing in its time or season.... So I look at the matter.

But Pettus did surprise him and the whole 7th Mississippi Regiment on February 24 by sending the men to Columbus, Kentucky, leaving the 3rd Regiment alone to deal with the vast army on Ship Island.

On March 1 sixty Yankees from the *New London* went ashore at Biloxi, refreshed themselves in the restaurants and beer halls, and then proceeded

With the occupation of Ship Island by Federal troops, Lieutenant John C. Palfrey, named successor to Prime, visited the wounded captain for a briefing on the status of the unfinished Ship Island fort. The Massachusetts native arrived at Ship Island on February 21, 1862, and, except for short periods of detached service, superintended the construction of the fort until he was relieved in October 1865. Courtesy, Gulf Islands National Seashore

across the bay to Ocean Springs. There they seized a cannon and 60 stands of arms and, over the protest of postmaster John Egan, cleared the post office of equipment, letters, and newspapers.

Colonel John Deason of the 3rd Mississippi Regiment, angered by these unopposed landings, posted seven companies of his troops along with the Seven Stars Artillery at Handsboro, ordered his other three companies to Pass Christian, and placed pickets from Ocean Springs to Mississippi City. One week later a Confederate sentinel spotted a Yankee gunboat making for Harrison's Wharf and rode to Handsboro to spread the alarm.

The 150 Yankee soldiers, delayed by gaps removed from the wharf for that purpose, had barely assembled on the beach when they saw the men of the Seven Stars Artillery detaching their guns and wheeling them into position in the nearby woods. The Yanks double-timed back down the pier to the whine of canister and ball. The only injury was a slight abrasion suffered by one soldier struck in the leg by a piece of spent canister, which then dropped into his boot.

The gunboat returned fire until the men were aboard and then cast off for Ship Island. The force, having been sent ashore to find a suitable campsite to alleviate the crowded conditions of the island, reported the Mississippi City area to be quite unsuitable for that purpose.

On March 20 General Butler himself arrived aboard a flagship leading a convoy of several thousand more troops for disembarkation at Ship Island. Three days later the general went ashore to witness a grand review of the massed regiments of the island, which, together with the ships and men of Admiral David Farragut's armada, constituted one of the greatest amphibious assault forces of the 19th century.

As Butler and Farragut planned their grand strategy for the capture of New Orleans, an incident regarding a child focused the general's attention on Biloxi. Four-year-old Alma Peniston of New Orleans, one of the few survivors rescued from a storm-smashed vessel in the Gulf, had been brought to Ship Island by a blockader. Butler, supposing her parents to have perished, ordered his chief of staff, Major George Strong, to deliver the child to the Biloxi town authorities for transshipment to relatives in New Orleans.

Major Strong arrived off Biloxi in a schooner flying a flag of truce on April 1 and duly delivered the child. In preparation for his return, the major unfortunately ran aground on Deer Island. While he was in this predicament, persons from the shore fired on him twice and then sailed out to demand his surrender. His refusal, together with his commands shouted to a non-existent company of soldiers below decks, frightened his antagonists away. Back at the island Strong reported the ugly incident. An incensed Butler ordered the *New London* and two other gunboats to stand by while a section of artillery and the entire complement of approximately 1,000 men belonging to the 9th Connecticut Infantry Regiment boarded a transport. Charged by Butler with securing written apologies for "cowardly conduct" from both the mayor of Biloxi and the commander of the 3rd Mississippi Regiment, the task force sailed.

This force arrived at Biloxi at sundown the next day, surrounded the town, and demanded to see the mayor. When Fewell did not appear, the Yankees held his daughter hostage until he did. Satisfied with Fewell's explanation and written apology, they looted a store belonging to one of the culprits suspected of firing on Major Strong, cut the telegraph line, and invited all slaves who wished to accompany them to board the boats. Prior to embarkation, the Yankees informed Fewell that another such outrage as had occurred against the flag of truce would result in the destruction of Biloxi.

The Yankee flotilla then sailed to Mississippi City to await the dawn with the intention of seeking a truce talk with Colonel Deason regarding the Strong incident. At 4:30 a.m. the *Oregon* and two other blacked-out Confederate gunboats muffled their engines, crept among the Union vessels, and opened fire.

In the following two-hour engagement the Federals suffered only one man

General Benjamin Franklin Butler (opposite page right, courtesy, HNOC) commanded the Federal army that occupied New Orleans in 1862. His notorious "woman order," which branded any woman who insulted a Yankee soldier as a "woman of the town plying her avocation," earned him the nickname "Beast." His Confederate detractors also labeled him "Spoons," referring to the disappearance of General David Twiggs' silverware while Butler occupied the former Confederate commander's New Orleans residence. Butler's wife Sarah (opposite page left, courtesy, LSM) lived on Ship Island for several weeks in a shack filled with captured furniture. In her letters she confessed her fears that some windy night she would be "swept off into the sea."

slightly injured, while the Rebels may have suffered as many as five dead plus considerable damage to all three of their gunboats. As the secesh boats broke off and fled westward, the Yankee steamers stayed in hot pursuit all the way to the Rigolets, where the Rebel steamers escaped into shoal water. Spoiling for a fight, the Union commanders then ordered an attack on the Rebel encampment at Pass Christian.

At the sight of Federal warships in the Sound, Confederate troops at Pass Christian ignited bales of hay on the wharves to destroy them and prevent a landing. The Union gunners, mistaking the smoke behind the bales for cannon puffs, opened up first on the wharves, and then on the entire town. Miraculously, as the populace fled the exploding buildings and ran for the woods, not one person sustained an injury.

The Yanks ceased firing and landed their entire complement of troops on the wharves and on the beach. The soldiers searched the town for military supplies under strict orders to respect private property and persons. Finding no military stores, they formed a column and headed up Red Creek Road (Menge Avenue) bound for the 3rd Mississippi encampment two miles away.

Half the distance to the camp the column drew artillery and musket fire. The Yanks then formed a skirmish line and drove the 300 Rebel soldiers back. When Lieutenant Colonel Thomas A. Mellon, the commander of the Pass Christian Confederate cantonment, realized he was heavily outnumbered and could expect no aid from the other seven Rebel companies then at Handsboro, he ordered a retreat, which turned into a rout. His only casualties were two men who were taken prisoner and several men who drowned attempting to swim Wolf River in full battle gear. The Yanks suffered one casualty—a private who was shot in the arm.

The 9th Connecticut plundered and burned the Confederate camp, shot all the horses there, and took the stand of colors left behind. As the victorious troops returned to Pass Christian flaunting the white silk ensign bearing a star and magnolia leaves, one woman who had helped make the first banner captured in the coast campaign wept openly in the street. According to a Federal officer present at the scene, the woman "said she didn't think the Southern soldiers were cowards but she couldn't see how they could allow that flag to be taken." The Yankee officers apologized for mistakenly shelling the town, cut the telegraph line, and departed with their entire force.

All through the month of April the buildup on Ship Island continued, and Farragut's fleet entered the mouth of the Mississippi to take up positions against the Confederate forts flanking the river below New Orleans. Following a week of bombardment, the armada launched its final assault.

As the Federal fleet ran the batteries of the principal forts on the river and approached New Orleans, the Confederate troops manning the fortifications guarding the other approaches to the city, now outflanked, spiked their guns and fled across Lake Pontchartrain in the Rebel gunboats. The *Oregon* and the other gunboats were then run up a river on the north shore of the lake and scuttled by their own crews. New Orleans surrendered, and Butler ferried 15,000 occupation troops into the city from Ship Island, reducing the number left on the island to 3,000.

With New Orleans in Federal hands, the 3rd Mississippi Regiment evacuated the coast and reported to Camp Moore, Louisiana. The coast inhabitants able to do so fled with them to take the New Orleans & Great Northern Railroad north to places of refuge. Only a few dozen families remained in each of the Six Sisters.

In the first flush of victory, Butler inaugurated a rather liberal policy of granting passes to schooners trading in consumer products along the coast. That action relieved the citizens remaining in the coastal towns.

The Confederate commander at Mobile anchored the western edge of his defensive perimeter at Pascagoula, providing adequate protection for that town. The only other effective Confederate force operating along the entire coast west of Pascagoula was Major Abner C. Steede's Mounted Partisan Rangers. Originally formed in Jackson County, this cavalry outfit established camps on the Wolf River in Harrison County and on the Pearl in Hancock. With only 200 men at his disposal, Steede necessarily resorted to hit-and-run guerrilla tactics. Steede centrally located his main base camp north of Pass Christian on the Wolf River and named it Camp Mayers in honor of Pizarro K. Mayers, one of his captains and the prewar editor of the *Handsboro*

Below left: Colonel Abner C. Steede of Jackson County commanded Steede's Rangers, the last organized Confederate force guarding the Mississippi Gulf Coast. Courtesy, Tommy Wixon

Democrat. On May 8 the Yankees paid a visit to Biloxi in search of the mayor, who was nowhere to be found. They raised the Stars and Stripes, administered the oath of allegiance to those who would take it, cut the telegraph line, and proceeded to Ocean Springs, where the "Union ladies" hosted a dance in their honor.

One week later Steede's Rangers ambushed the lead vessel in a four-gunboat convoy pushing up the Pearl near Gainesville. Although they inflicted only one casualty upon the enemy, the Rangers forced the expedition to turn back.

W.A. Champlin of Handsboro, collector of the Confederate War Tax, informed Governor Pettus that a great many traitors and spies existed among the population of the coast. He reported flagrant trading with the enemy and frequent visits of Federal officers stationed at Ship Island to Ocean Springs,

Above: On April 4, 1862, this flag was captured from the 3rd Mississippi Regiment at Pass Christian by the 9th Connecticut Infantry. On February 26, 1885 (designated "Connecticut Day" at the Cotton Centennial Exposition), members of the unit that captured the flag returned it with ceremonies to the survivors of the 3rd Regiment. Courtesy, Grady Howell

where "many women, some calling themselves ladies, entertain these Yankee officers and walk with them on the streets and load them with bouquets when they depart." He confessed his fear that he might be arrested by these collaborators.

In June 1862 General Butler, now called "Beast" by those of Confederate sentiment, ordered the commander at Ship Island to proceed to Pass Christian to arrest the mayor and other town leaders suspected of harassing Unionists in the vicinity. They were to be held hostage and hanged if such reports continued.

Two companies of troops aboard the *Creole* made a flying visit to the town and, unable to find the culprits, arrested members of their families. Proceeding up Jourdan River to pick up Union sympathizers, to destroy ferries and sawmills, and to steal cattle, the *Creole* ran headlong into one of Steede's ambushes set up at a bend in the river. A hail of bullets passed through the boat, piercing the uniforms of several soldiers but injuring none. The Federal soldiers drove off the attackers and put about, returning to Ship Island with their plunder and hostages.

In mid-July Lincoln gunboats hove to off Pascagoula and dispatched a launch of soldiers to cut the telegraph line to Mobile. That mission accomplished, they next attempted to enter the obstructed mouth of the river to capture two schooners loaded with cotton. A crowd of civilian onlookers on the shore suddenly scattered, and behind them stood 60 Rebel soldiers who fired directly into the launch, wounding 10 Yankees. In the return fire two men and a woman died on the shore.

Butler, outraged by these and similar incidents, instituted an avowed starvation policy, shutting off all trade with the Rebel coast. Even rowboats were no longer safe on the Sound, and attacks were ordered on the saltworks.

The South early displayed great ingenuity in the manufacture of ersatz replacements for many products cut off by the blockade, but no substitute existed for salt. Without it fresh meat could not be preserved. Consequently, the coast inhabitants constructed salt distilleries consisting of sugar kettles and old steam boilers filled with sea water and fired with lighter wood. At least 11 such plants existed on the Mississippi littoral, producing the white gold that took the place of money as a medium of exchange. Inland farmers came from as far away as Columbia to exchange their produce for salt. Despite the raids, the manufacture of salt continued throughout the war because it was the area's only really valuable resource.

With Federal New Orleans on the one side and Confederate Mobile on the other, the people of the Mississippi Gulf Coast found themselves in a no-man's land with neither contender willing or even able to protect the populace from the other. Subject to draconian requisitions of men and supplies from the Rebel side, destructive raids from the Union side, and demands of loyalty from both, various individuals swore fealty to one or the other, while many waffled between the two, and nearly all of them faced starvation.

Following a July 1862 raid on Pass Christian and Shieldsboro, a Union captain described what he saw to his wife in Connecticut. Regarding Pass Christian he wrote:

I strolled for some time about the place. The only discoverable inhabitants were half a dozen men and some scores of women and children. The women seemed rejoiced to see us, blessed God we had come, and begged us to hold the place. These poor people were on the verge of starvation. . . .They looked famished and in every way miserable; the women in shabby calico skirts clinging around their lean frames; the men without coats, and all as dirty as they were ragged.

We could find no food for sale but a few watermelons, a few stale ginger-cakes and a dozen loaves of bread. . . . If the war does not end soon, the South will starve to death.

These paupers expressed no hostility. On the contrary, they urged us to remain and protect them. They feared the guerrillas would hang them for speaking to us.

At Shieldsboro he found "about 35 families in a state of semi-starvation" who

habitually ate but one meal a day and were not sure of that. . . . Nearly all these people looked hungry, gaunt, ghostly and yellow. I noted one girl with very handsome features, but so pale and thin that she was pitiful to see. Some of the women begged us to take them to New Orleans, but of course that could not be done.

A few days later on August 4, J.F.H. Claiborne wrote Governor Pettus from his plantation near Shieldsboro:

Dear Sir:

It is my duty to inform you of the suffering condition of the people of this and the contiguous Sea-Shore Counties.

You are aware that scarcely one acre in 1,000 in these counties will produce corn. . . . Two thirds of our people, however, never plant corn, relying alto-gether on procuring it in New Orleans in exchange for wood and charcoal, tar, etc.

The sudden and wholly unexpected fall of that city has cut us off entirely, and for nearly two months many families have been without bread. There is not a pound of flour or rice for sale in the County. . . . We stand between starvation and military execution. We are now proving our loyalty by star-vation—by the tears of our women and the cries of our children for bread.

Claiborne closed his letter with an appeal to Pettus to use his good offices to strike a bargain with the Federals in New Orleans to reopen trade in foodstuffs. As for Claiborne, he had already struck his own bargain, becoming the most important Union spy in south Mississippi. He dutifully informed the Yankees of the precise locations of clandestine saltworks and tanneries, the better to direct their raids against his neighbors, whom he termed "essentially animal" in one report to a Federal general.

On August 15 Claiborne in another letter to Pettus complained that Steede's "utterly useless" cavalry consumed too much food and ought to be sent north to Lieutenant General John C. Pemberton's army at Vicksburg. A

Confederate General John C. Pemberton stripped the Mississippi Gulf Coast of supplies and the last of its troops in late 1862 in order to garrison Fortress Vicksburg. Courtesy, Confederate Museum, Richmond

few weeks later Steede received orders to do just that. In an October 29 letter of protest to Pemberton, Steede asserted that his troops, then numbering 640 men,

needed to protect their own homes from the minions of Beast Butler and his black allies, for this very day I am informed that ... the negroe regiments enlisted at New Orleans are to be stationed on Ship Island and to make descents on the Sea Coast of Mississippi.

Steede's information was remarkably correct. The Second Regiment Louisiana Infantry Native Guards, a black regiment formed in September and October, was to be sent to Fort Massachusetts on Ship Island and to Fort Pike on the Rigolets.

Pemberton sent an officer to the coast in November to investigate the situation. In his communique the officer praised Steede's Rangers and exposed Claiborne as a spy. He further reported that the white inhabitants were going over to the Federal lines for food in droves and that several hundred slaves had gathered on Cat Island and were engaged in making charcoal and turpentine for the enemy. He advised an immediate attack on Cat Island to retrieve the slaves and the retention of Steede's men in the area to harass the enemy and prevent their taking the large herds of cattle and sheep in the piney woods.

Pemberton ordered Steede's Rangers to leave the coast and join his army. Half obeyed, and the other half disbanded to stay behind and protect their families. When he heard about Pemberton's order, Alfred E. Lewis, owner of Oldfields Plantation in West Pascagoula, wrote Pettus: "There is nothing here now to prevent ten well armed Yankees to roam fifty miles in the interior, for there is not one old man in ten that has a gun load of powder."

Hired artisans, aided by escaped slaves, had greatly advanced the brickworks of the fort on Ship Island by December 31. That night the commandant confided in his diary:

...the darkeys had a New Years and Emancipation Ball in the dining hall of the Fort workmen. They had a gay old time of it. Most of the Captains of the fleet were present and I went in with them. I was some what afraid of a disturbance but everything went off quietly.

At the stroke of midnight January 1, 1863, those "darkeys" and all the others in the states still at war with the Union achieved freedom by the terms of Lincoln's Emancipation Proclamation. Nine days later elements of the Second Regiment Louisiana Infantry Native Guards under the command of white officers left New Orleans to occupy Fort Pike and Ship Island.

Since Ship Island was being used as a political prison by the Federal authorities in New Orleans, some of the black troops became guards while the rest continued construction work on the fortifications. Three months later their bored commander, Colonel Nathan Daniels, decided to liven things up with a raid on East Pascagoula.

Daniels loaded 200 black troops aboard the steamer *General Banks,* formerly the *Creole,* and sallied forth accompanied by a gunboat escort. At 11:30 a.m. on April 9 the troops landed on the town wharf and immediately seized the hotel, raising the Stars and Stripes above its cupola.

Confederate pickets stationed in the town by the commander of Mobile battled the invaders, while riders summoned reinforcements from the camp near the town. A large Rebel force arrived and quickly pushed the black troops back out on the wharf, killing two in the process. Artillery fire from the boats pinned down the defenders during the reembarkation, but, inexplicably, one Federal gunner lobbed a shell into the midst of the black column on the wharf, killing four and wounding seven. The Yankees retreated to Ship Island at 2 p.m.

In his after-action report Daniels claimed that his men had inflicted a large number of casualties upon the Confederates. Rebel sources listed three slightly wounded. Whatever the casualties, the East Pascagoula raid was one of the earliest actions of the Civil War totally conceived and executed by the officers and men of a black regiment. One month after this action the army cashiered Daniels for "conduct unbecoming an officer and a gentleman, in grossly insulting an officer of the Navy, while in the company of a lady," and the black troops of the coast were reorganized and rechristened the "Corps d' Afrique," a name derisively rendered "Corpse of Africa" by the Rebels.

On April 30 Major General Nathaniel P. Banks, Butler's replacement in New Orleans, published an order in New Orleans requiring all citizens of the city to swear the oath of allegiance to the United States or leave the city within 45 days. In the exodus that followed, thousands boarded Federal transports to be unceremoniously dumped on the beach at East Pascagoula to make their way along the 40-mile shell road to Confederate Mobile as best they could.

As these refugees poured into Mobile during the month of May, further straining the dwindling food supply, Major General U.S. Grant launched a *blitzkrieg* from the Mississippi River deep into the heart of the state of Mississippi. He burned Jackson, smashed Pemberton's army in the decisive Battle of Champion Hill, drove the tattered remnants back into Vicksburg, and laid siege to the "Gibraltar of the South." Refugees from central Mississippi then poured into Mobile from the north, while deserters from the shattered Rebel armies drifted south into the piney woods.

Considerable numbers of "slackers" (draft dodgers) and deserters had been hiding out in the swamps and pine barrens beginning as early as the fall of New Orleans. But Grant's march through Mississippi, culminating in the surrender of Vicksburg on July 4, 1863, with its attendant demoralization and defeatism, swelled their ranks considerably. Known as "jayhawkers," these armed and dangerous men gathered into bands and committed atrocities against the inhabitants of isolated farmsteads.

At least 1,000 jayhawkers infested the backwoods of the three coast counties, with their area of greatest concentration being the Honey Island Swamp in the Pearl River Valley of Hancock County. Thereafter the defenseless inhabitants of the coast had to contend with jayhawker raids from the backwoods as well as Yankee raids from the Gulf.

On August 6, 1863, at Mississippi City occurred one of those poignant oddities for which the Civil War is noted. Lieutenant Commander Henry A. Adams of the U.S. warship *Vincennes* lay offshore under a flag of truce and requested a parley with the ranking Rebel officer in the area. That officer turned out to be Christopher Adams of the Handsboro Home Guards—his brother. The two men, both natives of Virginia, talked for an hour and then

Admiral David G. Farragut, who lived for a time in Pascagoula, commanded the U.S. Naval forces that conquered the city of New Orleans and captured the Confederate forts guarding the mouth of Mobile Bay. HNOC

returned to the business of trying to kill one another.

In late 1863 the stranglehold of the blockade on Mobile, the South's last post on the Gulf, was tightened. On September 12 the *Fanny* (formerly the *Fox*), the last great blockade runner on the Havana-to-Mobile run, slipped into Mississippi Sound and headed east toward Grant's Pass. Cut off by the Federal fleet at East Pascagoula, the crew of the Rebel vessel rammed the shore in front of the town, fired the ship, and splashed ashore. Mobile would receive few supplies by sea after that.

In the last big raid of the year, the Federals, acting on information supplied by Claiborne, struck a tannery at Shieldsboro at dawn on October 15. They burned buildings, vats, and a large quantity of hides before withdrawing. Thereafter during the cold winter months they contented themselves with tightening the blockade and enforcing their grinding starvation policy.

With Rebel ranks thinned by desertion and outright opposition to conscription agents, the Confederate authorities planned a grand sweep of the piney woods for the spring of 1864 to flush out the jayhawkers and slackers. In late April a picket of Louisiana troops lined up from Shieldsboro to the north shore of Lake Pontchartrain and played anvil to the hammer of the 6th and the 20th Mississippi regiments, which swept through the pine barrens into Honey Island Swamp driving all before them. The jayhawkers who resisted or attempted escape were hunted down with dogs and summarily shot or hanged.

The Confederates conscripted all men aged 17 to 50 caught in the net, and the commander of the operation reported to Jefferson Davis that "over 1,000 of these men have been sent from the woods to their commands." Barely two months later the men thus taken had deserted once again and had returned to wreak vengeance on the informants who had aided the army. A correspondent in Gainesville described the town as a "paradise of deserters."

The Rebels had no opportunity to stage another action against the deserters, for in August Admiral Farragut's fleet shelled into submission the forts guarding the mouth of Mobile Bay. The city itself, 30 miles up the shallow bay, still held out.

The Federals first shipped many of the men taken in the Mobile Bay forts to New Orleans, but beginning in October they transferred them to Ship Island. By the end of the month more than 1,200 prisoners were on the island, guarded by the 74th Regiment, United States Colored Infantry (formerly the Corps d' Afrique), now commanded by Colonel Ernest W. Holmstedt. The Federals raided the Handsboro lumberyards in early November, partially to secure materials for sheltering the vast influx of prisoners.

Mobile's stubborn refusal to surrender resulted in a Union plan to cut the city's north-south communication lines. Accordingly, on November 27, 1864, four thousand blue-coated cavalrymen commanded by Brigadier-General John W. Davidson rode out of Baton Rouge with orders to cut the Mobile & Ohio Railroad.

Heavy rains forced the column to bridge swollen creeks and rivers with portable pontoons. Reaching the Pascagoula at Fairley's Ferry in an icy, blinding rainstorm on December 11, Davidson found his pontoons insufficient to bridge the raging torrent and ordered his men to turn south to the sea. By prearrangement the navy lay off the coast with food and supplies for the troops.

As the column slogged south along the muddy road leading down the river to West Pascagoula, units carrying canteens full of turpentine ignited bonfires of lighter wood along the way for the comfort of the freezing Federals. As discipline broke down, the Yankee soldiers fired houses, barns, bridges, and corn cribs, shot cattle and sheep, and gave way to rape and pillage. In at least one case a man died in a futile effort to protect his sister from them. Reaching West Pascagoula on December 13, they ran amok, smashing into burial vaults, robbing the bodies, and strewing the remains about.

As Davidson evacuated West Pascagoula, another Federal army 3,000 strong landed in East Pascagoula and drove 12 miles inland on the Mobile Road. That battle group fought a few skirmishes and captured a large sawmill on the Escatawpa River, confiscating a million board feet of lumber, together with the mill machinery. Six weeks later that force withdrew as well.

In exchange for a like number of Union prisoners, Federal authorities returned to Mobile from Ship Island on January 7, 1865, the 603 survivors of the 800 prisoners taken near that city during Farragut's attack the previous August. In four months of captivity, nearly a quarter of those men had died of disease and exposure, and one had been murdered.

In that case a guard shot to death a 16-year-old prisoner for putting a sweet potato on a stove out of turn. An eyewitness to the shooting related that the sentinel then reloaded his weapon, exclaiming, "I have killed one of the damned rebels and I'll kill another if I can get a chance." Colonel Holmstedt, commanding Post Ship Island, in the official communique regarding the matter, stated:

J.F.H. Claiborne, Mississippi's foremost historian of the 19th century and Hancock County's most distinguished citizen, was the son of General F.L. Claiborne of War of 1812 fame, and nephew of W.C.C. Claiborne, former governor of both the Mississippi Territory and State of Louisiana. Confederate authorities suspected the celebrated historian as a Union spy, but in the absence of hard evidence they never charged him with treason. MDAH

... I can attach no blame to Private George Rice, who only carried out the orders of his superiors.... George Rice, of Company K, 74th U.S. Colored Troops is a trustworthy soldier, and the shooting of Private J.C. Dunclin, prisoner of war, has had a good effect on the surviving undisciplined crew.

But the Ship Island prisoners did attach blame, and years later some of them spotted ex-Private Rice on a steamboat dock, kidnapped him, tied him to a rock, and rolled it from a high bluff into the Alabama River.

The ages of the Confederate soldiers repatriated to Mobile ranged from 11 to 75. The South had reached the bottom of the manpower barrel, and by March the suffering of the people of the Mississippi Gulf Coast had reached a stage of agony sufficient to melt the heart of a Yankee gunboat captain. Lieutenant Commander A.R. Yates, unnerved by the sight of such misery, landed in Biloxi and issued his ship's stores to the starving populace. While engaged in this mission of mercy he was given a letter which read:

Honored Sir:

I trust you will excuse a stranger intruding himself on your notice, and I only plead the urgency of the demands and humanity as my apology.

I am a resident of Mississippi City, on the Sound. We number about sixty families. Of these, about ten are self-supporting; the balance are in a starving condition. ...

We have subsisted by making salt, but owing to the rains during the summer and fall ... we have not realized more than one-third the usual yield.

Our soil is ... sterile ... and we have to rely on the back country 100 to 150 miles for corn and meat. Owing to the late rains, the whole country is overflowed beyond precedent, and a month or six weeks must elapse before the roads will be in a condition suitable for hauling.

In the meantime, there are fifty families, women and children, that will starve if the Government does not come to their relief. Many of them have not tasted meat for months. Many more are now living on roots and fish.

Under these circumstances we appeal to your humanity. ... I am, sir, in behalf of a starving community, your very obedient servant,

Edwin C. Mix

Yates sent a message to the admiral in charge of the West Gulf Blockading Squadron explaining his unauthorized issuance of food and enclosed the letter from Mississippi City. The reply empowered him to feed anyone who would take an oath of allegiance to the United States.

On April 9, 1865, General Robert E. Lee surrendered to General Grant at Appomattox, and on that same day 16,000 Federal troops launched the final assault on Mobile, sweeping through the city's outer defenses at Blakeley, and the South's final fortress surrendered three days later. The victorious Yankees loaded more than 3,500 Confederate prisoners aboard transports and dumped

Jefferson Davis, President of the Confederate States of America, spent his last dozen years at Beauvoir, where he wrote The Rise and Fall Of The Confederate Government. *He died on December 6, 1889, at the age of 81. Temporarily entombed in New Orleans, his body was permanently interred in Richmond's Hollywood Cemetery on May 31, 1893. MCM*

them on the sands of Ship Island to join the ones already there. In the words of one prisoner:

While on the island the news came of the assassination of President Lincoln. This was an unfortunate thing for the Southern country, and we felt the effects of it at once, the guards treating us very badly, abusing and shooting us whenever an opportunity offered. One night a man stood up to shake the sand from his blanket and was shot.

Within a month nearly all of these men were paroled and sent home.

In early May Federal troops occupied the dilapidated coast towns to begin a decade of Reconstruction. Over the following months the remnants of the coast units straggled in from far-off fields and prison camps. Of the men of the Live Oak Rifles who marched out of Ocean Springs 210 strong in 1861, seven returned. A like number of the Twiggs Rifles returned to Pascagoula. The other four Sisters had suffered similar losses. The coast would have to rebuild minus a generation.

Chapter Five

HARVEST OF THE LAND AND SEA

Mississippi had entered the Civil War as the fifth-richest state in the nation. It plummeted in defeat to last place. At war's end only two of the coast's antebellum sawmills still operated. The others had been dismantled or destroyed. Fortunately, with the exception of Pascagoula, the Six Sisters themselves had suffered very little war damage. Shops and homes showed the effects of five years of neglect, and grass choked the streets, but commerce and industry quickened as more and more townspeople returned from their places of refuge.

Erratic steamer service resumed between New Orleans and Mobile in June 1865. A few hotels and boardinghouses along the coast made a brave, if feeble, attempt at a "summer season," which largely failed because of the condition of the wharves and the general poverty of the inhabitants of the flanking metropolitan areas.

During that first postwar summer, the black garrison remained at Ship Island, and a mixed force of Federal troops still occupied Pascagoula. Army authorities defused the potentially explosive racial situation by confining the Ship Island troops to the island and evacuating Pascagoula altogether.

The civilian male population of both races carried arms, but remarkably few incidents occurred because of certain characteristics of the coast unique in Mississippi. In the first place, the coast possessed a small but significant class of black landowners and entrepreneurs with a history of enterprise and stability dating back to colonial times. The men of this group, some of whom had actually fought for the Confederacy, checked the excesses of their newly freed brothers. In the second place, only a few white coastians had been wealthy enough to own slaves. Thirdly, and most importantly, unlike areas such as the Delta, where blacks outnumbered whites 15 to 1, blacks accounted for a relatively small 25 percent of the coast population. Thus, even under Republican Congressional Reconstruction, when ex-Confederate soldiers were disfranchised, the white Democrats still usually won at the ballot boxes in the coast counties and towns. In the decade following the Civil War, the Mississippi Gulf Coast experienced some isolated incidents of racial violence, but these paled in significance when compared to the upheavals in other sections of the state; and the Ku Klux Klan exerted comparatively little influence in the area during the Reconstruction era.

In October 1865 the *General Banks* shed its armament and reverted to the gallant and peaceful old *Creole,* heralding the restoration of reliable steamboat service. Other boats soon joined in the coast trade with the surviving prewar captains, most notably A.P. Boardman and A.L. Myers, back in the pilothouses.

Other men prominent in the affairs of the area during the war period returned to positions of peacetime leadership and influence. In November Biloxians elected war hero and recent state legislator John L. Henley as their mayor. The following month Pizarro K. Mayers purchased equipment in New

The government withdrew from the Ship Island garrison in April 1870 and placed the fort in charge of a keeper. In 1901 the fort guns were declared surplus property and sold to a New Orleans scrap-metal dealer. Only one 15-inch Rodman remains. BPL

Beginning as a sawyer earning $45 a month, Henry Weston founded the Weston Company, one of the pioneer antebellum companies which became one of the largest organizations in the lumber industry. The company's sawmill was photographed around the turn of the century. MDAH

Orleans for the reestablishment of his prewar *Handsboro Democrat.* Mayers, who had served to the end as a captain in the Confederate cavalry, remained an "unreconstructed Rebel." He surrendered his sword but took up his pen in a private struggle against the carpetbaggers and scalawags.

The rafting of timber resumed on the rivers and creeks that winter, and 30 sawmills were in operation by spring 1866. Celebrating the reopening of the stores and one foundry at Handsboro, Mayers exulted in his newspaper, "Business of all kinds is looking up, and bids fair in a short time to eclipse its former mark of enterprise."

That summer the Christian brothers converted the Pass Christian Hotel into a boys' college, and the newly renovated Barnes Hotel at Mississippi City became the unchallenged leading inn of the coast, announcing year-round operations. The Ocean Springs Hotel reopened, and all the other towns offered at least boardinghouse accommodations.

Innovations and rumors of change filled the conversation of the people. A

New York firm set up the first large-scale turpentine distillery in coast history at Gainesville, and at nearby Logtown the Weston Lumber Company established the region's largest and most modern lumber mill. Most tantalizing of all, though, were the rumors of railroads. After 30 years of disappointment on that issue, few believed a railroad truly possible.

In March 1867, following nearly two years of uninterrupted Southern home rule, the Radical Republican Congress imposed military Reconstruction upon the prostrate South. The coast became part of the 4th Military District, and the U.S. Army established an occupation force at Pass Christian. Benjamin Orr, a Louisiana scalawag, set up office in that town as U.S. commissioner in charge of the Freedman's Bureau and voter registration. Black men now had the right to vote, and their children could now receive an education. In April 1867 a black Methodist minister opened a school for the children of freedmen at Bay St. Louis.

Despite the strictures placed on white voters and despite the registration of black voters, the former still outnumbered the latter. P.K. Mayers, learning of

the failure of Orr's voter registration drive, prophesied a "safe reconstruction." The printable portion of Orr's reply to that prophesy included the descriptive and colorful phrase that "Mr. Mayers can crow on his dung hill" in Handsboro and closed with the warning that a visit to Pass Christian would be injurious to Mayers' health.

The bitterness of Reconstruction slipped into the background as survey crews for the impending New Orleans to Mobile railway showed up at various points along the coast in June 1867. Cautious disbelief gave way to jubilation as railway officials went on record as predicting completion of the new line within two years. Coast economic recovery had already given reason for optimism, but it had been spotty and uneven. A massive works project like a railroad would prime the pump in every sector and set a general recovery in motion.

Reflecting the new festive mood, Bay St. Louis in August hosted the first official sailing regatta since the war. Barnes Hotel held a cockfight and another

The pine trees in this turpentine orchard have been "cupped" to collect the sap to make gum turpentine, the only turpentine derived from live trees. After the tree had been worked and cut for lumber, the resinous stump was then blown out of the ground with explosives and used to make commercial or wood turpentine. Courtesy, Tommy Wixon

contest never before witnessed on the coast and probably never after—a mule regatta. To the cheers of a large throng, three fashionably dressed gentlemen astride mules rode directly into the Sound, the object being the determination of the most seaworthy animal on the basis of greatest distance of penetration into the Gulf. Leander, with a distance of three-fourths of a mile triumphed over Parnassus and a gray mule misnamed Walk-in-the-Water.

Another new sport with a brighter future gathered crowds on October 3 at Pass Christian. The Pass Christian Yahaws played the Christian Brothers College Young Athletes in the coast's first baseball game to be reported in detail. The Yahaws, who already had the game sewed up at 17 to 10, magnanimously relinquished their turn at bat in the top of the fifth on account of rain. Top honors for the most number of runs (four) by a single player went to Henry Orr, son of the Radical Republican U.S. commissioner.

The political climate again turned nasty as the Republicans moved to consolidate their power in Mississippi. Proclamations against carrying concealed weapons were ignored by both sides, and on the eve of the June elections both sides resorted to intimidation, threats, and harsh language. In the *Handsboro Democrat* Mayers accused Benjamin Orr, then a candidate for the state legislature, of being a "liar, a scoundrel and a thief." The Republicans lost the election, and both Benjamin and his son Henry made numerous public threats to kill Mayers.

Matters came to a head on July 8, 1868, when Mayers accompanied his wife and sister-in-law to Pass Christian for the purpose of visiting friends. The following evening at 6 p.m., as he walked alone and unarmed back to the town wharf, he spied the Orrs lurking on the sidewalk some distance up the street. Forewarned of their intentions, Mayers entered Thomas Bond's store, borrowed a double-barreled shotgun, and resumed his stroll. As he neared his antagonists, Benjamin shouted, "You have denounced me as a liar and a thief." Mayers replied, "I have and you have threatened my life." Even as P.K. spoke, the elder Orr drew his pistol. The editor leveled the shotgun at Benjamin and discharged a load of buckshot into his side, killing him instantly. Mayers then turned the shotgun on Henry, who was pulling his revolver. When the second barrel misfired, the younger Orr put a pistol ball in Mayers' left wrist and emptied the revolver without further effect as the editor ran for cover.

A detachment of infantry surrounded the Harrison County Courthouse during the trial the following month. The verdict of the court was self-defense. When Mayers was re-arrested and retried by the military, the verdict remained the same. Mayers then resumed the publication of his newspaper without further harassment.

By May 1869 no one doubted the reality of the New Orleans, Mobile & Chattanooga Railroad. Hundreds of men, both black and white, worked at grading the roadbed and constructing immense bridges across Pascagoula Bay, Biloxi Bay, Bay St. Louis, the Rigolets, and Chef Menteur Pass. The lumber mills of Handsboro and those at the mouths of the Pearl and Pascagoula rushed to fill fat contracts for cross ties and bridge timbers.

A load of English rails arrived in Mobile in October, and on November 9 the track-laying commenced from Mobile westward. Soon thereafter crews began tracking from the foot of New Orleans' famed Canal Street eastward and at several points in between.

The 4th Military District ceased to exist in February 1870 with the restoration of Mississippi's Congressional representation in Washington, and the deployment of the Ship Island garrison to other commands then ended the military occupation of the coast. On the heels of that evacuation the people of Harrison County indicted their carpetbagger sheriff and other officials on charges of extortion and malfeasance, ejecting them from office.

That Fourth of July the men of New Orleans' Mississippi Fire Company Number 2 arrived by steamer in Biloxi for their annual outing, hosted that year by the Blessey family. Mayor John L. Henley, in his last official act, welcomed the group and joined in the festivities. As the celebration grew spirited, someone suggested the display of an American flag. In due time one flapped between two trees, and the firemen's brass band lined up to play the "Star Spangled Banner." The burst of patriotism ended one minute into the anthem as the unreconstructed coronets and trombones dropped into "Dixie."

Two weeks later New Orleans Volunteer Fire Company Number 14 journeyed to the Blesseys' in Biloxi for their outing and, following the celebration, boarded the *Creole* for the return trip. On the forward lower deck of the steamboat stood 30 black railway workers bound for another section of track. One by the name of Smith led the others in a serenade recounting the allegedly cowardly actions of the Confederate defenders of New Orleans during the recent unpleasantness. Other verses of the insulting ditty extolled the bravery and obvious superiority of black troops during the taking of that city.

An officer of the *Creole* descended to the lower deck, remonstrated with Smith, and suggested a less inflammatory ballad. As the officer returned to his post, Smith hurled a number of profane epithets describing that officer in particular and whites in general. In the midst of the tirade, one of the firemen went forward and inquired of Smith if members of his profession were included in the unflattering assessment.

Accounts differ as to exactly what happened next in this bloodiest race riot in coast history, but someone, not the fireman, struck Smith. In the ensuing melee, Smith practically severed the fireman's left arm with a straight razor. Simultaneously, a gunman standing behind the injured man fired three

Opposite page: Pizarro K. Mayers (bottom, courtesy, Tommy Wixon) was owner and editor of the Handsboro Democrat *(top, courtesy, BPL), the only newspaper on the coast during Reconstruction. His editorial column expressed his aggressive and often abusive opinions of certain "carpetbagger" politicians. Mayers took the paper to Pascagoula in 1878, where it became the* Pascagoula Chronicle Star.

Below: Eliza Jane Poitevent grew up in Hobolochitto, and, writing under the pseudonym "Pearl Rivers," submitted a number of poems to the prestigious New Orleans Daily Picayune. *Eventually she married the owner of the paper and upon his death became the first woman to own and edit a major American newspaper. In 1884 she succeeded in having the name of her hometown changed to that of her paper—Picayune. HNOC*

shots, instantly killing David Lot of Handsboro and Jim Daniels, the two black men flanking Smith. The entire fire brigade rushed to the aid of their fallen comrade and then turned on his antagonist, who belatedly attempted to apologize. The boat captain prevented the irate firemen from throwing Smith overboard, but they did beat him unconscious with cordwood and hog-tie him.

When the boat docked at Mississippi City the black men disembarked and stood on the wharf with shotguns, pistols, and clubs at the ready, while the captain called for the Harrison County sheriff. The sheriff and the coroner arrived and duly conducted an on-the-spot inquest involving more than 100 witnesses. Near midnight the officials rendered the verdict that the two deceased had died of gunshot wounds inflicted by "some party unknown." The firemen swore out an affidavit against Smith and delivered him to the sheriff's custody. The rest of the railway workers remained on shore as the boat proceeded to New Orleans.

Above: Fernando Upton Gautier, born in 1822 aboard a ship journeying to America, first settled in New Orleans. He came to work in Biloxi sawmills and in the early 1860s established his own mill near the mouth of the Pascagoula River, founding the town that now bears his name. Courtesy, Tommy Wixon

Above right: The Mexican Gulf Hotel, built in 1883, advertised such modern conveniences as electric bells and gas and steam heat. It was a favorite winter resort among people from Chicago, St. Louis, Cincinnati, and other points north and west. From the Antique Print Collection, BPL

Right: This map, published by the New Orleans and Mobile division of the Louisville & Nashville Railroad, shows the route between those two cities with stops at each of the Gulf Coast resorts along the way. BPL

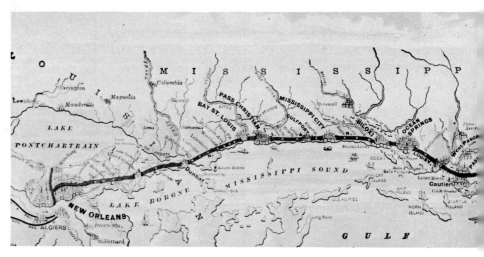

Three months after that sad affair wonderful news electrified the coast. On October 29, 1870, at 5 p.m. two trains, one from Mobile and the other from New Orleans, met near Chef Menteur Pass, 27 miles east of the latter city. Two representatives of the railroad drove in a gold spike and a silver spike joining the final rails that united the Gulf City with the Crescent City. The next day the first excursion train traversed the entire 139-mile run between the two cities. Regular official passenger and freight service officially began on November 21.

Without a doubt, the building of the railroad was the greatest single event in the next quarter-century of coast development. A *Handsboro Democrat* editorial aptly assessed its immediate impact:

We have had one great help—the railroad. It has literally clothed the naked and fed the hungry. It has given employment at high wages to every man who would work.

It has purchased enormous quantities of timber at high prices. It has built dredge boats and kept our saw mills and schooners in motion.

It has paid for fresh provisions, vegetables, milk, poultry, fish, wagon hire, water, fuel, sand, shell, even for dirt promptly and generously.

And if there be ... a man who cannot say from the bottom of his heart, God bless this great enterprise and all concerned with it, he must be a thankless fellow indeed.

In addition to pulling the coast economy out of the postwar doldrums, the construction of the railroad began the shift of industrial preeminence from Handsboro to the Pascagoula area. Much of the timberland accessible from the comparatively small streams converging on Handsboro had already been cut over, while the lands drained by the Pascagoula River lay relatively untouched. Handsboro mill owners began relocating their operations to the Pascagoula area, making it the beneficiary of the former town's expertise, talent, and hardware. Possibly the earliest migrant of this ilk, Fernando Gautier, moved his mill to West Pascagoula and eventually gave his name to that settlement.

Within a few years, Gautier became the site of a new industry spawned to solve a problem raised by the building of the railroad. Attacks by the teredo

The coast excursion trains from Mobile to New Orleans ran from 1870 until discontinued in 1969. The rail through-service ended in 1973. This engine was photographed in the late 1800s. MDAH

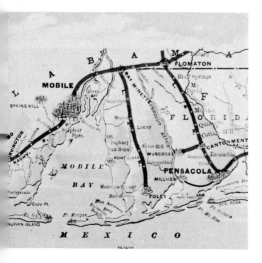

The David & Manning logging outfit of Jackson County was one of many such logging companies during the lumber boom. Logs were hauled by oxen to the streams and rivers of the piney woods to be rafted to the mills. Far better suited to the task than mules and horses, oxen were able to go through the low swampy country, making roads where there were none and bogging down less. Oxen were also cheaper to maintain, since they could graze on the open range when not working. Courtesy, W.E. David

worm on the untreated bridge pilings in the brackish bays resulted in the development and establishment of large and profitable creosote works as a mainstay of the incipient town.

The railway official in charge of naming the station on the east side of the bay, understandably confused by the profligate use of the word "Pascagoula" in reference to the bay, the communities, and various branches of the river, simply christened the station "Scranton" in honor of himself. For a half-century the inhabitants did battle over the two names, with the original finally emerging triumphant.

The town continued to drain the life's blood from Handsboro, resulting in the establishment of shipyards and foundries alongside its lumber mills. Even the redoubtable P.K. Mayers abandoned his hometown to establish the *Pascagoula Democrat-Star.*

The railroad bound the Six Sisters together with steel rails, establishing stations in each and at a number of other points. Two of these, Montgomery Station and Scott's Station, developed into sizable towns. The former became Waveland and the latter Long Beach.

Rapid rail transport to New Orleans and Mobile and access through them to the rail networks of the nation changed the lives of the coastal inhabitants in myriad ways. For the first time the coast became an exporter of foodstuffs. The production of vegetables, fruit, and pecans became big business all along the coast, and truck farming provided the basis for the growth of the new town of Long Beach.

"Big Jim," the Poitevent and Farve sawmill built in 1890, was an immense operation that cut 200,000 board feet of lumber a day. The lumber was loaded directly onto schooners to be carried out to deep water for shipment. The mill went out of business in 1904. From S.G. Thigpen, Pearl River County, 1965

The railroad practically ended the passenger, though not the bulk freight, service of the steamboats. By rail a passenger could travel the entire 139 miles between New Orleans and Mobile in six hours for five dollars—half the price and one-third the time of passage by steamboat. Denizens of the cities could commute daily to the coast if they wished or could enjoy a one-day weekend excursion from New Orleans as far east as Ocean Springs.

And that was not the end of it. The railroad inaugurated a second season for the watering places by enabling the inhabitants of Northern and Midwestern states to escape the rigors of winter. As more and more of these "snowbirds" flocked to the "American Riviera," the hotels remained open all year. In 1883 promoters in Pass Christian opened the magnificent Mexican Gulf Hotel, the first catering primarily to the snowbird trade.

The reawakening of the towns and sawmills of the coastal fringe by the railroad benefited the people of the piney woods as well. Following the Civil War they had resumed their former pattern of subsistence farming combined with the grazing of large herds of sheep and cattle, but the demand for forest products drew them more and more into the timber industry. By the early 1880s lumbering had become the main occupation of the back-country people.

The floating of saw logs to market continued throughout the year on streams of sufficient depth. On the smaller tributaries of the Pearl and the Pascagoula the choppers stockpiled logs in preparation for the heavy rains of late winter and early spring. When the freshets came, the men foresook their everyday chores and raced to the creek banks for the log drive.

A log drive had much in common with a cattle drive and echoed its terminology. Each landowner, chopper, caralog operator, and creek runner or drive foreman marked each log he processed with his own special brand. In time the L.N. Dantzler Lumber Company brand book at Moss Point listed more than 5,000 brands used in the Pascagoula River system. Thus protected, loggers herded their bawling, bumping charges down the stream courses together. The creek runner stationed some of his men at the bends armed with long spike poles to push the logs into the current if they tried to ground. Others outfitted with peavey hooks or even ox teams dragged strays out of low places and swamps when they overran the creek banks.

At the confluence of the creeks with the rivers, the men placed 10 or 15 logs parallel and pegged a hardwood pole binder across them to form a crib. A number of cribs roped together formed a raft, and one of these they designated as a sort of floating chuckwagon. The cook, who also took care of the bedrolls, prepared the meals in an iron pot over an open fire as the whole mass drifted south toward Moss Point or Gainesville.

Below right: "The very basis of his life, let it be noted, was his stand against compromise of principle. He would have no traffic where principle was involved. In this respect he was of course unusual; even extraordinary." Toney A. Hardy wrote these words of his father William Harris Hardy, railroad baron and "founder" of Gulfport and Hattiesburg. The elder Hardy is pictured around the turn of the century. Courtesy, Mrs. Roy Johnson

Above: After 1900 the caralog was outmoded by the eight-wheel log wagon developed by John Lindsey of Laurel, Mississippi. Lindsey's wagon retained the wide treads of the caralog, but decreased the diameter of the wheels by more than one-half and increased the number of wheels from two to eight. Courtesy, Wyndon "Buddy" Smith

From the headwaters of the Leaf and Chickasawhay, the journey to Moss Point might require weeks. From the mouth of Red or Black Creek, three to five days sufficed. At the mill the buyers broke up the rafts, read the brands, penned the logs, and paid the loggers accordingly. Burdened with flour, needles, calico, and something to warm them on the long trek home, the men returned to start the cycle once again.

The single-bit pole ax gave way to the double-bit ax in the 1870s and that to the crosscut saw in the 1880s. By the turn of the century the eight-wheel Lindsey log wagon replaced the Usan Vaughan caralog; but despite these improvements in felling and hauling logs, the economical strike zone extended but four miles from a stream. Only railroads could penetrate and conquer this last great virgin pine forest in the South. Two former Civil War captains (one gray and one blue), turned captains of industry, would lead the assault.

The year after his discharge from the Confederate Army, William Harris Hardy purchased the stock of the Gulf & Ship Island Railroad, defunct since

Above: This photograph shows a youthful Joseph T. Jones in 1864 when he was First-Lieutenant Jones of the 91st Regiment, Pennsylvania Volunteers. Jones went from being a Pennsylvania oil tycoon, to owning the Gulf & Ship Island Railroad Company, to being the "Yankee fairy godfather" of Gulfport. From Melodia B. Rowe, Captain Jones: The Biography of a Builder, *1942*

Left: These two photographs are scenes of the Gulf Coast turpentine industry. In the bottom photograph (courtesy, Mrs. Thurman Flurry), crude gum has been gathered in barrels and rolled on skids up into a wagon enroute to a distillery. The top photograph (courtesy, Celeste Allen), circa 1915, shows a group of turpentine workers. Turpentine workers were primarily poor blacks who lived in a company-owned-camp at the mercy of a boss or overseer. They were often kept completely dependent on the company for food and clothing as well.

the bursting of the Mississippi City bubble in 1837. Unable to secure the capital necessary to resurrect the project at that time, Hardy secured backing for another line.

This New Orleans & Northeastern Railway (later the Southern Railway), completed in 1883 from New Orleans to Meridian, penetrated the piney woods of the Mississippi Panhandle for the first time. Along its route the new railroad infused new life into some old towns and spawned entirely new ones. Principal among these were Picayune, Poplarville, and Lumberton.

While the New Orleans & Northeastern was still under construction, Hardy selected a point on that line 72 miles due north of the Ship Island anchorage as the junction for the other railway he intended to build from the coast to Jackson. On that site he erected a depot and platted a town that he christened Hattiesburg in honor of his second wife, Hattie Lott.

In 1887, just four years after he founded the Hub City, Hardy purchased 5,000 acres fronting for a mile on Mississippi Sound in the virtually empty

The "Four-Spot" was a Baldwin locomotive that pulled one of the first lumbering trains to Vancleave in Jackson County. Courtesy, Celeste Allen

strip between Mississippi City and Scott Station. He selected that particular site as the southern terminus of the Gulf & Ship Island Railroad because it most directly served the proposed dredged channel extension of the Ship Island anchorage and, incidentally, allowed his construction gangs to avoid a number of streams and high ridges in the interior. The coming town's locational and economic factors combined to suggest its name—Gulfport. By his site selection Hardy birthed a new coastal town and spelled the doom of Mississippi City-Handsboro.

By 1892 Hardy's engineers had graded the line from Gulfport to Hattiesburg and laid 20 miles of track. At that critical juncture a monetary panic similar to the one of 1837 halted construction again as it had done then. Even the rails in place were ripped up by the bankrupt company and sold to satisfy creditors.

Joseph T. Jones, a former Union officer, picked up Hardy's fallen standard. Following his recovery from wounds in both feet suffered in the Charge of Cold Harbor in the last year of the war, Jones had become a multimillionaire Pennsylvania oil tycoon. In the summer of 1895 he was present at a business meeting in Bradford, Pennsylvania, at which the defunct Gulf & Ship Island Railroad Company was offered for sale. Indulging a whim, he purchased the bankrupt company's stock and, by risking a great deal of his personal fortune, completed the line between Gulfport and Hattiesburg in October 1896. Years later, recalling those days, Captain Jones confided to a friend, "The two things I most wanted in life were a wife and a railroad." Then he chuckled and mused, "When I got them I found they were the very things I didn't want."

The penetration of the pine barrens by the Gulf & Ship Island Railroad attracted thousands of settlers into what one *Biloxi Herald* reporter termed a "howling wilderness." At average intervals of three miles, sawmills and turpentine stills sprang up beside the tracks to serve as the nuclei for a string of villages. Of these, Wiggins became the most important. Simultaneously, yet another railway, the Mobile, Jackson & Kansas City, snaked its way from Mobile through Jackson County to Hattiesburg. This line, as the others,

Dr. George A. McHenry brought 50 families from Michigan to settle on the right-of-way of the Gulf & Ship Island Railroad in 1889, founding the town which now bears his name. At the outbreak of the Spanish-American War in 1898, Dr. McHenry entered the service as a surgeon with the rank of captain and proceeded to Cuba (left). During his term of duty his immunity to yellow fever enabled him to render a valuable contribution to the final conquest of the dread disease. Dr. McHenry's Victorian home (below left) is one of the few structures remaining in the virtual ghost town. Courtesy, Dolores McHenry Mauldin

spawned a number of villages, with Lucedale becoming the most prominent.

By the turn of the century the railroads of the Mississippi Gulf Coast Panhandle formed two in-facing right triangles with the common side being the Gulf & Ship Island. At many points 30-mile-long "dummy lines" radiated out from these roads into the forests. The stands of trees still inaccessible could be reached by constructing feeders from stream banks. This new technology exposed the entire forest to the sawyer's blade and doomed it within a single generation.

In 1896, the same year he linked Hattiesburg and Gulfport, Jones built a pier in the latter that carried the tracks 4,500 feet into the Sound. The 12-foot depth at the end of the pier sufficed for lighters but not for ships. Only a dredged channel from the pierhead to the Ship Island anchorage could accommodate large vessels.

Even though Gulfport in 1898 "was just a nice bed of sand with a few shacks, two streets and a creek running through it," the legislature incorporated it as a city and the governor appointed Finley B. Hewes as mayor. Hewes, having entered military service at the outbreak of the Spanish American War that year, declined the commission and remained in military service.

The outburst of nationalism attending the "Splendid Little War of '98" dissipated much of the resentment left over from the Civil War. That year Congress removed the last political disabilities on ex-Confederates and that, together with news of stunning victories won by America's armed forces, deeply affected the people of the coast. Hundreds gathered at the Harrison County Courthouse on the Fourth of July, raised a huge American flag, and cheered as the bands played the "Star Spangled Banner," "Dixie," and other national airs. In that first "Glorious Fourth" in 38 years, the coast psychologically rejoined the Union.

Reference to Gulfport as a "Yankee upstart" lost much of its bite as the town's "Yankee fairy godfather" proceeded with his work. The government refused to dredge the Ship Island channel, so Jones bankrolled the project himself. The operation to cut the 24-foot-deep, 300-foot-wide trench began on May 9, 1899, in the face of pessimistic warnings that the next great storm would refill it with its own spoil.

On August 14, 1901, the dredge cut had reached a depth of 20 feet when the infant weather service, probably for the first time in coast history, forecast the approach of a hurricane. The forewarned citizens took cover as the wind howled and the waves mounted to 25 feet in the Sound. Not only did the blow fail to fill the channel, it bored its entire length three feet deeper. In the words of a *Daily Picayune* reporter:

The hurricane, the natural enemy of the people of the Gulf Coast, once again pounded the area on August 15, 1901. Biloxi residents survey the wreckage the morning after (below). Another view (below right) was taken during the storm, as the eye passed. Courtesy, Mrs. O.M. Smith

Left: The deep-water channel completed from Gulfport Harbor to Ship Island in January 1902 by Captain Jones allowed large ships to come safely into the port. Here the French vessel DeSaix is anchored at Gulfport in 1918. Courtesy, Blanche Saucier

Below: Captain Joseph T. Jones' dream of greatness for his city of Gulfport included not only dredging a deep-water channel, but also moving the Harrison County seat from Mississippi City to Gulfport. Jones donated the land and laid the cornerstone for the first Harrison County Courthouse in Gulfport, which opened on November 9, 1903. MDAH

The building of the Great Southern Hotel in 1902 was one of the many accomplishments of Captain Joseph T. Jones. The finest luxury hotel on the coast, the Great Southern stood proudly on the corner of Highway 90 and 25th Avenue until it was demolished in 1950, a victim of "progress." MDAH

This was an agreeable surprise to the officials and consequently president J.T. Jones has a broad smile on his face. This was as strong a test as the Channel will have to stand, and deep water is an assured fact.

The port opened for business in January 1902. When the underwriters refused to insure ships entering the untested port, Jones made Captain Aregino of the Italian steamer *Trojan* lying at Ship Island a deal he could not turn down. He personally gave Aregino $1,000 and promised to pay for any damage suffered by the ship. The *Trojan* berthed without incident.

As stevedores loaded the ship, Jones ordered a special train out of Jackson bearing a number of state legislators, the governor's wife, and William H. Hardy, the man whose dream he had fulfilled. Following shipboard festivities for these guests, Jones presented Captain Aregino with a new set of silverware to replace that stolen by the guests as souvenirs of the grand occasion, and the *Trojan* steamed out with a load of pine lumber. Thereafter, ships flocked to the harbor.

In June, Jones assembled Gulfport's 3,000 mostly male residents and out-

In its heyday the Great Southern Hotel employed these people as golf caddies. The elderly man in the center was at one time Jefferson Davis' personal valet. MDAH

lined his future plans. Among his gifts to his new city, he told them, was a lot for the location of the new Harrison County Courthouse. On August 1, 1902, the people of the county voted to remove the seat of government from Mississippi City to Gulfport.

By October Jones' three-story brick Gulf & Ship Island office building neared completion, and the material for an entire block of brick stores had been unloaded. Near the beach a large force worked diligently on the $250,000, 250-room, 125-bath Great Southern Hotel. That same month Jones broke ground for a General Electric light plant that would supply power for a 25-ton ice plant, a steam laundry, and the rest of the town.

In 1907 nine-year-old Gulfport became the world's leading exporter of yellow pine lumber. By the time of his death in 1916 at Buffalo, New York, Joseph T. Jones, a former captain of the Union army, had bequeathed to the Mississippi Gulf Coast a charming legacy. At a personal cost of $16 million, he had created out of lumber and locomotives a thriving all-American city of 8,000 souls on a formerly deserted strand in a land he had once fought to destroy.

Above: William K.M. Dukate, originally from Indiana, arrived in Biloxi in 1875. He joined in organizing the first seafood company on the Mississippi Gulf Coast. Dukate donated a school building in 1898 and took an active interest in Biloxi's development. BPL

Above right: F. William Elmer was born in Biloxi in 1847. His active role in the public schools, local and state politics, and the fledgling seafood industry, earned him the description "one of the most useful citizens Biloxi had ever produced." BPL

Above far right: William F. Gorenflo, born in 1844 in Bay St. Louis, moved to Biloxi as a child. He had been among the first to ship oysters to nearby towns. In addition to being a pioneer of the seafood industry, Gorenflo was an active civic and political leader and donated property and funds for building public and parochial schools. BPL

So the post-Civil War harvest of the timber resources of the "green sea" culminated in the birth of Gulfport. Likewise, the contemporaneous harvest of the blue sea aided in the economic recovery of the coast region and, incidentally, catapulted Biloxi into prominence.

Seafood had been a mainstay in the food supply of the coast from the beginning of human habitation. The Indians left vast middens as silent testimony to the importance of shellfish in their diet. Almost without exception the written accounts of early explorers and settlers pay homage to the bountiful harvest of oysters, shrimp, and fish of the Mississippi Sound, and advertisements for the antebellum watering places invariably extoll the excellence of the delicacies supplied daily by coastal fishermen. However, the fishermen serving New Orleans, Mobile, and the Gulf Coast often oversupplied the daily demand, and in the absence of methods of preservation, they lost as much as half their catch to spoilage.

Ironically, a New Orleans shoe-manufacturing family by the name of Dunbar pioneered the preservation techniques so necessary to the establishment of a profitable seafood industry. George W. Dunbar, the patriarch of the clan, prudently sent his two sons to Europe at the outbreak of the Civil War, and they whiled away the war years studying French canning methods. At the close of hostilities, the younger Dunbars returned to New Orleans and applied their new expertise first to fruit and then, in 1867, to shrimp.

A contemporaneous event that later had a far-reaching effect on the seafood industry was the appearance of the first artificial ice plant in New Orleans. Some boats were actually outfitted with ice boxes at that early date, but the product remained for some time too expensive for large-scale use. Consequently, unable to bring the shrimp to the cannery, the Dunbars took a floating cannery to the shrimp.

Anchored off Grand Terre Island, Louisiana, the Dunbars processed the shrimp and packed them in tin cans. When a chemical reaction inside the container turned their product an unappetizing shade of black, they solved the problem by first enclosing the shrimp in small cotton sacks before sealing the can. Improvements in ice manufacturing by 1875 enabled the Dunbars to

permanently locate their factory in New Orleans.

The Crescent City's innovations in the seafood industry portended well for the Mississippi Gulf Coast in general and Biloxi in particular. After 1870 rapid rail transport resulted in the shipment of small quantities of oysters in shells packed in buckets of ice from the coast to points as far distant as Memphis. The trade, however, remained negligible until a remarkable group of men formed a partnership in 1880 to construct Biloxi's first seafood cannery.

Of the five men only two, F. William Elmer and William F. Gorenflo, were native coastians. The other three were English-born John Maycock, a resident of Biloxi since 1839, Lazaro Lopez, an 1868 immigrant from Spain, and William K.M. Dukate, an Indianan who came to Biloxi in 1875 as an agent of the New Orleans & Mobile Railroad. None of them knew anything about the seafood industry, but all were willing to risk their capital to find out. Organizing as the firm of Lopez, Elmer & Company, they dispatched Dukate to Baltimore to observe canning operations and to purchase the necessary equipment to pack oysters and shrimp.

In 1881 the plant began operations on the bay, and its success proved contagious. The original corporation soon dissolved as the partners split up to form rival companies. News of the new coast industry spread rapidly, attracting the Dunbars and other canning pioneers to Biloxi. Within five years five large plants had sprouted on all three sides of the Biloxi peninsula— on Back Bay, at Point Cadet, and on the front beach. Subsequently, satellites of these and entirely new operations sprang up at Pascagoula, Ocean Springs, Mississippi City, Pass Christian, and Bay St. Louis.

Because of the seasonal nature of the industry, some of the firms switched to the canning of vegetables and fruit during slack periods. By 1885 the canning plants, together with the growing tourist industry, had so improved coastal economic life that one New Orleans newspaper reporter announced that the coast towns were "losing their Southern shabbiness" and "taking on ... the thrifty appearance of Eastern seashore cities."

Other writers of the time compared the area to more distant lands. The

Born in 1850 in Spain, Lazaro Lopez (above, courtesy, BPL) arrived in Biloxi in 1868, poor and speaking little English. He became an American success story in the coast's seafood industry and shared the fruits of that success with the city of Biloxi. Another of his businesses was L. Lopez & Company Grocers (top, courtesy, Mr. and Mrs. Julius Lopez), a department store located on the corner of Reynoir and Howard

sobriquets "American Riviera" and "American Mediterranean" were accurate descriptions not only of the environment and economics but also in large measure of the people, many of whom shared Southern European origins. The French and Spanish of colonial times had been joined early in the antebellum period by numerous Italians, a few Greeks, and some Balkan Slavs. As in their homelands, many of these engaged in fishing, but in light of future events the last mentioned became the most important single group in the modern seafood industry on the coast.

E.C. Jouillian moved his seafood business from Scranton to Back Bay in 1888. At the turn of the century the plant packed 150,000 cases of oysters and 25,000 cases of shrimp annually. Three hundred men, women, and children worked in the factory. Aside from the company-owned fleet of 35 boats, 200 or more boats gained employment from Jouillian. BPL

Even today when asked their origins, some of the descendants of this group may reply, "Austrian," but in truth their ancestors hailed from a conquered province of the Austrian Empire, which later became part of the nation of Yugoslavia at its birth immediately after World War I. That province, called Dalmatia, is a land of barrier island-guarded shores very like the Mississippi Gulf Coast.

The few who came in the early 19th century retained their Yugoslavian connections, and when the seafood boom of the 1880s opened the way, the former trickle of immigrants became a flood. Seeking to avoid conscription, which amounted to slavery for them in the foreign Austrian army of occupation, the young men came first. They went to work immediately, and as soon as possible they sent ticket money to Dalmatia. When the families entered the New York immigrant stations, the immigration authorities placed a tag on their coats directing the train conductors to route them to Biloxi. The Yugoslavs started out working in the seafood industry and wound up owning most of it.

In the decade of the 1880s Biloxi's population rose from 1,500 to more than 3,000, but even that labor force could not handle the seasonal glut at the canneries. Consequently, in 1890 a Biloxi firm imported the first contingent of seasonal workers by rail from Baltimore. Called Bohemians, these people were actually Poles. Housed in shotgun company houses on Point Cadet and Back Bay, the women and children picked shrimp while the men shucked oysters. Later contingents manned the factories in other coast towns, particularly at Pass Christian. This symbiotic relationship between the coast and Baltimore continued for more than 40 years. Apparently the Poles preferred this nomadic life, for despite invitations and inducements, only a few remained as permanent residents.

In 1887 the Artesian Ice Company began operations in Biloxi, increasing the range and cruise time of the fishing fleet. Two principal vessels served as the workhorses of the seafood industry—the lugger and the Biloxi schooner.

Above: In 1941 the Times Picayune *photographed and interviewed members of the Yugoslavian community at Biloxi for a feature story. The community has played an important role since it was established in the 19th century. Courtesy, Linda Gabrich Bourgeois*

Left: In antebellum days ice was shipped from New England to New Orleans packed in sawdust, and then hauled by steamboats to the watering places. The ability to manufacture ice in Biloxi was a boon to the seafood industry. Pictured is a turn-of-the-century stock certificate for Artesian Ice Company. Courtesy, Mr. and Mrs. Julius Lopez

Above: No law forbade the use of child labor in the seafood factories. "We got up at four o'clock in the morning—dressed and worked until seven o'clock or six-thirty—come home from school and changed those clothes—went back to the factory and worked until six o'clock in the evening" (excerpt from an oral history). Noted photographer and child-labor-law activist Louis Hines took this photo of a very young Biloxi worker early in the 20th century. From the Louis Hines Collection, BPL

Above right: Schooners are partially hidden by heaps of oyster shells in this circa 1900 photo. In cold predawn hours Biloxians were awakened by shrieks, wails, or moans as each factory steam whistle pierced the air with its own signal. Workers listened for their "whistle to blow" to know if schooners had brought in any work. BPL

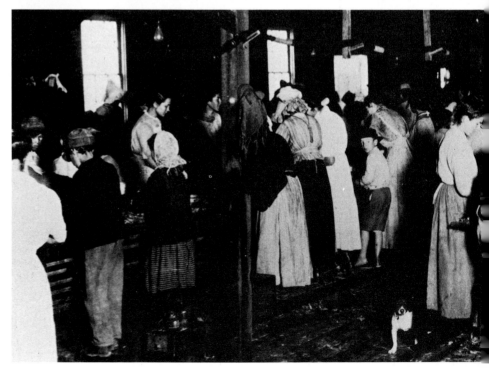

Right: The seafood industry dictated the lifestyle of many Biloxians. Schooner crews actually stayed on their boats for days and even weeks at a time. "Up on the back end of the boat we had a cabin. It was four men slept in the cabin, and the other two men slept in the front end of the boat that we called the foc'sle" (excerpt from an oral history). BPL

Below: Seafood factory workers labored long and hard. "You hold (shrimp) with one hand and pick them with the other. We took everything off the shrimp, the head and everything, clean. I used to stand in shrimp hulls up to my knees.... They just drop on the floor and you had to stand in them" (excerpt from an oral history). From the Louis Hines Collection, BPL

Above: Miniature railcars brought steamed oysters directly into the factories. From the Louis Hines Collection, BPL

Above: This oyster schooner is shown being unloaded by hand at a factory pier on Point Cadet, Biloxi, about 1920. MDAH

Right: Gentle breezes that powered his sails could without warning turn into the fisherman's greatest threat—the hurricane. The hurricane of 1893 caused more deaths than any other in the Gulf Coast's history and virtually destroyed the fishing fleet. From the Antique Print Collection, BPL

Both were broad-beamed, shallow-draft sailboats designed to negotiate the shoal waters of the Sound and the Louisiana marshes in search of oysters and shrimp. But the stubby, square-butted, two-man lugger contrasted sharply with the long, sleek, six-man schooner.

Depending on the season, the ice-laden boats sallied forth, outfitted with either nets or tongs. The crews pulled in the shrimp-filled nets with windlasses and sheer muscle power. In gathering oysters the men worked the reefs with the 12-foot-long, wooden-shafted tongs. The iron teeth at the end of this giant scissors-like contraption broke the oysters loose and held them until they were lifted into the boat.

The hot summer months of June, July, and August brought respite from toil as the seafood plants either suspended operations or turned to the canning of fruit and vegetables. For the fishermen this was a time for boat maintenance and net mending but also for celebration expressed in the form of schooner racing.

"Of course in those days we didn't have engines so we'd have to sail in what we call tack-up and down-in—in other words you had to tack up and down. You never had power to turn your schooners so you had to go forward and hold the gib to the windard so you could go about and then sail" (excerpt from an oral history). BPL

Beginning in 1888 each factory pitted its fastest schooner and best sailors against its rivals in fierce competition for glory and prizes usually consisting of $100 and a keg of beer. In preparation for the regatta, the crewmen crowded on canvas, transforming their work schooners into lovely "white-winged queens" scudding before the wind on the race course fronting Biloxi. These races, often marked by collisions and usually culminating in fistfights, were a Biloxi tradition for nearly half a century.

By 1893 Biloxi had emerged as a challenger to Baltimore, its mentor city, for the title of "Seafood Capital of the World." That same year E.G. Burklin, a recent arrival to Biloxi from Missouri, put in a horse-drawn street railway, a telephone system, and an electric light plant. In late September onlookers gasped as Burklin flipped a switch, illuminating a number of businesses on Pass Christian Street. One week later, on Sunday, October 1, the lights went out.

Statistics calibrating wind speed and storm surge for the October Storm of '93 seem unexceptional, but it dealt more destruction to the seafood industry and killed more people than any other storm in coast history. The 100-mile-per-hour winds and 15-foot storm surge caught the fishing fleet exposed in the Louisiana marshes between Lake Borgne and the mouth of the Mississippi. The wind-driven wall of water shattered scores of Biloxi schooners and luggers as it rolled inland, wiping out entire fishing villages, and entered the Mississippi River broadside.

The north fringe of the killer hurricane ground into the Mississippi Sound with a southeast gale at just the correct angle to render the buffer effect of the barrier islands almost negligible. Of 100 boats riding in the lee of Deer Island on Sunday evening, three remained afloat on Monday morning. Wind and waves destroyed outright the canning company buildings on the front beach and Point Cadet and detached a long section of the Biloxi Bay railroad bridge, hurling it as a battering ram against the canneries on Back Bay, crushing them like eggshells.

The canning factories and boats of all the other Mississippi Gulf Coast towns suffered similar fates. Sand and mud buried thousands of barrels of oysters at Mississippi City. At Bay St. Louis the storm destroyed the Dunbar's

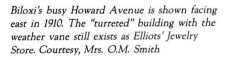

Biloxi's busy Howard Avenue is shown facing east in 1910. The "turreted" building with the weather vane still exists as Elliots' Jewelry Store. Courtesy, Mrs. O.M. Smith

Sons Canning Company.

Scarcely a wharf or a bathhouse was left standing, and all three coast railroad bridges were gone. Half the Bay St. Louis bridge lay beached on half of Ship Island, which itself had been sundered by the storm. Thousands of saw logs, washed from coast mills, bobbed in the Sound or littered the beaches.

Between Pascagoula and Grand Isle, Louisiana, more than 2,000 people died as a result of the storm. Exactly how many casualties were Mississippi Coast residents will never be known, but certainly they numbered in the hundreds. In just one area of the marshes, rescue workers counted 35 Biloxi schooners dismasted, upended, and abandoned. Of approximately 110 seamen known to have been on those boats, only five survived. Two of those, both from Biloxi, were rescued from two different islands as they fought for their lives against hordes of ravenous racoons.

Ten days after the disaster, Mayor John Bousquet of Biloxi appealed through the New Orleans newspapers for boats and tackle with which to resume the seafood industry. The generous response of the people of New

In another 1910 view, the circus parades along Howard Avenue. That year the population had grown to over 8,000 due to the prosperity brought on by the seafood industry. Courtesy, Mrs. O.M. Smith

Orleans and the American Red Cross set the coast on the road to recovery.

The introduction of steam- and sail-powered oyster dredges, a vast improvement over the tedious tonging method, accounted in part for the swiftness of the seafood industry's rebound. Actually the term "dredge" was a misnomer in that the contraption was a type of rake that scooped up the oysters in a wire basket as the boat passed over a reef. In addition to its superior gathering capability, the dredge also permitted the harvesting of deep-water oyster reefs for the first time.

Seafood production in 1896 far surpassed the 1893 levels, and the consequent economic boom in that industry, coupled with similar developments in timber and tourism, changed the lives of the people. Nowhere was the change more evident than in Biloxi.

That year the population reached 5,000, ranking Biloxi as the metropolis of the coast and the largest town between Mobile and New Orleans. The city's prosperity stemmed primarily from the five canning factories: Lopez, Dunbar's Sons and Company; Barataria Canning Company; E.C. Joullian Packing Company; W.M. Gorenflo and Company; and the Biloxi Canning Company. In addition to their canned products, which reached every corner of the civilized world, these firms daily shipped hundreds of thousands of dozens of iced bulk oysters via rail to the major cities of the South during the oyster season.

Oysters remained the basis of the industry, but the two-month shrimp season in the spring and the other two-month season in the fall filled the cash registers of the city with a lagniappe of shrimp nickels and factory tokens. Each worker received a nickel on the spot for peeling a five-pound cup of shrimp. The shrimp acid on the outstretched hand coated the nickel, turning it green—hence the term "shrimp nickel." Unable to keep enough

The original tabernacle at Seashore Methodist Campground at Biloxi (right) was built in 1872. At most Methodist campgrounds in the coast counties, revivals were held only one week annually. At Seashore there was year-round activity, with people coming on special trains from Tennessee, Louisiana and Alabama. Wesley Hall (opposite page, top) was Seashore's married men's dormitory. Men and women from visiting families were put in separate living quarters unless they owned their own cottages. Pearl Cottage (opposite page, bottom) was one of the many summer cottages built by families staying at the Methodist Campground that eventually became permanent residences. At first the cottages had only dirt floors spread with straw to remind visitors that they were on a spiritual retreat, not a holiday at the beach. Courtesy, Mrs. O.M. Smith

nickels to meet the demand, the companies issued five-cent tokens, which were accepted as cash in stores and banks until the government deemed the practice to be counterfeiting and halted it.

In 1896 Biloxi Electric's dynamo supplied power to three icehouses, 60 street lamps, and all business owners and residents wishing to subscribe. In April, People's Bank joined the three-year-old Bank of Biloxi in serving the commercial needs of the city's canneries, 55 mercantile establishments, and 28 hotels and boardinghouses.

The town's two shipyards turned out luggers and schooners, while off Pass Christian Street George Ohr spun out his eccentric genius in clay at the South's only art pottery studio. The 12-year-old *Biloxi Herald* supplied the citizens' thirst for news, and the men of two fire companies polished their new steam fire engines, confident that these, coupled to the plugs served by the city's artesian water mains, would enable them to handle any situation that might arise.

At 12:15 a.m. on Friday, November 9, 1900, a fire of undetermined origin began in the rear of Kennedy's Saloon on Reynoir Street. The engineer on duty at Biloxi Electric shrieked the plant's whistle almost immediately, alerting the fire fighters and citizens to the danger. Fanned by a strong north wind, the flames engulfed the saloon and spread along Reynoir.

As the clanging steam fire engines moved into position, the wind shifted first to the east and then to the west, spreading the conflagration beyond any possibility of control. *Biloxi Herald* employees stopped the presses and

fled into the street as the fire demon blistered the walls of their building. Once again the fickle wind shifted, driving the leaping flames southward. The fire gutted the business district and a posh residential area before burning itself out on the beachfront.

Holding the presses for the final tally, the *Herald* reported the loss of 90 buildings constituting entire blocks. Among them were several multistoried brick mercantile houses, the Catholic church, and seafood magnate Lazaro Lopez' palatial mansion. In summing up the calamity, the *Herald* predicted:

But as she has ever done Biloxi will rise Phoenix-like from the ashes, and will be inspired and encouraged to greater efforts than ever before to recoup her losses and obliterate the great wounds that have been inflicted on her.

Three years later Biloxi eclipsed Baltimore as the "Seafood Capital of the World" and Dukate Company weighed in as the largest cannery of its type on earth.

In the first half of the 19th century, the steamboat and tourism put the Six Sisters on the map. In the second half, the steam locomotive, together with lumber and seafood, enlarged five of them, killed one, and spawned a number of new towns. On the eve of a new century, the Mississippi Gulf Coast stood on the brink of a technological revolution unprecedented in its history. Not only would the modes, methods, vehicles, and dimensions of transport change, but also every aspect of the people's lives.

Chapter Six

T O W A R D A
N E W W O R L D

Gulf Park College students enjoyed swimming and boating at the college pier in the 1930. The school operated in Long Beach from 1923 until 1971. In 1972 it became a regional campus of the University of Southern Mississippi. MDAH

In 1896 a prominent railroad executive prophesied, "There will not be a vacant lot where it is possible to build between New Orleans and Mobile." While it would take the coast decades to come close to fulfilling that prediction, as he spoke the process had already begun. Evidence to that effect was collected in July 1896 by H.S. Evans, a *Daily Picayune* reporter. Traveling largely on the Louisville & Nashville, he sketched the nature of the settlements from the Pearl River to the Alabama line.

Compelled to leave the L&N to travel upriver by steamer to Pearlington, Evans found a town of 800 containing four stores and two large sawmills. Other mills were farther upstream at Gainesville, Logtown, and Napoleon, all served by the port of Pearlington.

In writing of Waveland and Bay St. Louis, Evans described them as "practically one city" of 3,000 persons, impossible to separate with "a diamond hyphen." The 10-mile beach drive, lined with palatial residences, schools, colleges, and churches, he termed the most beautiful on the coast. A 625-foot-deep artesian well served the residents and the electrified ice plant. Bay-Waveland's economy was based on tourism, in a number of first-class hotels, and the rebuilt Dunbar's Sons Canning Company, which canned oysters, shrimp, and figs. Two newspapers, the *Seacoast Echo* and the *Gulf Coast Progress*, served the citizenry.

Across the bay Pass Christian's 2,200 inhabitants shared Bay-Waveland's status as a tourist attraction, possessing three of the coast's largest hotels, which catered primarily to Northern visitors. A canning factory, designed to exploit the huge oyster reef just offshore, was under construction and expected to open in the fall. The town had its own artesian waterworks, a beautiful beach drive, and a racetrack.

Next down the line Long Beach (originally Scott's Station) had made its name as a vegetable shipping point for the surrounding truck-farming region. The village in 1896 claimed a permanent population of only 500, but rapid growth was assured by inexpensive fertilizers brought in on the L&N. In addition, a number of Italian families from the vicinity of Hammond, Louisiana, were even then purchasing property for expansion of their truck-farming enterprises. Increasing numbers of wealthy New Orleanians were building summer cottages in the area, and a cannery was under construction near the new ice plant.

Next door the future lumber capital of Gulfport was only beginning to stir. Evans noted only a few rude buildings and one sawmill. Mississippi City, which had maintained a static permanent population of 300 for decades, remained at that level in 1896. But as the Harrison County seat and the site of two grand hotels, it wielded an influence far beyond its size. Handsboro still retained its boat yards, sawmills, brickworks, and a sugar mill, but its population of 450 revealed its decline to half its former size as its losses to

The L&N depot at Biloxi is seen around the turn of the century. MDAH

the Pascagoula area continued.

Biloxi's commercial industrial economy and population far overshadowed all its rivals. In 1896 it was the coast's only real city, having attained the requisite 5,000 permanent inhabitants necessary for that designation.

Ocean Springs, incorporated four years earlier, claimed a population of just over 1,200. The town, despite its proximity to Biloxi, had not entered the seafood industry in any large way, preferring to rely upon the tourism engendered by its famous springs, together with the culture of fruit and pecans. In 1896, according to Evans, the town was "the central coast market for wool" and boasted a newspaper called the *Ocean Wave*.

At Gautier, Evans wrote, "The only thing of note at this place is a sawmill and the large creosote works." Across the bay he encountered the trinity of towns consisting of Moss Point, Scranton, and Pascagoula. The first he described as one of the great sawmill towns of the South, while the other two, really the same entity, relied mostly on tourism and served as a port.

As the 20th century dawned four years later, Biloxi was still racing for the position of the world's number-one seafood city, and Gulfport, having sprung up overnight, moved toward the same position in pine lumber exporting. The twin booms spawned unprecedented wealth and power. The coast entered a new world as it entered the new century. Nowhere was that more evident than in the realm of technology.

The first coast telephone exchange went into operation at Bay St. Louis in August 1899, serving 47 subscribers. Pass Christian followed in October. By mid-1900 Gulfport, Biloxi, and Ocean Springs had begun service. The lines reached Pascagoula-Moss Point in 1904, completing the trans-coast connection.

As the coast's first full-grown city, Biloxi led in nearly every innovation.

The pioneer electrification of the business district in 1893 paved the way for the replacement of the mule-drawn trolleys with electric ones four years later. Entrepreneurs immediately envisioned such a line running the length of the Harrison County shoreline. After several false starts, Captain Joseph T. Jones of Gulfport fame took charge of the project in 1905. The line reached Long Beach the next year and, with the electrification of Pass Christian in 1909, the trolleys ran bay to bay.

But the trolleys, along with the trains to a lesser extent, would eventually succumb to the greatest transportation revolution in American history—the advent of the automobile. By 1900 the city of Biloxi already led the coast with 24 miles of streets paved with shells and vitrified bricks "well adapted for Vehicles and Bicycles." Upon those avenues in July appeared the first automobile recorded in the state of Mississippi. Its owner, Frank Schaffer, crashed the noisy contraption into a tree on its maiden run, and it had to be laid up while a New Orleans machine shop repaired its bent wheel. On the road again it terrorized the horses of the vicinity, resulting in a number of wrecks. Many Biloxians expressed relief when Schaffer sold his automobile to a distant buyer. Exactly one year later the first "motor bicycle" appeared and amazed the citizens with speeds up to 40 miles per hour.

The first auto that came to stay in Biloxi showed up in May 1904 with Erena Lopez, daughter of seafood magnate Laz Lopez, behind the wheel. Thereafter, purchases by other affluent citizens made automobiles a familiar sight, but they suffered severe strictures at the hands of wary town authorities. A 1905 law required two lights for night driving, ordered the tooting of the horn at each street corner, and set the maximum speed limit at eight miles

Pass Christian's L&N depot is shown in the last decade of the 1800s. From there residents of the town could take the excursion train to New Orleans or other cities along the coast. Courtesy, Billy Bourdin

per hour. Penalties for noncompliance ranged from a fine—of between $25 and $100—to imprisonment.

Intercity roads other than cow paths and logging trails scarcely existed, but some hardy types made journeys anyway. In June 1908 Biloxi seafood tycoon W.K.M. Dukate took his family on a jaunt to Hattiesburg in a Thomas Flyer. The 80-mile trip via Gulfport, then north along the sandy roads connecting the villages flanking the Gulf & Ship Island Railroad, required a day and a half. The intrepid party spent a good portion of the first day using a mule team to haul the stalled vehicle out of Turkey Creek. The rest of the trip

To the left in this view of the shell drive on east front beach, Biloxi, is a "shoo-fly," which enabled people sitting around the oak to catch the Gulf breezes while escaping mosquitoes and flies. Built before 1896, the "shoo-fly" was destroyed in 1969 by Hurricane Camille. Courtesy, Mrs. O.M. Smith

The green bean was the first vegetable shipped from Long Beach in 1884 when W.J. Quarles and James Thomas started the truck-farming industry in the area. Quarles (left foreground) and W.H. Bouslog (right foreground) are seen inspecting beans circa 1880. By the mid-1920s, Long Beach was known as the "radish capital of America." Courtesy, Mary Ellen Alexander

Right: The "pecan boom" began in the 1870s in Jackson County where the finest varieties of grafted pecan trees originated. Pictured at right is Frank H. Lewis, the "Pecan Man," onetime mayor of Pascagoula and owner of major pecan orchards. Courtesy, Tommy Wixon

Above: These girls were participating in the annual Spring Festival at Gulf Park College in Long Beach. MDAH

Left: Ocean Springs contracted its first bonded debt in 1899 to build a school. Shown is the 1905 graduating class of Ocean Springs High School. Courtesy, Tommy Wixon

The busy intersection at 14th Street and 25th Avenue in 1908 Gulfport shows the amazing progress the city had made since its founding in 1898. MDAH

through Nugent, McHenry, Perkinston, and Wiggins was relatively uneventful until Dukate lost his bearings near Maxie. There he hired a pilot to Brooklyn, where the family passed the night, and then proceeded to the Hub City the following morning. The return required only one day, since only two hours were lost—one for lunch and the other for a flat tire. In their peregrinations the Dukate party covered 255 miles and burned 66 gallons of gas. The general route they ran would become U.S. Highway 49.

Accolades for the first successful automobile trip from the coast to New Orleans went to Pass Christian motorist Dr. Robert A. Strong. In December 1910 Strong drove his two-year-old Buick north through Poplarville and completely circumnavigated Lake Pontchartrain, entering New Orleans from the west 38 hours and 400 miles later.

The principles of gasoline propulsion were naturally applied to boats. In 1912 the *Bernardino,* the coast's first trawl, chugged into Biloxi, sounding the death knell of the "white-winged queens." Many schooner captains converted their craft by simply felling the masts and installing power machinery in the holds.

The heady, boom-town atmosphere of the opening years of the century brought changes not only in the realm of transport but also in every other facet of life—some serious, some frivolous. On March 15, 1907, King's Daughters' Hospital, the coast's first hospital, opened in Gulfport. Three days later surgeons at the facility successfully performed their first operation.

On March 4, 1908, Biloxi, following the lead of Mobile and New Orleans, gave the coast its first full-fledged Mardi Gras celebration. King John

Below: Shown here are the first electric linemen in city of Pascagoula. Courtesy, Tommy Wixon

Carraway and Queen Blanche Picard presided over a night parade of 17 floats, marching bands, and prancing horses down a Howard Avenue described as "black with people." Preceding even the royalty was a tableau

intended to be symbolic of the feast of Mardi Gras. A live white steer of immense size with gilded horns stood on a float decorated with the carnival colors. The executioner, as he might be termed, who was supposed to slay the bull for the feast, stood at his head with an immense gilded knife in his hand and four other masked figures stood as guards at the four corners.

A huge, golden electric crown surmounting the city hall flashed intermittently above the merry throng. Pate's Band of Bay St. Louis played in the ballroom that night, and "the gay maskers continued to trip the light fantastic until long after midnight." The Mardi Gras celebration would later spread to every coast town.

As early as 1900 another form of year-round entertainment reached the coast. In that year the first "five-cent flicker" played at Biloxi's Dukate Theatre. In 1909 the 10-cent "two-reel thrillers" appeared in Ocean Springs. These silent films, accompanied by a tinny phonograph record or a player piano, rapidly won a large following. The two-reelers gave way to five-reelers plus a cartoon and a serial. The serials, according to C.E. Schmidt of Ocean Springs, guaranteed repeat business, as each episode ended "with the hero or heroine ... either clinging to the edge of a cliff, or lashed to a log carriage approaching a buzz saw."

Blanche Picard served as the first Queen Ixolib in 1908. Mardi Gras had been a coast tradition beginning with the first French explorers of 1699, and early newspapers report masquerade parties, balls, and dinners; but 1908 saw the first official queen and parade. The charter of the Biloxi Carnival & Literary Association, drawn up in 1916, established Mardi Gras as an official annual event. BPL

In 1912 a traveler described the shore from Biloxi to Pass Christian as "one continuous town ... only separated by imaginary lines." Three parallel east-west connections, the L&N Railroad, the interurban trolley, and a shell road, ran the entire 22 miles, forming a trellis for urban growth. That same traveler journeyed into the piney woods and reported vast cut-over sections used as open range for huge herds of hogs, cattle, and sheep. The sheep industry in particular had increased dramatically after John Stigletts established a small town of 500 souls at the confluence of the Tchoutacabouffa and Big Biloxi rivers.

Woolmarket (formerly Coalville), located near the head of schooner navigation, served the sheepmen for 100 miles in the interior. Schooners out of Woolmarket hauled the shearings to New Orleans in 300-pound bags to the tune of half-a-million pounds per year. The boats returned from the Crescent City laden with groceries, cloth, shoes, and other stock for Stigletts' General Store which, in turn, disbursed the goods by the ox-wagonload to the sheepmen.

But the rise of the new industry essentially foreshadowed the decline of the old one. The cut-over lands so beneficial to the herdsmen resulted from Mississippi's *ad valorem* tax on standing timber that encouraged quick cutting and discouraged reforestation. Consequently, the millmen depleted the forests and left the land desolate. The introduction of the Clyde skidder as a replacement for the eight-wheel log wagon greatly increased the damage to the landscape. This steam-powered behemoth mounted on a spur track snaked its steel cables 1,000 feet into the forests to drag home 5 to 15 logs at a time, destroying even the grass cover in the process. In 1913, with more than half the "inexhaustible forest" felled, lumbering peaked and began a slow but inexorable descent.

The lumber boom and its coincident population explosion had wrought political as well as physical changes in the piney woods. North Hancock County, the first area penetrated by the railroad, detached from the southern section in 1890 to form Pearl River County with its seat at Poplarville. In 1910 north Jackson seceded to form George with its seat at Lucedale, and Wiggins became the seat of the new county of Stone, carved out of north Harrison in 1916. The penetration of the piney woods by the railroads in search of timber doubled the number of coast counties from three to six by pulling inland relatively large numbers of people for the first time in the history of the panhandle.

International as well as local events greatly influenced the changes already in progress. On Sunday, April 4, 1914, the interurban trolley ran a special excursion to Gulfport so that customers could witness what may have been the coast's first air show. Aviator T.T. Maroney staged a one-man aerodynamic exhibition above the city, climaxed by a nonstop flight to Biloxi. The high-flying 20th-century marvel sputtering in the sky that day was to add a new dimension to the war that would shatter the world four months later.

The outbreak of the Great War sent immediate shock waves through the coast economy. The export market for both timber and seafood nosedived with the interruption of European trade. The lumber mills suffered most, and within a year many of them temporarily shut down.

Compounding the economic woes, the worst hurricane since 1906 struck in September 1915. Like its predecessor, the storm leveled large stands of timber and washed out the shell highway and trolley line. At Biloxi the winds destroyed the brand-new amusement park on Deer Island. In Hancock County the wind demons blew Pearlington's Badon Saloon 10 miles upriver and sank it. In the aftermath of this storm, the coast cities for the first time seriously considered building a seawall.

The lumber mills were reactivated in 1916 as the Allies placed huge orders for timber needed in the construction of trench support structures on the Western front. The simultaneous preparedness program instituted by the U.S. government further stimulated both the lumber and the fishing industries.

Pascagoula-Moss Point benefited most from America's entry into the war in April 1917 because it was selected to be a shipbuilding center. Almost overnight the population quadrupled to 6,000 as huge firms such as the International Shipyard and Dierks Blodgett set up shop to build 34 military supply ships and other war vessels. For the first time, area yards produced steel-ribbed and steel-hulled ships. Celeste Allen, a schoolgirl at the time, still

Below left: In 1910 Cedar Lake was a thriving sawmill settlement on the banks of the Tchoutacabouffa River north of Biloxi Bay. This general store as well as all other signs of that era have long vanished. Courtesy, Mrs. James Lee

recalls the playground rhyme celebrating the launching of one of the iron monsters:

Here's to the steamer Boone
The best new ship afloat.
To cross the ocean she is doomed
To get the Kaiser's goat.

Above: Before their harvest, giant stands of majestic virgin pine stretched unbroken for 100 miles or more. MDAH

The other coast yards, particularly those at Handsboro, produced military craft as well, and Gulfport did its bit in another way. The buildings newly constructed on East Beach for the Mississippi State Centennial Exposition were converted into the Gulfport Emergency Training Camp. The installation trained thousands of yeomen in sailing, seaplane aerodynamics, wireless operation, and gunnery. A number of women filled noncombat posts. After the war the camp became a Veterans Administration hospital.

Above: One of the first planes to land at Leed's Field, also known as the Biloxi Fairgrounds, was piloted by Charles Banfil (center), who later distinguished himself in World War I and became a general. BPL

Right: Leed's Field once existed on Lee Street, where the Biloxi stadium is today. A large open field running from the railroad to Back Bay, the field was used by the army for military training around 1905. BPL

Far left: During World War I the idea of women entering the navy was, at first, shocking. However, in order to release more men for sea duty, "Yeomanettes" were recruited to fill office jobs ashore. Shown here are the first Yeomanettes at the Gulfport Naval Training Camp. From The Gadget, 1918

Left: General John J. "Black Jack" Pershing pins the Distinguished Service Cross on the chest of Private Henry Jetton Tudury of Bay St. Louis. "My head stopped the helmet from bending more," confided Tudury to his diary after being struck by a three-inch German shell in no man's land. The subsequent presentation of the Croix de Guerre by Field Marshall Henri Petain to the soldier made Tudury the coast's most decorated doughboy of the Great War. Courtesy, Elsie Benigno and Marie Johnson

On November 24, 1917, work began on the Gulfport Naval Emergency Training school. Buildings intended for use in the Mississippi Centennial Exposition were converted into camp quarters. Today the school is part of the Gulfport division of the Veterans Administration Hospital. Pictured are the camp's officers and enlisted personnel in 1918. From The Gadget, 1918

These two men are pictured in front of a charcoal kiln circa 1890. A staple commodity, charcoal was produced in large quantities and sold all over the country. A charcoal kiln, usually placed in a dry spot in a heavily wooded area near a railroad, was watched day and night. Wood needed to be burned 16 days to get a good product. Courtesy, Picayune Public Library

The Armistice of November 11, 1918, halted the coast war industries just as they were gearing up for full production. When the government dropped its contracts, the workers dropped their tools and departed as quickly as they had come. At Pascagoula-Moss Point huge ships' skeletons in various stages of completion were left standing on the ways at the mercy of the elements. The old established boat yards remained and continued to build fine fishing boats, some of which they modified to become the "best damn rum-running boats in the world." Rum-running would bolster the coastal economy for much of the interwar period.

Mississippi, which had declared itself dry in 1909, became the first state to ratify the 18th Amendment 10 years later. Thus, when national Prohibition went into effect on July 1, 1919, the coast's well-organized gangs of rumrunners and bootleggers did their best to slake the thirst of the entire country.

This new illegal, though locally respectable, industry came upon the scene at a time when many inhabitants of the seashore and the piney woods were seeking an alternative source of income. With the forests falling at a rate of a million acres per year, many a sawmill worker, cut out of a job, became a moonshiner. Whiskey stills secreted in old sawdust piles, swamp thickets, or underground bunkers poured forth a deluge.

Possibly the best-known Mississippi town in the North during the Roaring Twenties was the Hancock County village of Kiln, from which the Chicago-based Capone Gang secured vast quantities of "Kiln Lightning." From time to time "revenooers" discovered whole rail cars loaded with just enough pine lumber to conceal hundreds of cases of liquor or truckloads of "corn squeezings" nesting under egg cartons. In just one 1923 raid near Kiln, federal agents captured four cookers, one of them "a 300 gallon fellow—looking like the grandfather of all the stills."

The fishermen, too, entered the game, but served more epicurean tastes and made quick profits hauling the bottled-in-bond product. From Caribbean ports, chiefly Cuba, rum and every kind of European alcoholic beverage imaginable arrived aboard ships off the barrier islands. Gasoline powerboats and more prosaic fishing craft unloaded the goods on the high seas for the run through the Sound into the myriad bays, bayous, rivers, and coves of the highly indented coastline. The coast guard made some spectacular hauls, but the bulk of the stuff got through.

The machinations of the rumrunners sometimes resulted in consternation for innocent citizens. One ashen-faced deep-water pier owner showed a prominent Biloxi businessman an envelope containing $1,000 that had arrived anonymously in the mail. The businessman responded with some friendly advice: "They used your pier ... and they are paying for it. Go ahead and bank that thousand dollar bill and keep your mouth shut and you might get another one sometime."

High-powered cars roared along back roads carrying payloads throughout Mississippi and adjacent states while cargoes bound for the Midwest and East Coast rode the rails. A routine 1924 Biloxi safety inspection revealed 1,000 cases of whiskey and champagne camouflaged under mounds of chicken grit in a freight car marked "Pedigree Crushed Oyster Shells for Poultry."

Federal agents usually poured confiscated booze in the gutters or smashed the bottles, but after one particularly large Biloxi haul in 1925, they simply dumped the contraband into the Sound off Gulfport. Enterprising shrimpers

When the depleted forests no longer yielded sap, turpentine distillers applied their arts to grain, apparently with great devotion. Moonshiners racked up a 65-percent repeat arrest rate. One practitioner of the craft near Lyman, despite 42 arrests, continually reestablished his still in the same room of the same house. Courtesy, Biloxi Police Department

trawled the load back up and so saturated the local market that the price of a quart fell from $6 to $3. A similar situation occurred when a rumrunner grounded on a near-shore sandbar and sent out the call for all persons in the vicinity to lighten its load—free.

The attitude of local law-enforcement officers regarding the liquor business was quite casual, as one Gulfport incident illustrates. Four men in an automobile parked in front of the First National Bank. One of the men entered a nearby hardware store to purchase bullets, while the others waited outside with the motor running. Alerted, the Gulfport police arrested the quartet and found the auto to have a stolen license plate. The men vehemently protested the charge of attempted bank robbery, explaining that they were "on a mere rum-running venture." The police, apparently much relieved, fined the armed man $50 for carrying a concealed weapon and released all four.

The feds viewed the goings-on with a more jaundiced eye. By the mid-1920s the Gulf Coast had outstripped the Canadian border and the East Coast as an entrepot for liquor, and the government pegged the wholesale yearly value of the contraband passing through the area at $1.5 million.

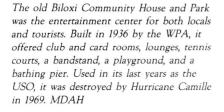

The old Biloxi Community House and Park was the entertainment center for both locals and tourists. Built in 1936 by the WPA, it offered club and card rooms, lounges, tennis courts, a bandstand, a playground, and a bathing pier. Used in its last years as the USO, it was destroyed by Hurricane Camille in 1969. MDAH

Recognition of the coast's status in the business made the game livelier through the introduction of more secret agents but scarcely dented the trade.

In 1923 Colonel J.W. Apperson, owner of Biloxi's Buena Vista Hotel, decided to provide gambling as well as drinking beyond the long arm of the federal law. He selected a small island beyond the 12-mile limit situated between Horn and Ship as the site of his new tourist attraction. In honor of its new role, he changed the island's name from Dog Key to the Isle of Caprice. Twice a day excursion boats ferried visitors to the island's combination casino and dance hall. There flappers and their beaux could sport hip flasks with abandon, play the one-armed bandits, and dance the blackbottom to red-hot jazz bands. The merrymaking lasted for nine years until construction and tourists removed the natural vegetation, turning the isle into a miniature Atlantis.

The real-estate and tourism boom of the 1920s fueled other ambitious projects. To battle the elements of erosion on the shoreline, the three coast counties at last began seawall construction in 1924. The hurricane of 1926 tested the half-completed wall and found it equal to its task. The storm did little damage other than knocking out all telephone and telegraph connections between New Orleans and Mobile, thereby proving "for the first time" the usefulness of WSMB (Saenger Maison-Blanche) Broadcasting Company. The New Orleans-based radio station beamed information to the beleaguered coast until ground lines could be restored.

On May 10, 1928, Harrison County dignitaries dedicated the 24-mile-long step seawall rimming the shore from Biloxi to Pass Christian. At its completion it was the largest reinforced concrete structure and the longest concrete seawall in the world. Contemporaneously, Hancock County walled 14 miles of the west side of the Bay of St. Louis, and Jackson County built two two-mile seawalls to protect the Ocean Springs and Pascagoula beachfronts.

These men were photographed in the 1930s shoveling oyster shells. Originally this by-product of the oyster industry had been used to pave roads. Later the shells were ground for poultry grit or returned to replenish reefs and create bottoms to grow more oysters. BPL

The seawall is shown being built in 1924. Instead of a straight, vertical barrier that would receive the direct force of the waters, the seawall was divided into a series of steps. Later the seawall itself needed protection when waters driven by hurricane force went under the wall, destroying large portions of it. BPL

One immediate result of the protective construction was the absorption of the Gulf & Ship Island Railroad by the Illinois Central system, "because the seawall program gave assurance that property values would be enhanced and general progressive development be put in motion." Development did follow, and summer homes and new subdivisions such as Gulf Hills and Bay Terrace sprang up on former truck-farm and orchard land.

The coming of the age of the automobile led to another construction project—a national highway system. By 1925 a ribbon of asphalt, part of the Old Spanish Trail National Highway from St. Augustine to San Diego, traversed the coast from the Alabama line to the Pearl. The road building spawned a number of new hotels, most notably the Pine Hills Hotel on the north shore of the Bay of St. Louis and Biloxi's Edgewater Gulf, the $2-million megahotel of the Gulf Coast. By 1930 bridges spanned every river and bay between New Orleans and Mobile, resulting in the first ferryless ride between the two cities.

But the crash of 1929 ended the coast real-estate boom and bankrupted many of the grand hotels. The onset of the Great Depression brought even worse privation to the piney woods counties. One now-retired George County logger summed up his memories of the time with the laconic statement, "Well, I never missed a meal but sometimes there was two days between 'em."

As the last of the virgin forests fell, one large mill after another closed. The repeal of Prohibition in 1933 added to the general misery by ending the coast's national standing as an illegal liquor supplier. The state and local trade, which continued for another 33 years of Mississippi Prohibition, furnished comparatively little opportunity to displaced workers. New government "alphabet soup" agencies, particularly the Civilian Conservation Corps, provided some relief. CCC camps stressing much-needed reforestation were established in 1936 throughout the coast panhandle, providing employment

On June 8, 1940, to cheering crowds, the largest all-welded steel vessel ever built in the United States—and the first ship launched at Ingalls—slid down the ways into the waters of the Singing River. The Exchequer, a perfectly "smooth-skinned" steamship, was the first of its kind on the high seas. Courtesy, Ingalls Shipbuilding

to hundreds of young men.

The sheep industry, so lucrative in the first two decades of the century when five million of the woolly creatures roamed the cut-over lands, fizzled out in the mid-1930s with the passage of open stock laws and the consequent sale of millions of them to Mexico. Gulfport, which had formerly devoted an entire street to the wool business, required only one block to accommodate the sheepmen in 1935. The loss of the wool trade, coupled with the rapidly dwindling lumber export trade, forced the port to find another reason for existence. At least as early as 1932 Gulfport began breaking New Orleans' virtual monopoly on banana importation from Central America. The desire to break a Chinese monopoly of 69 centuries' duration also augered well for both Gulfport and the piney woods. Certain landowners planted experimental tung orchards on sections of cut-over timberlands in the early 1930s.

The seafood industry underwent a number of changes between the World Wars, but in general suffered less than either timber or tourism. In the 1920s the seafood companies actively recruited large numbers of workers from the Acadian parishes of Louisiana. These people moved into Biloxi's Point Cadet factory camps to stay, and by the early 1930s they rendered unnecessary the importation of Bohemian seasonal workers.

Still, the Depression bankrupted many of the large original canneries. The Yugoslavs in particular, but also some of the Cajun French, bought the abandoned factories and even opened some new ones. Already united by the religious heritage of Catholicism, old world customs, and a common love of the sea, the Yugoslavs and the Cajun French melded through marriage, and rose to dominate the seafood industry. In 1930 the new owners inaugurated on Back Bay Biloxi the "Blessing of the Fleet," an old world Catholic custom.

Technological innovations like automated canning, refrigerated storage, and new distribution methods, combined with high demand for the products,

Before the advent of frozen foods, tins of fresh (not cooked or steamed) headed or peeled shrimp and gallon tins of fresh shucked oysters were packed into barrels with ice and shipped to all parts of the nation. A canvas piece between the lid and the barrel served as insulation, and the ice was replenished along the way as necessary. MDAH

Tung nuts hang in clusters—resembling large plums—on a tree in Picayune, the center of the "tung belt." Tung oil was used as the base for a high-quality, lightweight paint. Hurricane Camille completely destroyed the tung industry. Courtesy, Margaret Reed Crosby Memorial Library, Picayune

kept the seafood industry viable throughout the 1930s. Those same advances, however, completed the demise of the schooners. Newsreel cameras and newspapers throughout the nation covered the last Biloxi schooner race in 1932. Diesel-powered Biloxi luggers outfitted with trawl nets almost entirely replaced the schooners by the end of the decade.

Another casualty came in 1938 when the Dantzler Moss Point Mill sawed its last log and shut down, ending a century of large-scale lumber manufacturing on the Pascagoula River. But the Dantzler Pulp Mill, established nearly a half-century earlier to utilize the by-products of the sawmill and for a decade part of the International Paper Company empire, remained in operation.

In that same year Robert Ingersol Ingalls, lured by the promise of state "Balance-Agriculture-With-Industry" funds, came to Pascagoula and filled the industrial vacuum left by the demise of lumbering. The BAWI program, which awarded appropriations to approved industrial projects providing jobs to the unemployed, granted Ingalls $100,000. The wealthy Alabama industrialist, experienced in the fabrication of steel tanks and barges, leapt at the opportunity to apply his revolutionary concepts to shipbuilding. In a day when overlapping riveted plates dominated the metal fabrication industry, Ingalls favored the smooth, seamless welding method.

In November 1938 Ingalls began improvements on a 187-acre former World War I shipyard site on the east bank of the East Pascagoula. On June 8, 1940, the new yard launched its first ship, the *Exchequer.* That C-3 cargo vessel also happened to be the world's first all-welded oceangoing cargo carrier.

The yard, founded as a peacetime attempt to recapture America's former high status as a maritime nation, slid a number of passenger-cargo liners down the ways until December 7, 1941, when it retooled for war. With U-boat wolf packs blasting ships in the Gulf, some very near Pascagoula, the workers went on a nonstop production schedule that eventually contributed nearly 100 vessels to the Allied war effort. The blue-fired torches showered sparks even on holidays, in obedience to the exhortation of the *Ingalls News:*

This . . . is another Christmas gone haywire. . . . The fighters need those ships; their lives depend on them. So think of the fighters and stay on the job. Give Hitler and Hirohito a little more hell as a Christmas present. They asked for it.

The small town of Pascagoula burgeoned into a city of 35,000 as workers poured in from many parts of the nation and more women moved into the paid work force. "Rosie the Riveter" or, in Ingalls' case, "Rosie the Welder," wielded a torch with the best of them, freeing many men for the battlefront. Pascagoula's 19-year-old Vera Anderson defeated her rivals throughout the country to win the title "Championship Woman Welder of the World" and dinner at the White House.

At Moss Point the International Paper Pulp Mill converted to war footing with the production of paper products for the military. The 1940 repeal of *ad valorem* tax on standing timber had cleared the way for massive plantings of second growth timber, and International Paper Company alone reforested 115,000 acres of pine for use in its plant.

The severing of the China trade resulted also in the cultivation of thousands of acres of tung orchards throughout the panhandle, but particularly in Pearl River County. The military demanded large quantities of tung oil-based paint, invaluable for its lightweight waterproofing quality, for use in coating radar equipment, planes, tanks, guns, ships, and other war matériel. Quick-drying tung oil became even more valuable as a coating for steel cans when the tin stockpiles ran out.

In addition to priming the industrial and agricultural pump of the area, World War II also brought a number of new military installations to the Gulf Coast. Merchant marine officers trained at Pass Christian, and Gulfport built an air field and a Seabee hive, while Biloxi managed to land Keesler Air Force Base.

As early as 1938 President Franklin Roosevelt gave orders to expand America's fledgling air force with additional aircraft and bases. The following year the search for bases began in earnest with the outbreak of war in Europe. A group of Biloxians, aware that an air base would be a year-round economic boon to their city of 18,000 so dependent on seasonal industries, lobbied tirelessly to secure authorization for one of them. By way of enticement the city offered to donate an 832-acre site adjacent to the Veterans Administration hospital on Back Bay, containing a circa 1935 municipal airport, a country club, and three golf courses. The government responded with a $10-million construction contract, the largest in state history at that time.

The first cadre of officers and men pitched tents on June 12, 1941, thus activating the new base. Within three months nearly 12,000 workers poured in to labor on the project, and by Pearl Harbor day, 7,051 recruits were in basic training in Biloxi. Nearly half a million men and women would train at the Keesler facility during the war, and they would serve in every theater of conflict.

Just three weeks after the "day of infamy," the U.S. Navy responded to the exigencies of modern warfare with the constitution of new naval construction units unprecedented in American history. These Construction Battalions (their initials rendered "Seabee") sought three permanent bases or "hives"—one each on the Atlantic, Pacific, and Gulf coasts. In 1942 the navy picked a 1,150-acre site west of Gulfport. To the new base, known locally as Camp Hollyday, came a new kind of warrior—"a soldier in a sailor's uniform, with marine training, doing civilian work at WPA wages." Dispatched via ship or by plane from huge Gulfport Field, the Seabees wrought miracles of military engineering from the jungle hells of the Pacific to the mined beaches of Europe. In terms of local impact, the payrolls of the Seabee base and Gulfport Field helped to rejuvenate the area's sagging economy.

The rapid change that began at the turn of the 20th century accelerated during World War II. But the war did more than simply speed up a socio-economic revolution already in progress—it added new industrial and military elements to the crucible, changing the mix entirely.

Above: On October 8, 1918, Lieutenant Samuel Reeves Keesler of Greenwood, Mississippi, engaged four German Fokkers in a dogfight above the trenches near Verdun. He destroyed one before the others killed him. Keesler's home state honored the memory of the young Distinguished Service Cross winner by selecting his name for the Biloxi base.

Above right: These soldiers are in bayonet practice at Keesler Field during World War II.

Right: The site chosen for Keesler Field had once been the grounds of the Biloxi Country Club. The grounds are shown in 1939, consisting of a clubhouse (the present Keesler's Officers' Club), golf courses, the Biloxi Airport, and a ball park that had been used as a National League baseball training camp. Encamped on the field at the time this photo was taken was the Minnesota National Guard.

Above: The 310th School Squadron was the first student unit at Keesler Field in 1941.

Left: By late 1941 Keesler Field began to take shape and look like a military base. Despite labor problems, weather, and a shortage of structural materials, Keesler Field had grown into a functioning military facility by the time America found itself in World War II. All photos courtesy, Keesler Air Force Base

Chapter Seven

THE COMING MEGALOPOLIS

The Creole Queen—*a 1,000-passenger-capacity excursion boat custom-built by Halter Marine of Moss Point for a New Orleans firm—slides into the Escatawpa River in August 1983. The first of its type to use diesel-electric propulsion, the vessel recalls a bygone era when Jackson County shipyards built real steamboats for the New Orleans market. Courtesy, New Orleans Paddlewheels, Inc.*

The Mississippi Gulf Coast entered the Second World War as a peripheral province and in five short years joined mainstream America's military-industrial complex. In the ensuing two generations the area has undergone a transformation of "future-shock" proportions. In a mere 40 years the mechanical marvels spewing from the technological cornucopia together with attendant societal changes have reshaped and revitalized the entire region.

Most of the coast's war-born installations and industries remained intact even after the guns cooled as the United States, for the first time in its history, embraced the concept of "cold war" and consequent peacetime military preparedness. Big government soon rivaled seafood, tourism, and forestry as a major economic force in the lives of the people.

Keesler Field, even after demobilization, remained, with a population of 20,000, a city within a city in its role as the permanent electronics training center of the U.S. Air Force. Gulfport Field demilitarized but retained the barracks and matériel for instant reactivation. The Naval Construction Battalion Center mothballed its equipment but served as a stockpile area for mountains of strategic ores. Ingalls retooled for civilian production but retained its favored status as a ship fabricator for the peacetime navy.

Paradoxically, even nature aided in the early postwar development of the coast. No really damaging storm had struck for decades when the 1947 hurricane smashed the seawall in several places and menaced Old Spanish Trail (Highway 90). Government engineers, then engaged in transforming that road into America's first four-lane, coast-to-coast military superhighway, immediately recommended the construction of a sand beach as a buffer for the seawall.

Simultaneous construction of the superhighway and the 300-foot sloping beach along the entire shoreline of Harrison County began in 1951. Upon completion of the project four years later the sand beach proved to be the coast's greatest tourist attraction ever, and the new concrete highway provided rapid access to it for thousands in the neighboring cities and states. Huge neon signs advertising the restaurants and motels along the strip sprang up overnight, and the Deep South's oldest saltwater playground became its newest.

World War II exposed the need for transcontinental military roads, and it likewise highlighted the importance of protected highways of the sea. Beginning with the pioneering efforts of Captain John Grant in the antebellum period, individuals and private companies had made improvements from time to time in Gulf Coast offshore water routes. But the U-boat peril of the recent conflict focused governmental attention as never before on the need for a sheltered ditch for the use of water-borne commerce.

Frantic efforts by the U.S. Corps of Engineers to cut the 12-foot-deep, 125-foot-wide, 1,166-mile Intracoastal Waterway through the barrier island-protected shallows between Brownsville, Texas, and Carrabelle, Florida, brought

This young airman is training on a radar scope at Keesler Air Force Base. What began as a camp on Biloxi Back Bay has become the largest military electronics center in the world. Courtesy, Keesler Air Force Base

the project to virtual completion by war's end. Subsequent dredging operations perpendicular to this "Southern Erie Canal," which ran the entire length of the Mississippi Sound six miles offshore, widened and deepened preexisting channels or cut entirely new ones into Pascagoula, Biloxi, Gulfport, Pass Christian, and the mouth of the Pearl River. The Intracoastal Waterway sparked a veritable industrial revolution on the Gulf Coast and paved the way for space-age technology.

In the postwar era Pascagoula-Moss Point rose to the position of preeminent port and heavy industrial heart of Mississippi. Ingalls became the state's single largest industrial employer, and Moss Point's International Paper Company operation revitalized south Mississippi's failing forest industry by providing a ready market for second-growth timber.

In the mid-1950s Jackson County attracted even more industry with the establishment of the Bayou Casotte Industrial Area, Mississippi's largest planned industrial site. In 1957 liberal tax inducements, combined with the cheap transport offered by a location on the Intracoastal Waterway, lured to the park its first two multimillion-dollar industries—Coast Chemical Company and the H.K. Porter Company. Bayou Casotte's crowning achievement, though, was its selection as the site of the $125-million Standard of Kentucky Oil Refinery in 1961. Completed in 1964, the 2,500-acre plant was connected to the Louisiana oil fields 150 miles distant via America's longest underwater pipeline.

The other coast counties adopted the industrial park concept as well. In July 1960 Harrison County voters approved a bond issue to construct the Harrison County Waterway, designed to provide waterfront industrial sites north of Biloxi, Gulfport, and Pass Christian. Dredges cut a feeder canal from the Intracoastal Waterway through the entire length of Biloxi Bay and thence through the marshes to Gulfport Lake. Another such feeder entered the Bay of St. Louis and curved into the mouth of Bayou Portage in north Pass Christian. These new industrial parks provided factory locations protected from storms, hidden from the view of tourists, and, in the case of the sites in north Gulfport, easily accessible from Highway 49 and the proposed Interstate 10. Hancock County established a similar industrial area near the mouth of the Pearl on Mulatto Bayou.

Ingalls, with an impressive list of firsts, remained in the forefront of coast industrial development. By its 20th anniversary in 1958 the yard had launched more than 200 ships, including war transports, ice breakers, supertankers, and luxury liners. In 1959 Ingalls launched the USS *Blueback,* its first submarine and the nation's last diesel electric. Two years later, as the third-largest shipyard in the country, the yard christened its first nuclear sub, the USS *Sculpin.*

The Vietnam war spawned a vast new expansion program. On January 11, 1968, Ingalls celebrated its 30th anniversary with groundbreaking ceremonies on the west bank of the East Pascagoula for the "Shipyard of the Future," the nation's first new shipyard since World War II. The highly mechanized facility, the world's most advanced, secured the largest contract ever let by the U.S. Navy. The $2.14-billion work order authorized the construction of 30 destroyers as the backbone of the modern fleet and placed Ingalls on the threshold of becoming America's largest shipbuilder.

In late 1961 the Mississippi Gulf Coast entered the space age when the government chose Hancock County out of a field of 30 rivals as the site of

This rubble-strewn area near the intersection of Highway 90 and Reynoir Street in Biloxi shows the aftermath of the Hurricane of 1947. Sections of the highway buckled and snapped like matchsticks as the worst hurricane since 1915 pounded the coast on September 19. BPI.

the National Aeronautics and Space Administration's largest moon-rocket test facility. Proximity to New Orleans' Michoud rocket fabrication plant and easy access to it by water, coupled with the test area's sparse population, dictated the choice. The huge rocket engines could be built in New Orleans, tested in Hancock County, and shipped to Cape Canaveral for firing with all transportation aboard barges on the Intracoastal Waterway.

Right: A finished product is shipped through the Industrial Seaway barge canal. The canal handled two-million tons of cargo in 1983. Courtesy, Harrison County Development Commission

Below: This is one of the four industrial parks developed by the Harrison County Development Commission in the mid-1960s. Twenty-eight industries are located on the 1,500-acre park, providing 3,000 jobs for coast residents. Courtesy, Harrison County Development Commission

Above: On April 14, 1984, Ingalls Shipbuilding christened the guided missile cruiser Vincennes, *the fourth U.S. Navy vessel to bear that name. Almost exactly 121 years earlier the first* Vincennes *engaged in blockading Pascagoula. Courtesy, Ingalls Shipbuilding*

Left: Old and new come together as men use mules to build terraces in the vicinity of NASA's dual-rocket test stand. Courtesy, National Space Technology Laboratories

Radar tracks Hurricane Camille on its way to the Mississippi Gulf Coast. The storm did not take the predicted turn toward Florida, but instead stalled in the Gulf and then smashed into the Mississippi Coast with winds up to 210 miles per hour and waves cresting at 33 feet. MDAH

The selection of the site and the buffer zone around it spelled doom for five small historic lumbering communities inhabited by a total of 650 families. The families, many rooted in the area for generations, were ordered out of Gainesville, Santa Rosa, Logtown, Westonia, and Napoleon, and the villages were razed.

Thousands of construction workers and 1,200 permanent personnel under the direction of Dr. Wernher Von Braun, whose rockets had made such an impact on wartime London, completed work on the $500-million facility in late 1965. On April 23, 1966, south Mississippi shook as the site tested the second stage of the Apollo Saturn V space vehicle. The Mississippi Test Facility continued its work throughout Project Apollo, which culminated in a manned moon landing on July 16, 1969.

One month later the coast found itself in the grip of very earthly elements. Except for Betsy's glancing blow in 1965, the coast had not experienced a severe hurricane since 1947. Storm warnings sounded in mid-August 1969. Caribbean-born Camille savaged Cuba and moved into the Gulf where it stalled, took another gulp of warm, moist air, and headed straight for Pass Christian.

National Weather Service warnings, which led to mass evacuations to the interior coupled with quick action by Civil Defense and the National Guard, would later be credited with saving more than 50,000 lives from this worst

Thousands of military personnel representing the Army Corps of Engineers, Keesler Air Force Base, the U.S. Navy, and the Army National Guard—plus private contractors hired by President Nixon's Office of Emergency Preparedness—undertook the overwhelming task of clearing the storm-torn coast after Camille. MDAH

hurricane ever recorded. But many veterans of the 1947 hurricane and Betsy ignored the warnings, confident that they could ride out the storm in safety. Twenty-four residents of Pass Christian's spanking new Richelieu Apartments decided to have a party. Only one of them survived.

Camille thundered ashore Sunday evening, August 17, hurling a storm surge in excess of 25 feet over the seawall at Pass Christian and 20 feet high as far east as Biloxi. Buildings and cars exploded as the barometric pressure dropped to a record low of 26.6. Top wind speeds will never be determined because the gauges disintegrated at 230 miles per hour. Mountains of water pushed high up bays, bayous, and rivers, stood until the howling winds subsided, and then rolled over the peninsula towns carrying debris and bodies out to sea. The jackhammer effect of the more than 80 tornadoes contained within the storm shattered millions of acres of pine forests. In Pearl River County, Camille delivered the *coup de grace* to the tung industry, which had raised that county's per capita income from last to first in the state.

According to Red Cross statistics, 144 persons died, but many more were missing and presumed dead. Injuries totaled 9,472. Scarcely a home or business on the entire Mississippi Gulf Coast escaped at least minor damage, and bare concrete slabs served as the only memorial to thousands of others. Despite the measures taken to protect them, nearly 300 boats suffered destruction or heavy damage. Property losses ran into the hundreds of millions of dollars but the

A victim of Hurricane Camille, this lighthouse was built in the 1870s by Charles T. Howard, lottery king of New Orleans. It stood in the yard of the estate on front beach Biloxi and guarded second owner Baldwin Wood's beloved sailing schooner Nydia. MDAH

price in human suffering could not be calculated and neither could the worth of landmarks which had graced the coast since the antebellum period. The agonizing task of cleaning up and rebuilding began the day after havoc struck, but some marks of the storm remain.

In the wake of Camille a massive low-interest government loan program aided the coast seafood industry in making a relatively rapid recovery. That industry, with the 1947 discovery of new "shrimp bottoms" in the waters south of the barrier islands, together with the advent of larger technology-packed vessels able to harvest the sea on a year-round basis, had changed radically. The new boats infused new life into the seafood industry, but at the same time their high purchase price and staggering operational costs subjected the fishermen more than ever to the vagaries of climate and economics. Driven by the twin financial demons of high debt and intermittent recessions, boat owners overfished the waters of both the Sound and the Gulf.

Then, too, the industry has had to face a threat from a totally unexpected quarter. In 1932 the U.S. Corps of Engineers completed the Bonnet Carre Spillway, designed to protect New Orleans by diverting excess floodwater from the Mississippi River into Lake Pontchartrain, from whence it issues via the Rigolets into Lake Borgne-Mississippi Sound. While some of the earlier openings actually benefited the coast seafood industry, more recent ventings in the 1970s and early 1980s have upset the ecological balance. In particular, the large amounts of fresh muddy water released in 1979 and again in 1981 dropped the coastal salinity level, driving away the brown shrimp and silting up the oyster beds. Such frequent openings have left no time for nature to repair the damage. Although experts disagree as to the cost to the seafood industry, conservative estimates run into the millions of dollars.

Despite its problems, the seafood industry continues to play its historic role as the gateway for immigrant groups. The coast's latest influx of immigrants came with the exodus of South Vietnamese following the 1975 fall of

Vietnamese girls celebrate Mary's Day at St. Michael's Church on Point Cadet, Biloxi. The girls wear the traditional dress, the ao dai, *in white for a joyful religious occasion. While the Vietnamese are quickly being assimilated into the coast life-style, they still observe customs like this one brought from their homeland. Courtesy, the Vu family and Catholic Social Services*

South Vietnam to the communist regime of the North. Since many of these new arrivals had fished the warm waters of the embayed barrier island-girded shores of their homeland, they gravitated to America's nearest counterpart—the Gulf Coast. As early as 1977 a few arrived in Biloxi to perform much-needed labor as oyster shuckers and shrimp pickers. Those first few established a beachhead and sent word to the far-flung members of their extended families to join them. Present estimates place the number of Vietnamese on the Mississippi Gulf Coast at 2,000, with about 75 percent living in Biloxi.

In comparison to all the groups that arrived earlier, the Vietnamese experience seems most to resemble that of the Yugoslavs. Both groups emigrated, from environments similar to that of the coast, and both came seeking refuge from tyrannical domination of their native lands. Both were predominately Roman Catholic and maintained a strong sense of extended family loyalty. Both entered Biloxi through Point Cadet and started at the bottom in the seafood industry. Just as the Yugoslavs of a century ago sought first a boat

Above: Dr. Gilbert Mason, leader of the 1960 "wade-in" for civil rights on the Biloxi Beach, is currently president of the Biloxi branch of the NAACP. The first black member of the Biloxi Planning Commission, Dr. Mason is actively involved in the political and medical communities. He is also president of the medical and dental staff of Biloxi Regional Hospital. Courtesy, Dr. Gilbert Mason

Opposite: The setting sun silhouettes a pair of recreational fishermen near Biloxi. (Windsor)

and a house and then sent money to bring in family members from the old country, so have the Vietnamese. But there is an important difference as well. While the Yugoslavs entered on the shank of a seafood boom, the Vietnamese have entered during a period of decline, and the established commercial fishermen resent the competition of the large numbers of Vietnamese boats now taking to the waters.

This friction has led some Vietnamese to turn instead to tourism and the restaurant business. Lan Nguyen, proprietress of the Saigon Restaurant in Pass Christian, once worked for the American ambassador to South Vietnam. In the last days before the fall of Saigon, at the insistence of her boss she flew to Chicago. Lan Nguyen's co-workers who remained behind died before North Vietnamese firing squads. Considering that alternative, she considers her life in America wonderful.

The egalitarian legal climate fostered by black civil rights victories in the postwar era have made it easier for foreign immigrant groups, like the Gulf Coast's Vietnamese, to be accepted in the American mainstream. These civil rights battles, however, were hard won.

The military was integrated by Presidential order soon after the close of World War II. Because of the number of military bases in the coastal region, the area set an example found nowhere else in the state. Despite this positive example, racial violence sometimes flared. On April 26, 1959, a mob of hooded men lynched Mack Charles Parker, a black man, in Poplarville, igniting latent racial animosities throughout the coastal panhandle.

On October 5, 1959, a delegation of black citizens led by Dr. Gilbert R. Mason of Biloxi presented a petition to the Harrison County Board of Supervisors requesting unrestricted access to the sand beaches of the county on behalf of all black residents. By this act the black community for the first time officially challenged the Mississippi segregation laws—already declared unconstitutional in the landmark U.S. Supreme Court decision rendered in *Brown* vs. *the Board of Education of Topeka, Kansas* (1954). But the Board of Supervisors took no action on the petition. On the following night one of the signatories of the petition, a resident of Handsboro, awoke to find a six-foot-tall flaming cross on his lawn. In the ensuing days other members of the black delegation were harassed, and nightriders burned yet another cross, this time on the sand beach.

Beginning in mid-April 1960 blacks attempting to use Biloxi beaches were arrested, and cross burnings followed. On April 25, the eve of the anniversary of the Mack Charles Parker lynching, the tense situation exploded into what a *Daily Herald* reporter termed "near riot conditions." The score or more injured—none seriously—on the beaches and in the streets of Biloxi included six blacks and one white shot. In the wake of the violence, cooler heads prevailed, and the black coastians eventually gained access to the beaches.

The first Mississippi black child to cross the threshold of a previously all-white public school did so in Biloxi in August 1964. Mississippi Coast Junior College first admitted black students in 1965, the same year it divided into three campuses. Except for a few isolated instances, most public schools of the region were integrated by the end of the decade. The most notable exception was North Gulfport Elementary. That neighborhood school, by special court-sanctioned agreement, remained all black until reconstituted and integrated as the North Gulfport Seventh and Eighth Grade School in the fall of 1981.

Above: Historically the Gulf Coast—with its beaches and watering places—has been the playground for tourists from other states. In addition, coast residents enjoy celebrations of their own, from this small, impromptu concert on the sand to the spring's extravagant "Mardi Gras madness." (Windsor)

Above left: Anh Thi Vu, whose nickname is "America," poses in front of a photograph of her that appeared on the cover of the September 1981 National Geographic. *This photograph was taken at the celebration of Têt, the Vietnamese new year. Anh is wearing the traditional ao dai in red, the color for festive celebrations. Courtesy, the Vu family and Catholic Social Services*

Above: A gaily decorated shrimp boat takes part in the traditional Blessing of the Fleet, an annual event to mark the opening of the shrimping season. Photo by Charles Sullivan and Murella Powell

Opposite page, bottom: The Diocese of Biloxi, newly created on June 6, 1977, encompasses 17 southern counties and 42 parishes. At ceremonies at Nativity Cathedral in Biloxi, Bishop Joseph Howze became the first black bishop to head a diocese in the United States in this century. Courtesy, Commercial Appeal Magazine

Left: The Mississippi Coast Coliseum and Convention Center on Highway 90 in Biloxi was completed in 1977. The center, the largest in the state, can seat 11,500. It is used for many types of events, from rock concerts, conventions, and trade shows, to religious programs. Courtesy, Guice & Guice Advertising

Below: In the early 1970s at the conclusion of the Apollo Test Program, the Mississippi Test Facility began taking on new roles. The original test stands (pictured) were modified for the testing of space-shuttle engines. The MTF has evolved into NASA's National Space Technology Laboratories—a technical and scientific community comprised of federal and state agencies and industrial contractors engaged in space and environmental programs. Courtesy, National Space Technology Laboratories

These two photographs reveal the beauty of one of the Gulf Coast region's landscapes, the piney woods. In the view above, a mist clears in the woods. At left is a scene from the De Soto National Forest of the woods near the Big Biloxi River in Harrison County. Photos by Ed Longino

Right: Casting the net for mullet—also known as "Biloxi Bacon"—is a skill that has been handed down for generations. Courtesy, Guice & Guice Advertising

Below: The delicate Pearl River swamplands are another feature of the coast's varied landscapes. Photo by Russell Hatten

The stark beauty of Horn Island contrasts sharply with other types of Gulf Coast scenery. In the photo above we see a high dune and the sand beach of the island. At left the sun sets over an island tidal pool. Photos by Brent Funderburk

Former Harrison County Superintendent of Education Esco Smith, whose term of office spanned the years 1960-1972, recalled that the turbulence of the period stemmed not from integration but from demographic shifts that nearly tripled the school population of his district from 3,300 to 8,900 in just 12 years. According to Smith, only one "flare-up" of racial animosity occurred during his term as superintendent.

The Gulf Coast, though it failed in its 1837 bid to secure the site of the University of Mississippi, is today served by a network of excellent institutions of higher learning. Pearl River County Agricultural High School was established in 1909 at Poplarville, and Harrison County Agricultural High School was established in 1911 at Perkinston (now in Stone County). In 1921 the former became the first such institution in the state to offer college credit and the latter added a college curriculum four years later.

From those modest beginnings Pearl River Junior College evolved to serve a district composed of Pearl River and Hancock counties and four others north of but adjacent to the coast panhandle. In 1973 the Hancock County Vocational-Technical Center, located in the Hancock County Industrial Park, 10 miles north of Bay St. Louis, was created as a satellite of Pearl River Junior College.

In 1965 Perkinston Junior College, serving a district composed of Stone, George, Harrison, and Jackson counties, expanded to become the Mississippi Gulf Coast Junior College with the opening that year of Jackson County Campus at Gautier and Jefferson Davis Campus at Handsboro Station, Gulfport. In 1972 the system expanded once again with the construction of the George County Occupational Training Center at Lucedale. The following year, in cooperation with the United States Air Force, the Mississippi Gulf Coast Junior College inaugurated academic courses at Keesler Center on the base in Biloxi.

As early as 1947 Hattiesburg-based Mississippi Southern College (which became the University of Southern Mississippi in 1962) began intermittent course offerings at various points along the coast. Because they had a common goal, the university and the junior colleges formed a mutually advantageous link expressed in the sharing of facilities and even faculty. In 1972 the university purchased the campus of the defunct Gulf Park Junior College for girls at Long Beach and converted it into a regional campus. By one of those adventitious quirks of history, that campus occupied the former site of Rosalie, the home of John J. McCaughan, who had failed so valiantly in his attempt to secure a university for the coast 135 years before.

In 1976 the symbolic relationship of the University of Southern Mississippi with Mississippi Gulf Coast Junior College and with Pearl River Junior College was formally recognized in the announcement of the landmark Two-Plus-Two program. This agreement forged an alliance in which the junior colleges provide the first two years of college work while the university provides the courses for the second two years, thus enabling coast residents to remain at home and earn a college degree. That close relationship resulted in 1983 in the construction of a new university classroom building on the Jackson County Campus of Mississippi Gulf Coast Junior College for the purpose of serving the higher education needs of the residents of the eastern portion of the coast. This same sharing of facilities and sites exists at Keesler Center and other installations.

In addition to the Two-Plus-Two network, other higher-education oppor-

This rainbow curving over an open field could be a typical Midwestern scene. It is, however, another aspect of the Gulf region: a five-square-mile area in Stone County known as Big Level. Photo by Dave Davis, DeSilver

tunities were made available to coast residents by William Carey College in Hattiesburg. William Carey, a private Christian college, purchased the campus of the former Gulf Coast Military Academy in Gulfport in 1976. At present, Carey on the Coast offers four of the degrees offered by the parent campus.

The higher education network is just one of many manifestations of the single most important event in the history of the postwar coast—the evolution of the automobile from a luxury into a way of life. The rapid proliferation of cars, trucks, and buses on the coast detonated a transportation revolution analogous to, but far surpassing the railroad's overthrow of steamboats in the post-Civil War era. Commuter train service to New Orleans ended in 1969, and all rail passenger service ended in 1973. The competition for freight still continues.

By 1954 four-lane Highway 90 paralleled the Louisville & Nashville between Mobile and New Orleans. Subsequently Hattiesburg, long the junction of the three railroads serving the flanks and center of the coast panhandle, became also the hub of the three major paved highways built parallel to those railroads. Highways 11, 49, and 98 radiated from the Hub City to New Orleans, Gulfport, and Mobile respectively. A web of paved farm-to-market roads formed among these generally north-south tending arteries to provide rapid motorized transport to and from every point in the six counties.

In the mid-1960s Highway 49 had four lanes, and the construction of interstate highways began. Interstate 59, the coast's first interstate highway, was built parallel to Highway 11 in Pearl River County. By 1975 those portions of Interstate 10 passing through Hancock and Harrison parallel to and approximately five miles inland from Highway 90 were completed. Environmentalists concerned about the threat posed by I-10 to the habitat of the Sand Hill

On July 24, 1971, crowds cheered when the first blast failed to bring down the Edgewater Gulf Hotel. It took close to 475 pounds of dynamite to demolish the hotel, which had hosted thousands of visitors during its 47 years as one of the grand hotels of the coast. Courtesy, The Sun/The Daily Herald

Cranes in Jackson County held up the road until its final completion in 1982.

Prior to the Second World War an automobile trip between any two coast towns might and often did result in an item for the local newspaper. Today's road network makes it possible for any coastian to make a circuit of every major town in the panhandle between dawn and dusk and enables welders from Picayune to work at Ingalls.

In addition to revolutionizing socio-economic patterns, the automobile has remade the coast cities and towns. The rapid motor transport that made the flight to the suburbs possible brought inner-city decline as the tax base ebbed. The lack of parking places in the old downtown business districts birthed yet another automobile-age phenomenon that resulted in further deterioration of the city cores. On September 26, 1963, at 9:45 a.m. the snip of a red ribbon cleared the way for throngs of shoppers entering the coast's first regional shopping center. Edgewater Plaza, located on 40 acres between Gulfport and Biloxi, housed 20 initial stores on its air-conditioned mall and provided 3,000 parking places. Eight years later, demolition crews dynamited the grand Edgewater Gulf Hotel to clear space for 40 more stores.

In the years following the establishment of Edgewater Plaza, shopping centers large and small appeared in the suburbs of every coast town and city. In 1982 yet another giant regional shopping center, Singing River Mall, opened for business in Gautier. Some of the economically strapped cities developed downtown revitalization programs, and all of them moved to annex peripheral unincorporated suburban areas containing malls, shopping centers, and industrial plants.

Using a variety of funds originating at the local, state, and national levels, Pascagoula, Gulfport, and Biloxi led the way in city-core revitalization programs. Gulfport has given its downtown area a face-lifting complete with fountains and a multilevel garage, while Pascagoula has converted its old business district into a mall surrounded by acres of parking.

Biloxi undertook the most ambitious project of all. In the aftermath of Camille, armed with Urban Renewal funds, the city transformed its obsolete business district into the Vieux Marche. The "Old Market," roughly in the form of a "T," consists of the four-block-long canopied Howard Mall at the top and the Magnolia Mall shafting southward to Highway 90. The Vieux Marche's architectural mix contains specimens from nearly every period of coast history, culminating in the ultra-modern million-dollar Biloxi Library, completed in 1976.

Annexation of choice areas, though, proved to be a simpler, more efficient answer to the cities' woes. Legal opposition by suburban residents fighting the higher taxes that come with incorporation, and by the counties whose tax bases the expanding cities are shrinking, have clogged the courts for years. Some court cases have even resulted in three-way suits involving two cities seeking the same area with the county opposing both.

The coastline of Harrison County is now virtually one single unbroken strip of settlement composed of Biloxi, Gulfport, Long Beach, and Pass Christian, with certain streets designated as boundaries. These cities, unable to grow to the east or west, are now moving north.

Biloxi leaped Back Bay with the annexation of Sunkist and is presently in hot pursuit of D'Iberville. Gulfport, having absorbed the former towns of Mississippi City and Handsboro, is engaged in a sharp legal duel with Harrison County regarding its proposed takeover of a vast area containing Orange

Confederate reenactors fire a volley as a medal of honor is presented to the Unknown Soldier of the Confederate States of America at Beauvoir Cemetery on Sunday, May 1, 1983. Photo by Herb Welch. Courtesy, The Sun/The Daily Herald

Grove and large plants along the Industrial Seaway.

In the east, Pascagoula, blocked to the north by Moss Point, is likewise entangled with Jackson County authorities concerning its proposed annexation of Gautier. Adding to the confusion, a strong separatist movement calling for the incorporation of Gautier by the Gautierers has surfaced. Not to be outdone, southward-blocked Moss Point is casting its net northward toward Escatawpa. On the western front Waveland, in a series of spirited moves, has pinned Bay St. Louis against the bay, leaving that town no growing space. Waveland, on the other hand, continues a wide-open westward movement.

A sequence of time-lapse photography showing the Mississippi Gulf Coast Panhandle from 1945 to the present would reveal a wisteria-like growth east and west all along the shoreline from Waveland to Pascagoula and a northward clambering of that same growth up the trellis formed by Interstate 10 and the north-south arterial highways. At present the only unsettled area of any consequence is the rapidly closing gap between Ocean Springs and Gautier.

It seems likely that the 1896 prophecy that there would someday be one continuous city from New Orleans to Mobile will come to pass in time for the 1999 tricentennial of the Iberville landing. Even now a nighttime satellite photo encompassing the 140-mile arc from New Orleans to Mobile reveals only two major darkened areas—one between Slidell and Waveland and the other from Pascagoula to Mobile. Not long from now the last gaps will close, and the Mississippi Gulf Coast will fulfill its destiny as the centerpiece in a vast Southern megalopolis.

Despite 300 years of growth and change, certain characteristics, traditions, and commemorative events remain that would be familiar to denizens of almost every period of coast history. One of the threads woven through the coast's historical fabric is smuggling. Any indented shoreline is a smuggler's paradise, and the Mississippi Gulf Coast certainly fits that description. In every period of coast history contraband has been run in or out or both.

In the colonial and antebellum period the illegal trade items ranged from charcoal to slaves. In the 1920s the item was alcohol. Today it is drugs. The large-scale piney woods moonshine manufacturing and coastal rumrunning of the Prohibition era correspond in large measure to the backwoods marijuana-growing and cocaine- and marijuana-running in the Gulf at present. If the historic cycle continues, some other contraband article may replace drugs in the future.

Nostalgia buffs may choose to attend or engage in a number of public events highlighting coast history. Each year Ocean Springs' 1699 Historical Society stages the Iberville Landing Celebration on the beach in front of reconstructed Fort Maurepas. Periodic living history encampments and ceremonies open to the general public are held on the grounds of Beauvoir and at Fort Massachusetts. Participants are drawn from a number of Civil War reenactor units located on the coast and in adjacent parts of Louisiana and Alabama. Principal among these are Stanford's Mississippi Battery of Pascagoula, Boone's Battery of New Orleans, and the 21st Alabama Infantry C.S.A. of Mobile. The Beauvoir Chapter of the Sons of Confederate Veterans has recently resurrected the Seven Stars Artillery, originally formed by the owners of Grasslawn during the War Between the States. All of these and many others gather each May for the Battle of Champion Hill, Mississippi's premier reenactment, hosted by Stanford's Mississippi Battery.

One annual event in the piney woods possesses time-machine qualities— the Methodist camp meeting. Every fall since 1826—except during the last year of the Civil War, the hurricane of 1906, and the influenza epidemic of 1918—descendents of 22 original founding families have gathered at Salem Campground in what is now south George County for a week of "Old Time Religion." The camp meeting originated as a combination thanksgiving and harvest festival and remains for its member families the biggest religious and social event of the year. In the beginning the families lived in tents arranged in a square about a central brush-arbor tabernacle. In time the tents gave way to rough plank cabins carpeted with pine straw, but the nomenclature remained. Many of the "tents" of today sport all the conveniences of home, but others retain their crunchy flooring and "Methodist pallets"—straw ticks.

Three other camp meetings on the Salem model still flourish in the panhandle. After Emancipation, black Methodists, many of whom had attended Salem camp meetings as slaves, established themselves nearby at Mt. Pleasant Campground. In Jackson County near Vancleave a number of families, some with a former Salem connection, organized New Prospect Camp Meeting in 1880. Three years later the last presently active campground was founded at Palmer Creek in North Harrison County.

Nineteen eighty-four was a year of nostalgia on a grand scale for the coast. In 1884 New Orleans hosted the World Cotton Exposition. In 1984 the city hosted the World's Fair. In honor of the May-November grand event, the Mississippi Gulf Coast geared up to play its traditional role vis-a-vis the metropolis. Amtrak restored commuter-train service, deleted more than a decade before, on the Mobile-to-New Orleans run to provide easy access to the fair for citizens and guests of the Gulf City and those of Gulf Coast. And for the fair a Moss Point shipyard launched a steamboat whose name, whether by fortuitous accident or by design, recalls that of the most famous of the coast boats in the golden age of steam—*Creole Queen*. As Mark Twain said, "history does not repeat itself, but it rhymes."

Right: The city hall at Gulfport, built in 1906, has been renovated as a part of an overall city revitalization program. The restoration was completed in February 1981 and included extensive work on the annex building. Photo by Charles Sullivan and Murella Powell

Left: This is the tabernacle tent at Salem Methodist Campground in George County, one of the four campgrounds still used each year for camp meetings in the piney woods. Photo by Charles Sullivan and Murella Powell

Above: An aerial view facing east shows Highway 90 along the longest man-made sand beach in the world. Thousands of visitors each year come to the beach at Biloxi for fun in the sun. Courtesy, Guice & Guice Advertising

Right: Fire Chief Guy Roberts and Lieutenant McGivary of the Biloxi Police Department prepare to put to the torch 603 bales of marijuana confiscated from a shrimp boat on Point Cadet. Courtesy, Biloxi Police Department

Chapter Eight

PARTNERS
IN PROGRESS

During the 1920s, after spending days in the Gulf, fishermen unload their catch from an oyster schooner at a Point Cadet factory in Biloxi. The seafood industry is only one of the many successful economic endeavors in the Gulf Coast region. MDAH

Over a century had passed since Pierre LeMoyne and his valiant men trod the beaches of Noveau Biloxi, and the echo of their axes in the forests had long been silent, but in the little settlements that remained in the early 1800s these adventurous ancestors had not been forgotten.

In 1811, in the territory that now comprises the Gulf Coast counties of Mississippi, there were only about 770 people and most of them were of French descent. By 1818, however, the influx of settlers from the North and East brought in a new pattern of living that fostered the establishment of small inland settlements, usually built around a single family-owned industry: a sawmill, lumber port, or turpentine still.

By 1830 New Orleans had discovered the Gulf Coast. Small family-owned hotels and boarding houses sprang up and elaborate homes were built. Steamboats plied the coast from Mobile, Alabama, to New Orleans, making scheduled stops at the small towns, and the tourist business was born.

Lumbermen from the Northeast brought their dollars to the area and timber was sent downriver on small boats and carried to Ship Island, there to be loaded on ships bound for foreign shores.

The arrival of the railroads in 1870 also signaled the coming of prosperity: Transportation would play the prime role in creating new employment, new customers, and tourism. Communities that once depended on one industry would now become diversified.

Keesler Air Force Base, soon to be known throughout the world as the Electronics Training Center of the Air Force, came into existence in Biloxi in 1941, bringing an influx of new people and ideas. The demand for warships, and the availability of a deep-water port along with a large labor force, brought Ingalls Shipbuilding to Pascagoula the following year.

The National Aeronautics and Space Administration (NASA) brought its technology to the area in 1964, and the Edgewater Mall, now consisting of four major department stores and over 100 specialty shops, was built in Biloxi.

The land that once knew only the Indian and his bark canoe has now become a cosmopolitan community with people from every land working together. It has progressed from the time of small wooden boats carrying lumber and charcoal down the bayous to nuclear submarines that plow the ocean's depths and to rockets that search the heavens.

The organizations whose stories are detailed on the following pages have chosen to support this important literary and civic project. They illustrate the variety of ways in which individuals and their businesses have contributed to the growth and development of the Mississippi Coast.

MISSISSIPPI COAST HISTORICAL & GENEALOGICAL SOCIETY

"We are here because we have a past. We preserve because the fabric of the moment has been made by the past. We exist only because there is a past.

Without family, friends, lovers, something, someone to tie ourselves to, there is only a vacuum for the soul, and it must surely die. There can be no present or future without a past."

James Biddle, president of the National Trust Historical Preservation, addressing a group of college students in 1969.

A group of people who realized the necessity of preserving what is left of the past, and the present, met at the Old Spanish House in Biloxi and by acclamation adopted a constitution and by-laws for an organization to be named the Mississippi Coast Historical & Genealogical Society. In 1969, after meeting for several years, the group obtained a charter. It would be a nonprofit organization dedicated to "collect, process, preserve, and disseminate material of a historical and genealogical nature" in the six southernmost counties of Mississippi: Jackson, Harrison, Hancock, Pearl River, Stone, and George, as these counties represented the earliest settlements along the coast.

The group adopted an official emblem, which incorporates Mississippi's state flower, the magnolia, the six coastal counties, and the Biloxi Lighthouse, which is generally considered the most characteristic historical landmark on Mississippi's coastline.

Enthusiastic members, families, and friends sifted through dust and cobwebs in attics and found many treasures—old, forgotten family Bibles, trunks filled with yellowed newspaper clippings, pictures, and

The architecturally renowned Biloxi Public Library is the headquarters of the Mississippi Coast Historical & Genealogical Society. The cottage in the foreground, built around 1836, became the state's first free library in 1900. Courtesy, Guice & Guice Advertising

letters brittle with age. They braved snakes, searching for graveyards in open fields and in churchyards to obtain the bits of information that help bridge the gap between the present and the shadowy generations of the past.

In addition to a journal that is published three times a year and distributed to members, the Society has published the Harrison County census records, several Gulf Coast family histories, and Harrison County marriages and wills.

The volumes of historical and genealogical material that have been accumulated by the Mississippi Coast Historical & Genealogical Society over the years have now become permanent archives for those that follow, and are housed in the Biloxi Public Library, headquarters of the Society.

The most ambitious "Stories on Stones" undertaking, a project of the Mississippi Coast Historical & Genealogical Society, was copying the 1,500 headstones in the Coalville Cemetery at Woolmarket. Mississippi Gulf Coast Junior College/Perkinston Campus history students Laurie Taft (kneeling), Lorre Bradley (standing), Beth Farris, and Karen Farley participated in the project.

THE PEOPLES BANK

Biloxi was already known throughout the United States as an oyster- and shrimp-canning center on April 2, 1896, when seventy-four people met at the Fireman's Hall for the purpose of organizing another bank. It was decided to name the institution The Peoples Bank, and opening day was set for April 15.

The first Peoples Bank building was erected on the northwest corner of Howard and Lameuse streets, and the bank remained there until moving to its present location on the southeast corner of Howard and Lameuse in 1925.

The current site is the old Harrison County Bank, which The Peoples Bank took over in a 1914 merger. The present bank lobby retains the 1914 marble fixtures and grillwork, along with several matched additions (completed in

The bank moved to its current location on the southeast corner of Howard and Lameuse streets diagonally opposite its original structure in 1925.

1924, 1952, 1957, and 1975).

The Swetman family of Biloxi has been associated with the bank since its inception in 1896. J.W. Swetman was one of the original founders. His brother, Orcenith George Swetman, joined the bank as assistant cashier in 1903; he became the president and chief executive officer in 1951, and served in that capacity until his death in 1963.

Glenn L. Swetman, son of O.G. Swetman, is currently the chairman of the board. Glenn Swetman first became associated with the bank in 1917. On the death of his father, Swetman assumed the presidency of the bank in 1963, and served in that capacity until he was succeeded by his son, Chevis C. Swetman, in December 1983.

The Peoples Bank of Biloxi is proud of its growth. Over the years the institution has taken a genuine interest in the community. Guided by its chairman, the bank has been the driving force behind the preservation and restoration of several local structures of historical

The first Peoples Bank building was erected on the northeast corner of Howard and Lameuse streets in 1896. This old witch weather vane topped the structure and has provided eighty-eight years of service.

significance. Some notable accomplishments include the refurbishment of the old Magnolia Hotel, built in 1845; the relocation and restoration of the oldest free library in Mississippi; the restoration of the Saenger Theater of the Performing Arts; and the listing of The Peoples Bank's present building on the National Register of Historic Places.

To ensure its continued efforts, in 1981 the bank established the Peoples Heritage Foundation, one of the few private foundations of its kind in the Southeast. Some of the projects on its calendar are the establishment of a Mardi Gras Museum, the formation of a Seafood Industry Museum, and the preservation of several additional historical sites.

By all accounts it would appear that The Peoples Bank of Biloxi and the Mississippi Gulf Coast are true partners in progress.

BILOXI PRESTRESS CONCRETE, INC.

Biloxi Prestress Concrete, Inc., spans thirty acres in Clay Point.

A red-and-white tugboat gives two short whistles and starts pushing a string of steel barges laden with huge prestress concrete girders toward the drawbridge that crosses Back Bay from Biloxi to Ocean Springs. Two huge red cranes lift massive concrete beams onto a long trailer truck, and a flat-bottom railroad car waits at the siding for a load of the company's products.

Rows upon rows of concrete beams and pilings stacked high and wide cover thirty acres of land that extends to Biloxi Back Bay. Casting beds are hives of activity.

Prestress concrete was fairly new in 1959 when J.B. Michael, Sr., a contractor from Memphis, Tennessee, received the contract to build the Biloxi-Ocean Springs span over Back Bay.

Michael bought five acres of land near the proposed bridge for his headquarters and for the manufacture of the prestress concrete products that he would use.

Prestress concrete, a structural material of great strength, is a combination of high-strength concrete and high-tensile-strength steel.

Prestressing is done by stretching special steel cable (strands) between two anchoring points. These strands may be tensioned to as much as 31,000 pounds each and some members may have as many as 100 of these strands, thus creating more than three million pounds of stress.

These strands are positioned within the specific form or section that is desired and then high-strength concrete is poured into the forms. Once this concrete hardens, the strands are cut loose from the anchors and the stress is induced into the concrete—thus the term prestress concrete. The strength of prestress concrete is created by putting the concrete under compression and creating a built-in resistance to the loads the members will be subjected to.

After the Biloxi-Ocean Springs span over Back Bay was completed, the plant did not expand until after Hurricane Camille in 1969. Camille's heavy winds and high tidal wave destroyed all buildings in her path and twelve feet of water covered the area.

To rebuild the plant and to allow for further expansion, twenty-five acres of land was purchased from the Harrison County Industrial Park and J.B. Michael, Jr., became president of the organization.

When I-10 was started in 1970, Biloxi Prestress received the contract to supply all major bridge components in Harrison County and the plant went into full production.

Other projects built by the firm include the Gulf Breeze Bridge over Santa Rosa Sound at Pensacola, Florida; the Back Bay Bridge from D'Iberville to Biloxi; and many bridges in Louisiana.

Biloxi Prestress is now furnishing box girders for the Westbank Expressway in New Orleans, Louisiana. Approximately 900 girders, most of them 132 feet long with some weighing up to 145 tons, have already been delivered.

Biloxi Prestress Concrete, Inc., was started in 1959 with only 10 employees. It now employs about 150 workers with an annual payroll well in excess of one million dollars.

Barges are loaded with concrete beams and pilings at Biloxi Prestress Concrete's docks.

MARY MAHONEY'S OLD FRENCH HOUSE RESTAURANT

Would you like to eat in a small dining room that had once been part of the slave quarters in a house built in the eighteenth century, and sample gourmet dishes like Lobster Gorgo—lobster served with a cream sauce of shrimp, mushroom, cheese, and brandy—or enjoy the deliciousness of petite soft-shell crabs fried to a golden brown, and seafood gumbo made as only the old Creole cooks knew how? Would you like to revel in Mary Mahoney's special bread pudding made with a rum sauce, and then, with an aged bottle of wine, watch the candles burn low?

A dream evening, an unforgettable experience.

This is only a part of Mary Mahoney's Old French House Restaurant. There are other dining areas in the old house—intimate rooms for a few guests, larger rooms for groups, and the beautiful garden dining room that overlooks the Vieu Marche. There is the Daily Herald room and the Carriage House. Then there is the lovely old courtyard where young couples gather to exchange their marriage vows, and where receptions and parties are held.

A high wall encloses the courtyard, the entrance to the restaurant, but a wooden gate stands open and bids you enter. You enter and step into the past. Visions of Creole beauties and courtly cavaliers haunt the area. Scarlet hibiscus, like dancing butterflies, sway in the gentle breeze. Blue and pink hydrangeas lift their heads to a hummingbird, and a fountain tinkles. A majestic oak whispers and time stands still.

The "Patriarch" has been judged by foresters to be over 500 years old. It was here when d'Iberville claimed this land for the King of France, and when the little French

Mary Mahoney has fulfilled a lifetime dream as proprietress of her nationally famous landmark restaurant.

town of Biloxi was born. The giant oak was here when Louis Frazier, a French colonist, built his home under its sheltering branches. The house, constructed of handmade bricks with wooden pegged columns of cypress and floors of polished pine boards, remained in the family until 1820. Other residents lived there until 1962, when the estate was purchased by Mary and Bob Mahoney and Mary's brother,

Andrew Cvitanovich.

The Old French House is not just another good restaurant. It is a dream come true for a young Yugoslavian girl who desired to create a perfect dining atmosphere—a place of beauty and charm serving foods that would be delicious and different, a restaurant that would be nationally famous—and the Old French House has become just that.

Only three years after its opening it was featured in *Ford Times* magazine. Mary Mahoney has also become famous. Hundreds of articles in leading magazines have extolled her charms, and honors by the dozens have been bestowed upon her. But Mary remains Mary. She loves her restaurant; it is her world and she loves the people that enter there.

Mary Mahoney's Old French House Restaurant and Old Slave Quarters Lounge at 138 Rue Magnolia in Biloxi.

GULF NATIONAL LIFE

The siren call of adventure and the dream of making a new home in America led young Edward O'Keefe to leave Tipperary County, Ireland, in the 1840s and settle in Ocean Springs where he started a small livery and drayage business.

The family business prospered, but in the early 1920s the advent of the newfangled automobile led the O'Keefe family in another direction; J. Ben O'Keefe established an undertaking concern in Biloxi in 1923.

Jerry O'Keefe went to war and became a highly decorated Marine Ace. After returning to Biloxi and his new wife, Annette, he attended Loyola University where he completed four years of college within two and a half years. After college Jerry returned to work with his father.

When J. Ben O'Keefe suffered a stroke in 1952, Jerry took over the management of the funeral home and later merged with an established and respected firm, creating the Bradford-O'Keefe Funeral Home.

Drawing on their personal knowledge of the funeral home business, Jerry and Annette O'Keefe founded Gulf National Life in 1958 and started selling insurance policies along the Mississippi Gulf Coast. In 1960 Gulf National began a series of acquisitions of small funeral home insurance companies.

In spite of the demands of the growing Gulf National, Jerry became active in civic matters and his leadership was evidenced by his selection as both the Outstanding Young Man and Outstanding Citizen of Biloxi. Jerry was elected to serve in the state legislature, and while there was selected as the Outstanding Freshman Representative.

In 1973 Jerry was elected mayor of Biloxi, and in 1977 reelected for a

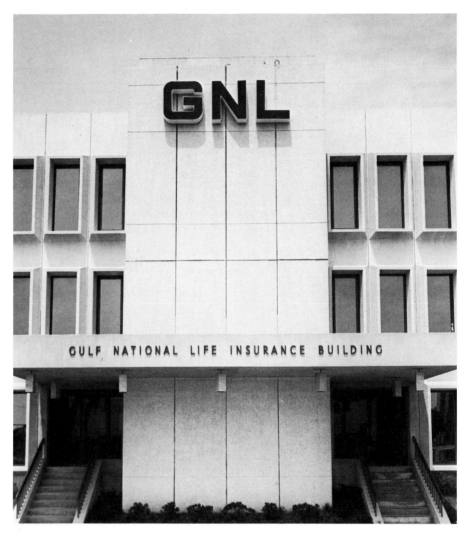

The home office of Gulf National Life, located in Biloxi, was completed in 1974.

second four-year term. After serving eight years he chose not to run again, but to devote his full time to the life insurance business.

Wright & Ferguson Life Insurance had been purchased by the firm in 1975, and in 1979 the Mississippi Insurance Company was incorporated into Gulf National.

The firm expanded into Texas in 1981, acquiring the Dependable Life Insurance Company of Waco.

In Mississippi, Gulf National offices are located in Biloxi, Jackson, Southhaven, Columbia, and Hattiesburg, in addition to the offices of ninety-five affiliated funeral homes throughout the state.

Since 1975 Gulf National assets are up 161 percent. Premium income has grown by 149 percent. Insurance in force has increased 98 percent from $76 million to over $150 million.

This impressive growth has been the result of the company's key personnel, all of whom work under incentive plans, and the affiliated funeral homes in Mississippi and Texas who know Gulf National Life's strength offers real protection for their hometown folks.

PACECO, INC.

Paceco, Inc., began in Oakland, California, on November 5, 1923, as the Pacific Coast Engineering Company for the purpose of manufacturing hydraulic suction dredges. In late 1941 the business moved to Alameda, California, where it remained until 1981.

Pacific Coast Engineering Company officially adopted its abbreviated name, Paceco, in 1967. About that time Paceco's success in the container crane market began to attract the attention of larger corporations.

At the same time Paceco recognized an increasing need for expansion capital. Its Alameda facilities were limited and demands for its products were quickly outgrowing its production capacity.

In 1968 Fruehaf Corporation acquired Paceco as a wholly owned subsidiary, giving the firm the financial ability to expand its potential. After much study, a 100-acre site was selected in the Harrison County Industrial Seaway Park at Gulfport, which offered excellent water, rail, and interstate

The Paceco world headquarters complex is located in the Harrison County Industrial Seaway Park in Gulfport.

highway connections. The $9-million plant was put into operation in 1971.

By the late 1970s the decision was made to expand its Gulfport facility and move Paceco's world headquarters and all manufacturing facilities to Gulfport. The $26-million expansion program was completed in 1981. Today Paceco's computer integrated manufacturing complex is one of the most modern in the private industry, with over 450,000 square feet of under-roof fabrication area and the world's largest environmentally controlled blasting and coating facility. The plant employs between 250 and 500 people with an annual payroll of about six million dollars.

Paceco has become recognized throughout the world as the leading manufacturer of container-handling cranes as well as other large, custom-fabricated, heavy-steel machinery. Currently there are several thousand Paceco-designed and manufactured products in operation around the world, serving the power-generation, aerospace, defense, shipping, mining, and offshore-drilling industries.

Other accomplishments include the first nuclear reactor vessel for commercial use; the *Alameda,* one of

the world's most powerful dredges; the *George Ferris,* the first offshore platform manufactured on the West Coast; Daring class tugs; dam gates and hoists; 325-ton-capacity revolving barge cranes; and polar, bridge, and gantry cranes.

Mississippi Governor Williams Winter presented a proclamation issued by the Harrison County Development Commission to Paceco in 1982 for the firm's "material expression of confidence in our community, represented by its substantial investments at its headquarters here."

On May 5, 1983, in a ceremony at Encinal Terminals in Alameda, California, the American Society of Mechanical Engineers dedicated the world's first high-speed, dockside, container-handling crane, produced by Paceco, as an International Historic Mechanical Engineering Landmark. The crane went into operation on January 7, 1959, and set the standards for container-handling cranes around the world.

Paceco's multipurpose Portainer^R crane and catenary continuous unloader (shown here) is used to unload ships at the Port of Gulfport.

MISSISSIPPI POWER COMPANY

Mississippi Power Company was created by a group of enterprising businessmen and civic leaders who saw electric power as essential to the economic progress of south Mississippi.

At midnight, December 31, 1924, the Gulfport and Mississippi Coast Traction Company, which operated a small generating plant and an electric interurban railway system stretching from Biloxi to Pass Christian, ended with the old year, and Mississippi Power Company was born.

Initially, limited electric service from small isolated generating plants was available to 5,493 customers in thirteen communities primarily along the Gulf Coast. In some small towns upstate, electricity was available only at night, but growth was to come rapidly.

"Our entire interests are in Mississippi," declared Barney Eaton, Mississippi Power Company's first president, "and we will develop a system to meet the needs of a growing Mississippi."

Eaton began developing an efficient electric system, acquiring and modernizing existing operations and constructing new facilities in communities that had no electric service. By the end of 1929 the company was serving 38,900 customers located in the eastern half of Mississippi from the Gulf Coast to the Tennessee state line.

The 1930s were difficult years for Mississippi Power. Following passage of the Tennessee Valley Authority Act, the construction of transmission lines duplicating company facilities in northeast Mississippi was announced. This plan for government duplication forced Mississippi Power to sell or salvage its properties in northeast Mississippi in 1934 and 1939. The firm's service area was reduced to its

Mississippi Power Company's Gulfport Steam Plant was once located on the current site of the firm's general office building. The old bus barn can be seen in the background of this photo.

present twenty-three counties in southeast Mississippi.

During the early years hydro-electric power was transmitted from Alabama into eastern Mississippi. During the Depression the first company-owned generating plant was planned for construction near Hattiesburg. Following delays because of material restrictions and manpower shortages during World War II, Plant Eaton, named in honor of the firm's first president, began operating in 1945.

As the state's first modern, high-pressure steam plant, Plant Eaton was called "a major milestone in the progressive development of a

power system that has helped implement industrial and rural growth."

Mississippi Power's second generating plant, named in honor of Lonnie P. Sweatt, the company's second president, began producing electricity in 1951. A second generating unit was added in 1953, the first year Mississippi Power generated one billion kilowatt-hours.

Realizing that its growth depended on the economic development of its service area, Mississippi Power established the state's first full-time industrial development department to attract new industry. The growth that southeast Mississippi and the company experienced from 1925 to 1955 was a prelude to the extensive industrial development that occurred in the years that followed.

To help meet growing energy demands, construction began in

184

Transportation, utilizing buses such as this one, was once a sideline of the firm.

early 1955 on a third generating plant. This facility, between Gulfport and Biloxi, began operating in July 1957. Today Plant Jack Watson, named in honor of A.J. Watson, Jr., who was elected the firm's third president in 1958, is the largest generating plant on the utility's electric system.

Tropical storms have always been a potential threat to the Gulf Coast. The night of August 17, 1969, Hurricane Camille, one of the greatest recorded storms, struck southeast Mississippi. Damage to Mississippi Power's electric system was extensive. Tens of thousands of customers were without electricity, and property damage and other losses to the corporation exceeded ten million dollars.

To restore essential power as soon as possible, Mississippi Power's 850 employees were joined by 1,600 men and women from other electric utilities and private contractors. By September 1, two weeks after the hurricane struck, electric power had been restored to every customer

able to receive service. For this achievement, the Edison Electric Institute awarded Mississippi Power the Edison Award, the electric utility industry's highest honor.

In 1972 Victor J. Daniel, Jr., became the firm's fourth president. Meanwhile, construction had begun on a coal-fired generating plant in Jackson County. The plant, later named in honor of Daniel, went into commercial operation in September 1977.

The energy crisis of the 1970s

directed Mississippi Power's attention to conservation and the efficient use of electricity. In 1978 the company initiated a computerized home energy inspection program, one of several additional programs to help customers conserve energy.

In May 1980 Alan R. Barton became the fifth president of Mississippi Power. Today the organization's generating capacity exceeds 1.9 million kilowatts, with coal being used as primary fuel. Electricity is provided to more than 169,000 customers. Residential customers in 1984 used an average of 10,814 kilowatt-hours.

Mississippi Power Company begins its sixtieth year of service in 1985. New opportunities for service lie ahead. Electric power will continue to play a leading role in the development of southeast Mississippi, and Mississippi Power Company will continue to meet the energy needs of its customers.

Mississippi Power Company's general office was located in the Kremer Building from early 1925 until 1935.

HANCOCK BANK

On the evening of August 29, 1899, the prominent businessmen of Bay St. Louis, Mississippi, gathered at the Hancock County Courthouse to organize a bank for their fast-growing city. Nineteen subscribers were present, representing a total of 198 shares, and these shareholders elected a board of directors.

A small frame building located on South Beach was rented for the sum of seven dollars a month, and on October 9, 1899, it was formally opened as Hancock County Bank. Opening-day capitalization was $10,000 and deposits amounted to $8,277.41.

Within a few weeks the board purchased a site at the corner of Main Street and South Beach and began planning a new building.

On March 1, 1900, a contract was given to John T. McDonald to construct a facility, including a vault, for the sum of $5,100. When completed in September of that year it was the first two-story brick building in Bay St. Louis, and when occupied it housed the bank, post office, and U.S. Customs Office.

Illinois Central Systems purchased the Gulf & Ship Island Railroad in 1925 and created a real estate boom along the coast. Business flourished and the Hancock Bank grew as well. Then came the stock market crash in 1929. Financial institutions failed throughout the United States, and eventually Gulfport had no bank.

Hancock weathered the Depression, and a delegation of Gulfport citizens headed by Mayor Joe Milner, editor Clayton Rand, and Chamber of Commerce president J.C. Rich appealed to the bank to open in Gulfport.

The institution agreed to the move and on August 15, 1932, an office was opened on the corner of Thirteenth Street and Twenty-sixth Avenue. Hancock occupied this

Hancock Bank's new fifteen-story corporate headquarters is located at One Hancock Plaza in Gulfport.

The first Hancock Bank was formed in 1899 in Bay St. Louis.

facility until moving to Twenty-fifth Avenue and Fourteenth Street in July 1939.

Under the leadership of its five presidents—Peter Hellwege, Eugene Roberts, Horatio S. Weston, Leo W. Seal, Sr., and Leo W. Seal, Jr.—Hancock from its beginning has been involved in public projects. It was the first bank along the Mississippi Coast to establish a branch and was first to offer drive-in facilities.

Hancock's beautiful fifteen-story corporate headquarters at One Hancock Plaza, completed in 1982, has the distinction of being the tallest coastline building between Port Arthur, Texas, and Tampa, Florida.

From a little one-room office with a capital of $10,000 to a magnificent edifice towering to the sky, with total capital accounts of $39,069,958, deposits of more than $500 million, and over 600 employees, Hancock Bank has become the largest bank on the Mississippi Gulf Coast.

BROADWATER BEACH HOTEL

Overlooking a beach of glistening white sand and an expanse of green gulf waters that stretch into the far horizon, the Broadwater Beach Hotel stands in a lush tropical garden of thirty-three acres.

A soaring white concrete canopy rises over the circular drive that fronts the hotel's entrance. Across the way is the hotel's own marina, one of the most modern and complete in the world. It has 136 berths jutting out into the Gulf of Mexico, home for sleek seafaring yachts, charter fishing boats, and sailing crafts with colorful sails. A 65-foot lighthouse stands guard over the marina and its powerful rays guide the sailor into port.

This luxurious beach resort is the fruition of the dreams, planning, and hard work of an imaginative and astute businesswoman, Mrs. Joe W. Brown.

In 1958 Joe W. Brown, owner of the fabulous Joe W. Brown's Horseshoe Club in Las Vegas, well-known sports personality, and prominent New Orleans businessman, purchased the old 44-room Broadwater Beach Hotel from the estate of Pete Martin and T.W. Richardson. Joe Brown died in 1959 and the hotel became his widow's chief interest. Plans for expansion were made, and Mrs. Brown envisioned the Broadwater being transformed into a beautiful, luxurious, warm, and hospitable hotel, one that would be a wonderful and exciting experience to the young at heart as well as a haven to the weary traveler.

To create this dream hotel, Mrs. Brown enlisted the help of her nephews, T.M. Dorsett, a graduate of Texas A&M with a degree in mechanical engineering, to be supervising engineer for the project, and W.C. Dorsett, to act as general manager.

Joe W. Brown, well-known sports personality and prominent New Orleans businessman, purchased the old, 44-room Broadwater Beach Hotel in 1958.

Largely through the efforts of Joe W. Brown's widow, the Broadwater Beach Hotel has grown into a luxurious beachfront resort with 360 rooms. Three golf courses, tennis courts, three swimming pools, and two clubhouses cater to the sportsman.

Leaders in the fields of architecture, construction, design, and interior decoration were hired. The renovation began in 1959, and within the next two years more than five million dollars had been invested in the old hotel's refurbishment.

Mrs. Brown was actively involved in the activities. She personally designed the award-winning three-tiered swimming pool, decorated the garden room area, and selected the main items to furnish her Dorothy Brown's Ladies' Shop.

Today the resort has 360 rooms, including garden cottages. Three golf courses, tennis courts, three swimming pools, and two magnificent clubhouses cater to the sportsman. An elegant ballroom, seven meeting rooms planned to accommodate any size group and any style function, and four lovely dining areas combine to make a very special hotel.

Mrs. Brown became one of the most prominent women along the Gulf Coast and was the first woman ever to be elected to the board of directors of the Biloxi Chamber of Commerce.

After the death of W.C. Dorsett in 1978, Jack L. Stanford, who had been with the hotel since the early days of its expansion, became general manager.

E.I. DU PONT dE NEMOURS AND COMPANY

Aerial view of the Du Pont plant in DeLisle.

Founded in 1802 in Wilmington, Delaware, E.I. du Pont de Nemours and Company is one of the premier manufacturers in the world.

For its first 100 years the firm specialized in explosives production. Early products included black powder, gunpowder, and dynamite. Following the turn of the twentieth century, Du Pont began to diversify into fields such as basic chemicals, plastics, textile fibers, synthetic rubber, pigments, agricultural chemicals, pharmaceuticals, and electronics.

Today more than 165,000 employees work in the plants, laboratories, offices, oil fields, mines, refineries, and other facilities worldwide. Du Pont's acquisition of Conoco in 1981 made it the eighth-largest industrial corporation in the country today, adding petroleum, coal, and minerals operations to its business portfolio. Du Pont now has eight major product segments, ranging from biomedical, industrial, fiber, and polymer products to products of petroleum refining and exploration.

In December 1979 Du Pont dedicated its DeLisle, Mississippi,

In 1983 the firm became the first chemical plant in the country to receive the U.S. Occupational Safety and Health (OSHA) Star Award, and its employees helped celebrate the event.

plant to the manufacture of titanium dioxide. This facility, the firm's fourth such plant, currently provides employment for more than 580 people, with an annual payroll of over $18 million. The plant's rated capacity is 150,000 tons of titanium dioxide annually and construction costs exceeded $150 million. The facility is located on 200 acres of a 2,280-acre site on the Bay St. Louis, about five miles north of Pass Christian.

The site's history can be traced to 1850, when William A. Witfield founded Shelley Plantation. Prior to that, stories of local residents tell of

an ancient Indian tribe harvesting oysters and fish from the coastal waters. Mounds of oyster shells and burial mounds remain intact on the site.

The plantation continued until 1925, when the land was purchased to build a luxury hotel, clubhouse, and golf course, named Pine Hills, Inc. The $1.3-million facility opened in 1926, but only a small portion of the 2,300-acre site was ever developed.

In 1983 Du Pont purchased the adjacent eighty-acre hotel site for two million dollars to be used as a "good neighbor" buffer zone between manufacturing operations and the surrounding community.

Actual construction on the Du Pont site began in 1976. Many factors made Harrison County, Mississippi, attractive, including a high-quality work force, shipping access through the Port of Gulfport, a good road network, potential for rail shipments, ample fresh water, attractive construction costs, available utilities, and community facilities to attract and hold employees.

Of the 580 employees who work around the clock to produce

The company's DeLisle plant has the capacity to produce 150,000 tons of supreme titanium dioxide annually to meet its customers needs.

titanium dioxide, 97 percent live in the coastal three-county area. In addition to salaries and wages, Du Pont employees enjoy a benefits package that includes a savings and investment plan, medical and dental coverage, pension, and paid vacation. Du Pont is an equal opportunity employer.

The DeLisle plant has had and continues to have positive economic impact on the local community and the state of Mississippi. In addition to the $18-million payroll, local goods and services purchased contribute another $16 million to the local economy. It has always been Du Pont's policy to pay its fair share of taxes where it operates a plant. In 1984 the DeLisle plant paid $1.2 million in taxes. Conoco operations in Mississippi also paid more than $2 million in 1983. In addition, gasoline and product taxes collected by Conoco for the state were nearly one million dollars.

Being a good neighbor means that Du Pont and its employees promote and participate in the civic, social, and cultural activities of the community. In 1984 the 580 DeLisle employees donated $33,000 to the United Way.

The DeLisle plant's only product, titanium dioxide, is an inert, non-toxic white pigment widely used in paints, inks, paper, textile fibers, and plastics to impart whiteness, brightness, and opacity. Surface-coating paints, varnishes, and lacquers account for approximately 50 percent of the titanium dioxide consumed in the United States each year. Paper accounts for another 10 percent and plastics, rubber, textiles, and many smaller uses account for the rest.

More than 700,000 tons of titanium dioxide are used annually in the United States. The finished product is packed and shipped to all parts of the country and all regions of the world.

Safety has always been one of the highest priorities at Du Pont. This concern has helped the firm achieve the best safety record among all large manufacturing concerns in the United States.

Dedication to safety is much in evidence at the DeLisle plant. Its best record is nearly three million exposure-hours without a time-losing injury. In 1983 the plant became the first chemical facility in the United States to receive the U.S. Occupational Safety and Health, (OSHA) Star Award.

A wide-ranging industrial hygiene program at the DeLisle plant features evaluation of chemical exposures with air-monitoring devices, and prescribes engineering and operational control of exposure to materials handled during titanium dioxide manufacturing. Employees use protective equipment such as acid suits, respirators, and goggles. A comprehensive program of medical surveillance is provided. Du Pont's objective is to produce titanium dioxide without harm to its employees or to the environment.

At DeLisle, in addition to maintaining the natural beauty of the environment, there is an on-site wastewater treatment and state-of-the-art deep-well disposal systems engineered to dispose of all wastes economically and safely. Capital committed to pollution-abatement facilities at the plant is $40 million, and the annual operating and maintenance cost for this investment is $1.2 million.

Du Pont DeLisle Plant employs over 580 mechanical, laboratory, production, and office and clerical workers.

RIEMANN FUNERAL HOMES

Ernest T. Riemann grew up in Richmond, Michigan, and until he enlisted in World War I, worked as a boy in the local funeral home.

When he left the service in 1918, he established his first funeral business in Memphis, Michigan. In 1920 a friend, C.E. Holmes, who had a home on the beach in Gulfport, encouraged him to move there.

Ernest Riemann and his wife, Ruth, settled in Gulfport in 1920, and established the Riemann Funeral Home at the corner of Fourteenth Street and Twenty-fourth Avenue. With the help of one other person, Ernest and Ruth serviced thirteen funerals during that first year. In 1926 the mortuary business was moved downtown to Twenty-fifth Avenue.

In 1931, during the Great Depression, Ernest and Ruth formed the Riemann Insurance Company to provide a program enabling families to pay funeral expenses. Along with other businesses along the coast, Riemann struggled through the 1930s, but in the early 1940s the situation began to brighten financially.

The funeral home furnished mortuary services to the Air Force, Navy, and U.S. Marine Corps units along the coast. Riemann currently services Keesler Air Force Base, the U.S. Construction Center in Gulfport, the local U.S. Marine Reserve Unit, the U.S. Naval Home, and over the years has worked with the Veteran's Administration in Biloxi and Gulfport.

Following a heart attack in 1950, Ernest turned over the managerial reins to his son, Robert, who had been associated with the firm since 1945.

Years of expansion followed. In 1947 Riemann had established its first branch funeral home, in Pass Christian. In 1961 the Fahey-

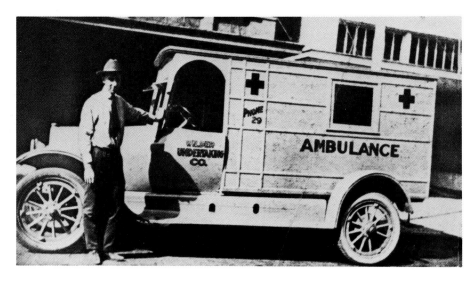

Whitfield Funeral Home in Bay St. Louis was purchased and immediately redecorated. Riemann built the first funeral home in Long Beach, on Jefferson Davis Avenue, the following year. In 1964 a funeral home on Debuys Road in Biloxi was established.

The old funeral home on Twenty-fifth Avenue in Gulfport was completely renovated in 1965, and a lovely colonial mansion, complete with lavish furnishings, crystal chandeliers, costly antiques, and ornate mirrors, emerged. Deep, luxurious carpets and huge vases of flowers helped create a sense of tranquillity.

The funeral home in Bay St. Louis was moved in 1972 and a larger one was built on Highway 90, the first all-new funeral home for the community.

The Family Guaranty Life Insurance Company was organized in 1973 to better allow the public to meet family funeral expenses. In addition to the Biloxi-Bay St. Louis area, Family Guaranty furnishes insurance to Pascagoula, Moss Point, Laurel, and Ellisville.

As a memorial to its founders, Ernest (who had died in 1965) and Ruth Riemann, Riemann Memorial

Ernest T. Riemann, Sr., who had been in the funeral business in Michigan until he moved to Gulfport, established the first Riemann Funeral Home in 1920.

Funeral Home was built in 1974 on Highway 49, just north of the Interstate 10 exit.

In 1977 Lang Funeral Home, which had been established on the Gulf Coast since 1884, was purchased; with that addition, Riemann Funeral Homes became the largest funeral establishment in the state of Mississippi.

In 1975 Riemann founded Family Care Inc. to offer a prepayment funeral trust program for those who feel the need to preplan and prepay for their funeral. This program has been widely accepted by the citizens of the Gulf Coast.

Robert M. Riemann, sole owner of Riemann Funeral Homes, Lang Funeral Home, Family Guaranty Life Insurance Company, and Family Care Inc., was born in Gulfport on August 8, 1924. He finished high school in Gulfport and entered the U.S. Army in World War II, serving for three and one-half years. He completed his mortuary education after the war, and became a partner in Riemann Funeral Homes in 1950.

Robert married the former Frances Files in Gulfport, and they became the parents of three sons, R. Mack, David, and Michael. Robert was named to the board of trustees of the National Foundation of Funeral Service in 1984 for a term of three years. The foundation has been the pioneer education facility for the funeral industry since 1945.

Other positions in which Robert Riemann has served his industry include immediate past president of the Mississippi Funeral Directors'

Association, 1982-1983; past president of the Order of the Golden Rule; and finance committee member of the National Selected Morticians' Group.

He has also been active in community affairs, serving as chairman of the board of the First Methodist Church of Gulfport, president of the Gulfport Lions Club, director of the Gulfport

The old funeral home on Twenty-fifth Avenue in Gulfport was completely renovated in 1965, and this lovely colonial mansion emerged.

Chamber of Commerce, director of the Gulfport Yacht Club, director of Hancock Bank, and director of the American Funeral Assurance Company.

Robert partly retired in recent years and his sons took over: David as president and general manager of Riemann Funeral Homes, and Michael as president and general manager of Family Guaranty Life Insurance Company, which has approximately 120,000 policies serving approximately 1,000 families a year in funeral services.

In 1983 Michael and David Riemann bought Cardinal Flower and Gift Shop in Gulfport as a convenience to those they serve.

The Riemann-Fahey Funeral Home on Highway 90 in Bay St. Louis.

DIOCESE OF BILOXI

On March 8, 1977, Archbishop Jean Jadot, apostolic delegate to the United States, announced that, by order of Pope Paul VI, the Diocese of Natchez-Jackson, which had encompassed the state of Mississippi for 140 years, would now be divided into the Diocese of Jackson and the Diocese of Biloxi. Archbishop Jadot also announced that Bishop Joseph Lawson Howze would become the ordinary of the new Diocese of Biloxi.

On June 7, 1977, in the Cathedral of the Nativity of the Blessed Virgin Mary, the oldest cathedral in Mississippi, over 2,000 lay people, 40 bishops, and 200 priests participated in ceremonies creating the new Diocese of Biloxi and installing Bishop Howze as its first ordinary.

The Most Reverend Jean Jadot, personal representative of the Pope, presented the documents from Rome proclaiming the existence of the diocese and the commission of Bishop Howze.

The Papal Bull decreeing the establishment, read by the Reverend Monsignor Kevin Bambrick, and the Papal Decree of appointment, read by the Reverend Monsignor James McGough, were signed by bishops Hannon and Howze to become official.

Bishop Howze, after taking his seat in the Episcopal Chair, was adorned with a miter, the bishop's crown, and handed the crozier, the symbol of his role as the chief shepherd of the new Biloxi Diocese, and became officially the first black Catholic bishop to head a diocese in the United States in this century.

The Biloxi Diocese consists of seventeen counties—Jefferson Davis, Covington, Jones, Wayne, Walthall, Lawrence, Marion, Lamar, Forrest, Perry, Greene, Pearl River, Stone, George, Hancock, Harrison, and Jackson—with forty-four parishes, sixteen missions, and twenty-three schools. The three coast counties—Hancock, Harrison, and Jackson—

The Cathedral of the Nativity of the Blessed Virgin Mary, built in 1902, is the oldest church in the Diocese of Biloxi.

have the largest Catholic population.

When Bishop Howze assumed his duties as ordinary, there were forty-three diocesan priests and twenty-six religious priests. Today there are fifty-three diocesan priests, twenty-seven religious priests, and six permanent deacons. The majority of priests working within the diocese are natives of Ireland.

Bishop Howze, ordained on May 7, 1959, in Raleigh, North Carolina, celebrated his Silver Jubilee Mass and the seventh anniversary of the Biloxi Diocese at St. Michael Church in conjunction with the Mass of the Shrimp blessing on June 2, 1984, and the Blessing of the Fleet on June 3. The Blessing of the Fleet, dating back to 1929, was part of the week-long celebration by the clergy and people for the Diocese of Biloxi.

St. Michael Church was dedicated in 1964 in Biloxi.

GULF PUBLISHING COMPANY

In 1922 the Daily Herald *moved into this new plant in Gulfport.*

Over 100 years ago George W. Wilkes and M.B. Richmond started a weekly paper in the small fishing village of Biloxi. One year later, in 1885, Richmond sold out to Wilkes, who became sole owner and publisher of the *Herald.*

Despite two fires, the little newspaper thrived, and in 1898 became a daily. The first paid editor during the early years was Joseph R. Davis, nephew of President Jefferson Davis of the Confederacy, who then lived at Beauvoir.

In 1912, after having editorial offices in Biloxi and Gulfport for two years, the *Herald* moved its printing plant to Gulfport.

George Wilkes died in 1915, and the family, who included his wife, Laurie Wilkes, sons Charles, Walter, and Eugene, and daughters Thelma and Beryl, inherited the paper.

Family members eventually sold their shares to Walter and Eugene, who operated the business as a partnership until 1929, when it was incorporated.

Gene Wilkes, born in August 1885, was only ten when he started working with his father. Over the following years he held virtually every job at the newspaper, from carrier to publisher, and learned every phase of the newspaper

business.

Wilkes continued for several years as editor of the *Herald* after its purchase by the State-Record Company of Columbia, South Carolina, in July 1968.

Gulf Publishing Company was formed as a wholly owned subsidiary of the State-Record Company, and Roland Weeks, Jr., was named president and general manager.

In early 1970, five months after Hurricane Camille had devastated the Mississippi Coast, the *Herald* launched its Sunday edition. One month later ground was broken for the new, $2-million plant. By October 1970 the plant was finished and operations were moved from the

Gulfport plant to the new facility on Debuys Road.

At that time the content of the paper was expanded, with new features added to the daily and Sunday papers. News bureaus were opened in Ocean Springs in 1969, in Bay St. Louis in 1971, and in Jackson in 1973. The *Daily Herald* was the first Mississippi newspaper to operate a news bureau in the state capital.

Gulf Publishing Company founded *The Sun* in October 1973 as a morning complement to the afternoon *Herald.*

GPC's growth has not been confined to publishing newspapers. In March 1982 the firm established a telecommunications department and formed the Sun-Herald Cable Network, producing local news programs and commercials for cable subscribers. The Sun-Herald Cable Network adds to GPC's status as the area's leading provider of news and advertising.

Gulf Publishing Company today is a leading employer in Harrison County, with an annual payroll of about four million dollars. The number of employees is over 300.

In 1970 this $2-million plant was finished, and operations were moved from the Gulfport plant to the new facility on Debuys Road.

PATRONS

The following individuals, companies, and organizations have made a valuable commitment to the quality of this publication. Windsor Publications and the Mississippi Coast Historical and Genealogical Society gratefully acknowledge their participation in *The Mississippi Gulf Coast: Portrait of a People.*

Mary M. Bankston
Beauvoir, The Jefferson Davis Shrine
Biloxi Prestress Concrete, Inc.*
Leonard A. Blackwell II
Bookland of Biloxi
Albert Breeland
Broadwater Beach Hotel*
J.B. and Louise Brown
Cleophan Club

Mrs. L.O. Crosby, Jr.
Diocese of Biloxi*
E.I. du Pont de Nemours and
  Company*
Mrs. Bettye Jane McCaughan
  Edgington
Gulf National Life*
Gulf Publishing Company*
Hancock Bank*
Hancock County Historical Society
Dr. J.J. Hayden, Jr.
Howell Insurance Associates, Inc.
Jackson County Historical Society
Jackson-George Regional Library
McBride Library
Mary Mahoney's Old French House
  Restaurant*
Mississippi Gulf Coast Junior
  College

Mississippi Power Company*
Moody Grishman Agency, Inc.
Munro Petroleum & Terminal Corp.
Paceco, Inc.*
The Peoples Bank*
Hazel and Bob Portwood
Riemann Funeral Homes*
William H. Wilson, Sr.
Wixon & Co.

*Partners in Progress of *The Mississippi Gulf Coast: Portrait of a People.* The histories of these companies and organizations appear in Chapter Eight, beginning on page 177.

SELECTED BIBLIOGRAPHY

Most of the information in this book came from the M. James Stevens Collection. The collection itself consists of approximately 53,000 documents arranged chronologically in large, loose-leaf binders, each containing an average of 300 pages.

One set of 6,000 documents runs the entire gamut of coast history, while another set of equal length chronicles the Civil War years alone. Numerous subsidiary volumes explore such specific topics as the growth of individual cities, industries, and cultural movements.

The bulk of the documentation consists of newspaper dispatches, letters, portions of diaries and memoirs, and official government reports. Interspersed with these are magazine and journal articles and portions of books illuminating particular subjects.

In many cases Stevens typed the document he wished to preserve and placed a synopsis of its contents in the upper right corner. Much of the 19th-century documentation consists of reports sent by coast correspondents to newspapers primarily in New Orleans. Only rarely were these correspondents newspaper employees; rather, most were well-educated inhabitants of the coastal towns writing under pseudonyms. Their dispatches were not mere "letters to the editor" but were full slices of life published as a matter of general interest in that pre-radio and television age, since the metropolitan editors viewed the Mississippi Gulf Coast settlements as satellites. These letters and reports, preserved in Crescent City files, thus survived the hurricanes and other disasters that destroyed such material on the coast.

In addition to the Stevens Collection, the files of the various newspapers of the Mississippi panhandle contain a wealth of information. The most complete and comprehensive is that of the *Daily Herald* which celebrated its centennial in 1984.

The three most important periodicals used in the preparation of this work were *The Journal of Mississippi History, The Journal of the Mississippi Coast Historical and Genealogical Society,* and *Down South Magazine.* From its inception in 1951 to its discontinuation in 1981, this magazine chronicled coast history from its beginnings. Scores of *Down South Magazine* articles, particularly those by Ray Thompson and Hazel Holt, were used by this author.

In the realm of published works the best source dealing with the coming of the French is Richebourg McWilliams' translation of *Iberville's Gulf Journals* (1981). At last the question regarding the original landing site can be answered and laid to rest. Marcel Giraud in his excellent *History of French Louisiana: The Reign of Louis XIV, 1698-1715* (1974) weaves Iberville's journals and a number of other accounts into the best secondary source on the period.

The finest single secondary work dealing with a broad overview of one aspect of the history of the coast panhandle is Nollie Hickman's *Mississippi Harvest: Lumbering in the Lone-leaf Pine Belt, 1840-1915* (1962). Perhaps the title has led potential readers to misjudge this work as a dull rendition of board-feet production statistics, and it does contain such information. On the whole, though, *Mississippi Harvest* is a literary and historical classic deserving a wide audience. Hickman's perception of the human condition and his epic descriptions of log drives and life in the piney woods are superb. This book should stand at the top of every reading list in every school in the panhandle.

Of the historical publications concerning various portions of the panhandle, the best is Cyril Cain's *Four Centuries on the Pascagoula* (1953-1962). This two-volume work, recently reprinted, contains a number of chronological lists that render it invaluable to librarians and researchers throughout the district.

The best chronicle of black contributions to coast development by a black writer is Etienne William Maxson's *Progress of the Races* (1930). Although this small book deals with the black experience primarily in the Pearl River Valley, its uniqueness commands district-wide interest.

The following abbreviated list of published works can serve as a guide to those wishing to pursue knowledge in depth.

Alexander, Mary Ellen. *Rosalie and Radishes: A History of Long Beach, Mississippi.* Gulfport: The Dixie Press, 1980.

Arthur, Stanley C. *The Story of the West Florida Rebellion.* Baton Rouge: Claitor's Publishing, 1975.

Bartram, William. *Travels through North and South Carolina, Georgia, East and West Florida.* New York: Dover Publications, 1955. Originally published 1791.

Bay St. Louis, Mississippi: *Commemorating 100 Years of Incorporation.* Bay St. Louis: Bay St. Louis Centennial Corporation, 1958.

Bearss, Edwin C. *Decision in Mississippi: Mississippi's Important Role in the War Between the States.* Jackson: Mississippi Commission on the War Between the States, 1962.

_____. *Historic Resource Study: Ship Island, Gulf Island, National Seashore.* Denver: U.S. Government, 1984.

_____. *Historic Structure Report, Administrative and Historical Data Sections: Fort on Ship Island (Fort Massachusetts), 1857-1935; Gulf Islands National Seashore, Harrison County, Mississippi.* Denver: U.S. Government, 1984.

Brown, Wilburt S. *The Amphibious Campaign for West Florida and Louisiana, 1814-1815.* University of Alabama Press, 1969.

Burns, Zed H. *Ship Island and the Confederacy.* Hattiesburg: University and College Press of Mississippi, 1971.

Carter, Hodding and Anthony Ragusin. *Gulf Coast Country.* New York: Duell, Sloan and Pearce, 1951.

Carter, Samuel. *Blaze of Glory: The Fight for New Orleans, 1814-15.* New York: St. Martin's Press, 1971.

Christmas, J.Y. (ed.). *Cooperative Gulf of Mexico Estuarine Inventory and Study, Mississippi.* Ocean Springs: Gulf Coast Research Laboratory, 1973.

Cox, W.A. and E.F. Martin. *Facts About the Gulf Coast: The Book of Harrison County, Mississippi, Gulfport, Biloxi, Pass Christian and Other of its Thriving Cities.* Gulfport: Cox and Martin, Publishers, 1905.

Dyer, Charles L. *Along the Gulf: An Entertaining Story of an Outing Among the Beautiful Resorts on the Mississippi Sound From New Orleans, Louisiana to Mobile, Alabama.* Gulfport: The Dixie Press, 1971. Originally published 1895.

Eleuterius, Charles K. and Sheree L. Beaugez. *Mississippi Sound: A Hydrographic and Climatic Atlas.* Ocean Springs: Physical Oceanography Section, Gulf Coast Research Laboratory, 1979.

Eleuterius, Lionel N. *An Illustrated Guide to Tidal Marsh Plants of Mississippi and Adjacent States.* Ocean Springs: Mississippi-Alabama Sea Giant Consortium, 1980.

Greenwell, Dale. *Twelve Flags: Triumphs and Tragedies.* Ocean Springs: 1968.

Guice, Julia Cook (ed.). *The Buildings of Biloxi: An Architectural Survey.* Biloxi: City of Biloxi, 1976.

Gunter, Gordon. *The Relationship of the Bonnet Carre Spillway to Oyster Beds in Mississippi Sound and the "Louisiana Marsh," with a Report on the 1950 Opening.* Port Arkansas, Texas: Institute of Marine Science, 1953.

Gutierrez, C. Paige. *The Cultural Legacy of Biloxi's Seafood Industry.* Biloxi: City of Biloxi, 1984.

Hancock Bank, Gulfport. *The Coast of Mississippi: Its Past and Progress.* Baton Rouge: Moran Publishing Corporation, 1982.

Hardy, Toney A. *No Compromise with Principle: Autobiography and Biography of William Harris Hardy in Dialogue.* New York: American Book-Stratford Press, 1942.

Hayden, Julius J. "The History of Pass Christian, Mississippi." Master's thesis: Mississippi State College.

Higginbotham, Jay. *Fort Maurepas: The Birth of Louisiana.* Mobile: Colonial Books, 1968.

_____. *The Journal of Sauvole.* Mobile: Colonial Books, 1969.

_____. *Pascagoula: Singing River City.* Mobile: Gill Press, 1967.

Hines, Regina R. *Ocean Springs, 1892-1979.* Pascagoula: Lewis Publishing Co., 1979.

Holt, Hazel. *History of Biloxi.* Biloxi: First National Bank of Biloxi, 1968.

Jackson, W. Harvell. *By the Rivers of Water: History of George County, Mississippi.* Pascagoula: Lewis Printing Services, 1982.

Lang, John H. *History of Harrison County, Mississippi.* Gulfport: Dixie Press, 1936.

Latour, Major A. Lacarriere. *Historical Memoir of the War in West Florida and Louisiana in 1814-15.* Gainesville: University of Florida Press, 1964. Originally published 1816.

Margy, Pierre. *Journal of the Frigate LeMarin.* Ocean Springs: Blossman Printing Co., 1974.

Otvos, Ervin G. *Coastal Geology of Mississippi, Alabama and Adjacent Louisiana Areas.* New Orleans: The New Orleans Geological Society, 1982.

Penicaut, André. *Fleur de Lys and Calumet Being the Penicaut Narrative of French Adventure in Louisiana.* Baton Rouge: Louisiana State University Press, 1953.

Pitts, J.R.S. *Life and Confessions of the Noted Outlaw James Copelan.* Jackson: University Press of Mississippi, 1980. Originally published 1909.

Prindiville, Alice Bell. *Trinity Episcopal Church, Pass Christian, Mississippi, 1849-1974: An Historical Record.* Pass Christian: 1974.

Romans, Bernard. *A Concise Natural History of East and West Florida.* New Orleans: Pelican Publishing Co., 1961. Originally published 1775.

Rowe, Melodia B. *Captain Jones: The Biography of a Builder.* Hamilton, Ohio: Hill-Brown, 1942.

Schmidt, C.E. *Ocean Springs: French Beachhead.* Pascagoula: Lewis Printing Services, 1972.

Sheffield, David A. and Nicovich, Darnell L. *When Biloxi Was the Seafood Capital of the World.* Edited by Julia Guice Cook. Biloxi: The City of Biloxi, 1979.

Thigpen, S.G. *Next Door the Heaven.* Kingsport, Tennessee: Kingsport Press, 1965.

_____. *Pearl River: Highway Glory Land.* Kingsport, Tennessee: Kingsport Press, 1965.

Titler, Dale. *Keesler Field: Inception to Pearl Harbor, 1939-1941.* Keesler Air Force Base: Keesler Technical Training Center Office of History, 1981.

United States Coast Guard. *Lighthouses and Lightships of the Northern Gulf of Mexico.* New Orleans: Department of Transportation, 1976.

Wixon, Thomas. *Jackson County, Mississippi: Photographs from the Past.* Pascagoula: Falcon Publishers, 1982.

INDEX